The Canterbury and York Society

GENERAL EDITOR: PROFESSOR R. L. STOREY

ISSN 0262—995X

DIOCESE OF EXETER

CANTERBURY AND YORK SOCIETY VOL. LXXXII

The Register of

Walter Bronescombe

BISHOP OF EXETER

1258–1280

VOLUME I

EDITED BY

O.F. ROBINSON

READER IN LAW
UNIVERSITY OF GLASGOW

The Canterbury and York Society

The Boydell Press

1995

First published 1995

A Canterbury and York Society publication
published by The Boydell Press
an imprint of Boydell & Brewer Ltd
PO Box 9, Woodbridge, Suffolk IP12 3DF, UK
and of Boydell & Brewer Inc.
PO Box 41026, Rochester, NY 14604–4126, USA

ISBN 0 907239 51 X

British Library Cataloguing-in-Publication Data
Register of Walter Bronescombe, Bishop of Exeter, 1258–
1280. – Vol. 1. – (Canterbury & York Society Series,
ISSN 0262-995X; Vol. 82)
    I. Robinson, O. F.   II. Series
    262.0242356
    ISBN 0-907239-51-X

Details of previous volumes available from Boydell & Brewer Ltd

The paper used in this publication meets the minimum requirements
of American National Standard for Information Sciences –
Permanence of Paper for Printed Library Materials, ANSI Z39.48–1984

Printed in Great Britain by
St Edmundsbury Press Ltd, Bury St Edmunds, Suffolk

CONTENTS

ACKNOWLEDGMENTS

In the first place I owe a considerable debt to the late Rev. F.C. Hingeston Randolph. While his edition is defective in very many ways, he was a local parson who was also an antiquarian with a deep knowledge of his subject. I would dearly love to have been able to discuss the Register with him.

I also owe thanks to: the lord bishop of Exeter, the Right Rev. Dr G. Hewlett Thompson, for permission to publish the Register; the Dean, the Very Rev. R.M.S. Eyre, and Chapter of Exeter Cathedral for permission to publish their statutes; Joan Sinar, former Devon County Archivist; Mrs M.M. Rowe, the present Devon County Archivist; Audrey Erskine, formerly the Cathedral Librarian; Professor R.M.T. Hill, my supervisor; the successive General Editors of the Canterbury and York Society, Dr Alison McHardy and Professor R.L. Storey, who have bullied me gently for my own good; and, above all, to Sebastian, who really should be reckoned as assistant editor rather than mere husband. From the days when this was being worked on for submission to the University of London for a Ph.D., I remember the friends in 1965 who helped me have the manuscript ready on the appointed day, and, in her private capacity, Joan Sinar, who allowed me to keep my new-born daughter on a shelf in the Record Office, and looked after me like an elder sister.

It is expected that the Register will be completed in two further volumes, with the Appendixes and Indexes appearing in the third.

March 1995   O.F.R.

ABBREVIATIONS

C.C.R	*Close Rolls: Henry III*; *Calendar of Close Rolls: Edward I* (HMSO, 1902–38; 1900–08)
Cal. Fine R.	*Calendar of Fine Rolls, Edward I 1272–1307* (HMSO, 1911)
Cal. Inq. Misc.	*Calendar of Miscellaneous Chancery Inquisitions* (HMSO, 1916)
C.L.R.	*Calendar of Liberate Rolls: Henry III* (HMSO, 1917–64)
C.P.L.	*Calendar of entries in the papal registers relating to Great Britain and Ireland: Papal Letters*, vol. I, ed. W.H. Bliss (HMSO, 1893)
C.P.R	*Calendar of Patent Rolls* (HMSO, 1891–)
C & Y	Canterbury and York Society publications
Councils and Synods	*Councils and Synods, with other documents relating to The English Church, Part II 1205–1313*, ed. F.M. Powicke & C.R. Cheney (Oxford, 1964), Part i 1205–65; part ii 1265–1313
D & C	Devon and Cornwall Record Society publications
Hingeston-Randolph	*The Registers of Walter Bronescombe and Peter Quivil, bishops of Exeter*, ed. F.C. Hingeston-Randolph (London/Exeter 1889)
Quivel	see Hingeston-Randolph
Pecham	*The Register of John Pecham, archbishop of Canterbury 1279–92*, vol. I ed. F.N. Davis and others, vol. II ed. D. Douie (C & Y vols. 64 & 65, 1969 [reprinted] & 1968)

INTRODUCTION

1. THE MANUSCRIPT

(a) Physical appearance

The register of Walter Bronescombe is nowadays included in a folio book[1] of about 140 vellum leaves, which is held in the Diocesan Record Office – now part of the Devon County Record Office – in Exeter; the volume also contains the register of Bronescombe's successor, Peter Quivel (or Quinel[2]). It is the first of a series in which only the register of Thomas Bitton, bishop 1292–1307, is missing.[3] It was written in a brownish ink on parchment measuring roughly 10¼ in. by 6¼ in. (26cm by 16cm), and it is now enclosed in covers dating probably from the end of the nineteenth century, though marks on the endpapers suggest that there was an earlier cover. Bronescombe's register seems to have been stitched together at least as early as the middle of the fourteenth century when a hand, perhaps that of Bishop Grandisson (1327–69),[4] numbered its folios throughout.

The manuscript is in good condition. Splits in the parchment have been neatly stitched up with what appears to be hair thread; there are a few small holes – presumably the remnants of warbles or some similar parasite – and in a few places the edge of the page has become worn.

The quires are grouped together somewhat irregularly: first, four unnumbered pages, probably bound in when the volume was enclosed in its covers, and then f.1 which was originally the fly-leaf; thereafter the separate gatherings run from f.2 to f.9 (8 folios), 10 to 21 (12 folios), 22 to 33 (12 folios), 34 to 42 (9 folios), 43 to 64 (23 folios), 65 to 76 (12 folios), 77 to 100 (24 folios), 101, 102, 103/109, 109b to 110 (2 folios), 111 to 131 (20 folios), 132, 133 to 143 (11 folios), and various endpapers. Altogether there are twenty-three deeds or charters stitched in, while seven of the regularly numbered and entered folios are also stitched in. (These deeds are here called f.1c and f.1d, etc. after the folio they follow.) Most of the deeds have spike marks in the top corner, so were presumably filed before being included in the register; some have slits for seal tags, but no seals have survived.

A framework for the entries is commonly formed by a double line around the sides of the folios. These lines are approximately ¼ in. apart, and approximately 1in. from the top and bottom, ¾ in. from the outside edge and,

---

[1] See M.T. Clanchy, *From Memory to Written Record* (London, 1979), p.54.

[2] There is no certainty which is the correct form; I have chosen to follow Hingeston-Randolph and use 'v'.

[3] Though a grant to Bishop Bitton of land at Kelly has been stitched in at the beginning of the register (f.1e). Hingeston-Randolph attempted to compile a record of Bitton's episcopate at the end of his edition of the Registers of Bronescombe and Quivel.

[4] Hingeston-Randolph, p.viii.

presumably because of the binding and rebinding, have about ½ in. as inner margin. There is also a horizontal line about ⅜ in. from the top throughout most of the register; on this line, as far as f.53, is written, often across the double spread, the year of the episcopate and, usually, the month(s) of the year mentioned on the page beneath. From f.54 on, except on 82v and 83, only the year is given, and that only occasionally; the year of the Lord is given as well on ff.90v and 95v.

The folios are numbered throughout with Roman numerals in the top outer corner; ff.2–11 were also numbered with rather small Roman numerals at the top centre. The numeration is consistent, except where two consecutive folios are each numbered 62. To ease the task of anyone consulting the MS, I have called them 62a and 62b. At some date, almost certainly later, Arabic numeration was added, also in the centre, above the date line.[5] In the Arabic, f.37 was misnumbered as 38, and from then on the Arabic numerals stay one ahead of the Roman until the Roman misnumbering of 62b, which the Arabic, quite consistently, calls 64, and so remains two ahead until the end of the register.

The register is written mostly in a small neat hand, or series of them; minor variations may be due to fresh quills, the presence or absence of adequate light, the temperature, the scribe's state of health, etc., and closely related hands could result from pupillage or a common background. Clearly identifiable as well are a small and spiky hand (entry nos. **51, 821–24, 1294–96, 1299–1305**), and a large untidy hand (**943–53, 998–1000, 1293**); there is also a large and tidy hand which may be distinct (**1315–23**). Other possible changes occur (**186, 201, 212, 219, 222, 243, 296, 300, 330, 931, 936, 943, 954**), and the presence of a new scribe is sometimes highly probable, as **646–49** (on f.35) where it seems as though some other clerk on the registrar's staff inadvertently repeated **637–40**. At the very top of f.36 is written in a very small hand: *Hic incepi* (Here I began); this may refer to a new clerk, or perhaps more probably to a new registrar. Several times, especially for the taxation of vicarages, one hand, almost certainly that of the registrar himself, wrote the marginal heading and opening phrase of an entry (e.g. **819**), and the rest was then filled in by some other hand.

(b) Its history

It seems likely that the registers normally accompanied the bishops on their journeyings, for this volume was lost when Walter Stapledon, bishop 1308–26, was murdered by the London mob,[6] and it appears to have gone missing there. Grandisson[7] somehow recovered it, and wrote on f.1, the fly-leaf: 'A certain register of the first Walter, bishop of Exeter from 1257 [O.S.]. You are to know that cancellations were made[8] or entries blacked out in it by some ignorant or improper person who bought the register after the death of the

---

[5] The numbers appear thus: １ ７ ３ ２ ４ ６ ∧ ８ ９ ０
[6] Hingeston-Randolph p.vii, citing the register of Walter Reynolds, archbishop of Canterbury 1313–27, f.150, 26 November 1326.
[7] Identified by Hingeston-Randolph, p.viii.
[8] E.g. the deposition of Abbot Chubbe (**733**).

second Walter and kept it for a long time'.[9] Who this person was and for what purpose the register was acquired, and indeed by what means, must remain unknown. Perhaps during this period, and almost certainly in the fourteenth century, what appear to be extracts from canon law were entered on ff.44v (in the margin), 78, 79v, 80 and 109v.

At the beginning of the volume there is a note indicating that Bishop Brantingham (1381–97) made use of it, and on f.109v there is an entry relating to his period of office inserted by a sixteenth century registrar, William Germyn. The latter, at least, clearly had antiquarian interests because he copied into the register a number of documents relating to the thirteenth century,[10] with the remark, on f.37: 'Note that the aforesaid document[11] was handed to the right reverend father the bishop, John Wolton by name, to be entered here by the hand of the dean, Sir Stephen Townsend,

[9] Quoddam registrum primi Walteri episcopi Exoniensis de A.D. mcclvii. Et sciendum quod cancellationes hic facte vel per nigrum tracte ab aliquo ignorante vel non pertinente fiebant qui registrum post necem secundi Walteri emit et retinuit multum diu.

[10] He took them from various cartularies (chiefly that of St Nicholas' Priory, Exeter, according to Hingeston-Randolph). They include: on f.35v the appropriation of Lanlivery in 1202 and of St Austell between 1138 and 1155 to Tywardreath Priory; on f.91v a grant by Bishop Briwere to the bishop of Salisbury of the prebendal church of Kingsteignton; on f.98v a composition, between 1214 and 1223, between the cathedral chapter and St Nicholas' Priory, Exeter, over the tithes of the chapels of St Clement and St Olave, and also the taxation of Cadbury vicarage; on f.99 a composition (1214/1223) between St Nicholas' Priory and the rector of Thorverton over the tithes of that parish; on f.99v early charters to the cathedral by kings Aethelred, Cnut, and Edward the Confessor; on f.102 King Henry III's inspeximus (26 November 1243) of King John's grant to the bishops of Exeter of the royal chapel of Bosham, together with the churches of Colyton, Braunton, Plympton, St Stephen's Exeter, Perranzabuloe, ?Little Petherick ('ecclesia S. Petroci' – Padstow? Petrockstow?), Probus, St Stephen's (? in Brannel), and 'Thohou' – perhaps St Kew (*Roscarrock's Lives of the Saints: Cornwall and Devon*, ed. N. Orme (D & C vol. 35, 1992) pp.127 & 145) or St Tudy; on f.103/109 – a case of faulty numeration with a single stitched-in folio – an assize of darrein presentment from 1203 over the advowson of St Just in Roseland, and a previous settlement, 1186–91, in the royal courts; on f.110 a copy of Pope Gregory I's bull to St Augustine of England on the foundation of the provinces of Canterbury and York, and a composition, 1214/23, f.110v over the chapel of Nether Exe between Bishop Simon of Apulia and St Nicholas' Priory, Exeter; also on this folio, and written above, are two entries, both from 1281, relating to Bishop Quivel's episcopate: his acknowledgement of a debt of £113 12s 8d to R. Tantefer, burgess of Exeter, and the sequestration of the goods of the late H. de Montfort; on f.102v are a further two entries for 1281, Quivel's acknowledgement of his debt to Bronescombe's executors, Roger de Dartford and Gervase de Crediton, and a grant of wardship and marriage; on f.138 is recorded the grant by Bishop Briwere in 1242 of land at Crediton to the hermitage he had founded near St Laurence's chapel there; on f.141 (which has a spike mark in its top left-hand corner) at some time after 1236, a grant by the prior of Montacute to the bishop and church of Exeter of the churches of Altarnun and Crediton.

[11] The entry concerns the appropriation of Braunton, Bishop's Tawton, Swimbridge, and Kea to the deanery of Exeter.

12 May 1585. William Germyn, registrar.'[12] And perhaps in his hand, there is at the beginning of the volume an index to the vicarages established in the registers, and at the end, on ff.144, 145v and 146, a fragmentary index to the registers as such. Otherwise the volume presumably simply sat on a shelf, for all the other entries, outside the registers proper of Bronescombe and Quivel, date from their episcopates or earlier.

(c) Contents

Bronescombe's register runs from f.2 to f.98, and that of his successor, Peter Quivel, 1280–91, from f.111 to 133. The rest of the volume is filled with miscellaneous entries on the blank folios or stitched-in documents; all those not yet mentioned belong to these two episcopates or are earlier.

The stitched-in documents which relate to Bronescombe's episcopate are printed as Appendix I to this edition. The entries added from earlier times or from Quivel's episcopate include the record of the taxation of the vicarage of Holbeton, and the admission of a vicar in 1256 (f.1f); the foundation charters of the hospitals of St John Baptist and St Alexius at Exeter, which were united c.1230 (f.17c);[13] the grant by Edmund, earl of Cornwall, in 1284, to the bishop, dean and chapter of lands at Hexworthy (f.19d); a composition, made c.1285, over Harpford vicarage (f.130c); a list in Grandisson's hand (f.134v) of the documents in the cathedral treasury in Bronescombe's time, which is printed as Appendix III; and at the end of the volume a copy is bound in of the 1291 taxation of Pope Nicholas IV as it related to the diocese.

(d) Method of compilation

The register may have been written up in its gatherings. Some entries were clearly written in advance, at least so far as common form could be used, to save time when a large number of similar entries had to be made, in this way looking forward to the subject classification of later registers. The most notable example of this is the long series of assignations of suitable portions to the vicars of parish churches carried out by the bishop in August 1269. *Taxatio vicarie . . .*, or more often simply the name of the parish to be taxed, was written in the margin at regular intervals, and on the body of the page was entered the date and the words: *vicariam ecclesie de S. Senaro* (e.g.), *assignantes vicario nomine vicarie . . .* in the registrar's hand, after which a gap was left that was usually more than sufficient for the details of the taxation.

The register was obviously assembled from a variety of sources. There may have been a rough preparatory version, but it seems more likely that it was compiled from minutes or letters on file, and from such other records as the bishop's visitation, ordination or court rolls.

---

[12] Notandum est quod memoratum scriptum traditum fuit reverendo patri domino Iohanni Wolton, nomine et cognomine, hic inserti per manus domini Stephani Townsend, decani, xii die mensis Maii, anno 1585. Willelmus Germyn, registrarius.
[13] The only paper used in the whole volume; cf. Clanchy, *op. cit.* p.92. On the hospitals, see D. Knowles and R. Neville Hadcock, *Medieval Religious Houses* (London, 1953), p.270.

It seems unlikely that entries were made every day or even every week, although this must sometimes have happened. The entry concerning Crediton (**926**), dated 22 October 1272, which begins on f.50v, is continued extremely untidily on f.51. The bottom part of 51, and 51v, goes on to deal with other matters, on various dates ranging from 23 October to 7 November; then the lower part of 51v is filled in with a corrected version of what was crossed out on 51. F.52 resumes with an entry (**937**) dated 16 December. This suggests a time lapse in making entries of between three and six weeks. On the other hand, on 7v an entry (**135**) dated 20 September 1259 appointed a date for the prior of Launceston to make his submission within eight days, and in the margin was added 'at Tregony'; this submission is in fact recorded as having taken place at Tregony on 30 September (**143**). If the marginal amplification was felt necessary, it seems fair to assume that the two entries were not written at the same time, though the interval between their insertions could well have been less than the ten days between the acts they record. It would also be interesting to know if there was any relationship between the date on which the bishop performed some act, the date on which the formal notification was sent out from his chancery, and the date on which the necessary details were entered in the register. For example, the bishop settled a dispute about tithes at Kingsteignton on 12 November 1259; the letter about the settlement was dated 15 November (**181**). Again, the release from the bishop's service of Peter Dureman took place on 29 December 1259, and it was published on 1 January (**208**); a proctorship granted at Bayonne on 10 November 1273 was sent out on 12 November (**964**). This raises the question of whether the register was abroad with the bishop at this period. No further entry is dated from England until 23 August 1274 (**985**). But the fact that the register rarely departs from strict chronological order, no matter how various its contents, suggests that it was filled in quite frequently and regularly, even if blank spaces were sometimes left, and then filled in at some odd time, just as the blank space at the bottom of two adjacent leaves might be used to supply omissions (e.g. **1114**).

(e) Note on editorial method

In the text, I have simply marked each new folio by its number, with v[erso] for where the page turns; only where it seems necessary for clarity have I referred to f.00 r[ecto]. The order of the paragraphs has been followed just as they appear in the MS, ignoring insertions from other episcopates. They have been numbered from beginning to end of the register (with stitched-in deeds from the period of Bronescombe's episcopate listed separately in an appendix). Where (rarely) an entry was repeated word for word, I have omitted the repetition, but duplicate entries which show any variation, unfinished entries, and those entries that were later cancelled – usually with *va --- cat* – have been included. Similarly I have left out the occasional words which were erased or expunged, unless the change seems significant. Holes or wear in the parchment have been noted.

The punctuation is my own, as is the use of capital letters, since convention in these matters has changed so much; I have used far more punctuation than the original for ease of understanding. Spelling has been standardized; for

example, I have chosen the normal mediaeval littera, although the word is sometimes spelled with a single 't'. Square brackets are used for conjectural readings or where I have, for example, supplied a marginal guide, or expanded a proper name for clarity. Etc. is so transcribed where it appears in the MS, as also are initials. The dots . . . (as in **304** or **332**) represent deliberate gaps left in the text, gaps usually big enough for later insertion of the missing name or names. I have noted where there are marginal signs giving cross-references, sometimes with *supra* or *infra* added, or correcting the order of entries with an 'a' and 'b', and occasionally a 'c' and 'd' as well.

As appendices I have included, first, the contemporary documents stitched in to the register in their approximate chronological order, second, the two sets of statutes issued by Bronescombe in 1268 and 1275 to the dean and chapter of Exeter, which are in the Cathedral Library, and, third, the list of cathedral archives which Grandisson noted as contemporary with Bronescombe. As a final point, it is worth making explicit that this is a most unusual register. It contains a far wider range of material than was soon to become normal; since it is one of the earliest known in England, and the first in the diocese of Exeter, the registrars had no model to follow. It is not laid out by archdeaconry or ordered by subject, but provides something more reminiscent of a working diary. There was as yet no convention for the registrar to follow; this does, however, make it more interesting, more illuminating, than the standardized registers of bishops a scant generation later (such as that of Oliver Sutton, bishop of Lincoln 1280–99[14]). Nevertheless, the register's function was to record what was necessary for the administration of the diocese. That is why the references to Bronescombe's affairs outside the diocese, even if fairly frequent compared with later registers, tend to be fragmentary. Recorded relations with the archbishop are somewhat scanty; moreover, no register for the metropolitan see of Canterbury existed until the last two years of Bronescombe's life. Relations with the papacy must also be gleaned from scattered information, though the papal records can be helpful.

2. THE TRANSLATION

The translation is fairly literal. I have, however, usually broken down very long Latin sentences. Where a semi-colon in the Latin marks a new thought, I have thought fit to start a new sentence, repeating the governing verb in square brackets if necessary. I have preferred to avoid double punctuation, such as 'etc.'. The dates are all given in New Style, bringing the year back to start on 1 January; e.g. Bronescombe was consecrated bishop on 10 March 1257 by his reckoning, but I have preferred to call it 10 March 1258. *Dominus* is translated sometimes as 'lord' – the lord bishop – and sometimes as 'Sir', but it must be remembered that the term implies what one might call the status of a gentleman rather than having been knighted; similarly *domina* can normally be translated 'the lady'. *Magister*, a graduate in arts, is abbreviated to M. in the translation, but I have used MA in this Introduction.

---

[14] Ed. R.M.T. Hill, 8 vols., Lincoln Record Society, 1948–86.

Unidentified place names are given within inverted commas in the translation. Christian names are given in modern form where there is one. Proper names have usually been expanded, without square brackets, as being easier on the eye and less potentially ambiguous; square brackets are used to give additional information where a footnote is not necessarily appropriate, for example, where a document simply refers to Bishop W. I may have expanded to 'William [Briwere]'. I have standardized surnames under the place-name from which they are taken; an indication of the county is given in the Index (to come in vol. III) except in the cases of Devon and Cornwall. Surnames which are probably place names, but cannot be identified, are given a conventional form or translation, for example, John 'de Esse', since 'Esse' is probably Ash, but could be, e.g., Saltash. I have followed the *Handbook of British Chronology*, and then various works of Powicke,[15] where they prefer a particular version of a name – such as Raleigh – but all variants are collected in the Index. Similarly, since mediaeval persons were primarily known by their Christian name, everyone is indexed by that as well as by any surname. In a few cases I am not sure whether the second part of a name is a surname or a description, for example, Robert le hosteler, but it seemed prudent to include it as a surname in the Index.

3. BRONESCOMBE'S LIFE

Walter de Bronescombe seems unlikely to have been born much before 1205, since he died in 1280 and there are no references to his being of great age; it is improbable that his birth was after c.1220, since he was rector of Coningsby in the diocese of Lincoln by 1243[16] and archdeacon of Surrey by 1245.[17] The tradition is that his birth was very humble, and in Exeter, according to the inscription on his tomb.[18] There seems no positive evidence for either of these assertions, but a relatively humble birth seems likely, since we hear nothing of any family before his lifetime.[19] After his episcopate various Branscombes and Brunescombes are found holding land by knight service in South Devon.[20] But

---

[15] *Handbook of British Chronology* 1986³, ed. E.B. Fryde, D.E. Greenway, S. Porter and I. Roy (Royal Historical Society, London); F.M. Powicke, *Henry III and the Lord Edward* (Oxford, 1947); *The Thirteenth Century* (Oxford, 1953).

[16] *Rolls of Robert Grosseteste*, ed. F.N. Davis (C & Y, 1913), p.67.

[17] J. Le Neve, *Fasti Ecclesie Anglicane 1066–1300, II, Monastic Cathedrals*, ed. D.E. Greenway (University of London Institute of Historical Research, 1971), p.94.

[18] J. Hooker, *The Description of the City of Exeter* (D & C vol. 11, 1947), p.230 calls him 'but a poor mans sonne'. The birth in the city of Exeter may be due to poetic exigency, see footnote 78.

[19] B.F. Cresswell, *An Armory of Exeter Cathedral* (privately printed ?Exeter, 1908), pp.14f, suggests that Bronescombe, not coming from an armigerous family, had to invent his own coat of arms.

[20] Richard de Brankescomb' is recorded as among the wealthiest ten per-cent of tax-payers in the parish of Littleham in the hundred of Shebbear and also among those who held land in Colyton hundred (in which Branscombe lay): *The Devonshire Lay Subsidy of 1332*, ed. A.M. Erskine (D & C, 1969), pp.21 & 42. The same Richard is recorded as having married his daughter to Hugh de Courtenay, member of the

if he was not born in Branscombe, why (since he never seems to have held the living there) was he called after the place? The occasional reference to him in records from outside the diocese as Walter of Exeter seems more likely to spring from benefices or dignities that he held there – the chancellorship,[21] for example – than any particular knowledge of his birth. Moreover, Branscombe had been a manor belonging to the bishops of Exeter since before the Conquest; Bishop Leofric had held it in the time of Edward the Confessor according to the Devonshire Domesday.[22] If Walter was born on an episcopal manor, this could explain how his abilities were recognized and how he first won preferment. Bishop Briwere might have sent him to university, for we know he was an MA.[23] Such a connection could also explain his recommendation to the bishop of Winchester, either Peter des Roches, 1205–38,[24] or more likely William Raleigh, 1244–50 (whom Briwere must have known as a member of another great landowning family in Devon), for it was in the diocese of Winchester that the archdeaconry of Surrey lay.

The first probable record of Bronescombe as archdeacon of Surrey shows that he was already successful, since it is a papal dispensation to hold three other benefices with cure of souls, together with the living of Farnham which was attached to the archdeaconry.[25] A few years later he was granted a licence to hold by commendation the chapel of Blosworth in Dorset.[26] Shortly afterwards his benefices and dispensations were confirmed and, furthermore, he was described as a papal chaplain.[27] In 1251 he was granted a faculty to resign one benefice and receive another, canonically offered in England, in its place,[28] and in the following year he was licensed to hold Clandon Abbots, in the diocese of Winchester, probably under this faculty.[29] Later in the same year he obtained a dispensation to hold an additional benefice or dignity with cure of souls[30] and, a few months after, the confirmation of an old dispensation

prominent Devon family: *Calendarium Genealogicum, Henry III & Edward I*, ed. C. Roberts (London, 1865), vol. II, p.758.

[21] *C.P.R. 1247–58*, p.618.

[22] *The Victoria History of the Counties of England, Devon*, vol. I, ed. W. Page (London, 1906) – chapters on the Devon Domesday by O.J. Reichel – p.417.

[23] A.B. Emden, *A Biographical Register of the University of Oxford to AD 1500* (Oxford, 1957), vol. I, p.279, suggests that he was an Oxford graduate.

[24] Who, according to Powicke, *Henry III and the Lord Edward* (Oxford, 1947), p.76, was present on Crusade with Bishop Briwere, when the Emperor Frederick II ratified the treaty with the Sultan el Kamil.

[25] *C.P.L.* 14 August 1245, p.219; his name is not given, only his office.

[26] *C.P.L.* 23 August 1250, p.261.

[27] *C.P.L.* 3 September 1250, p.261; it is not known when he could have visited the Curia, but he was in a position to obtain favours, for on 12 September 1250, at his request, William de Stanway, MA, canon of Exeter, was allowed an additional dignity or benefice with cure of souls, *ibidem*.

[28] *C.P.L.* 31 January 1251, p.266; *ibidem*, 26 November 1250, there was a mandate to two canons of Salisbury to settle Bronescombe's claims concerning his archidiaconal jurisdiction, which he alleged was being intruded upon by G. de Foring, MA, and other men of the late Bishop William Raleigh.

[29] *C.P.L.* 23 January 1252, p.275.

[30] *C.P.L.* 8 March 1252, p.275.

permitting him to hold Farnham in plurality.[31] In 1253 he was granted a privilege of protection from excommunication by papal or legatine letters which did not specifically mention this privilege;[32] this seems to be linked with the indult granted him to retain Farnham and his other benefices when Aymer de Valence, the bishop elect of Winchester, was disputing his rights in them.[33] Also in 1254 he received a dispensation to hold a parsonage or dignity at Exeter beside those he already had.[34] In 1256 he again received a faculty, valid for five years, empowering him to replace one benefice with another.[35] The following year he was confirmed as a prebendary of Chalgrove, Oxfordshire, in a canonry of Wallingford, in the diocese of Salisbury, in addition to his other benefices;[36] in the previous month he had been given licence to hold one more benefice with cure of souls.[37] Thus in the ecclesiastical world of the thirteenth century he was doing well. Moreover, he must have acquired extensive experience of administration as an archdeacon; it is possible, although there is no direct evidence, that, if he was indeed Briwere's protégé, he had served his apprenticeship in his household, or that of the bishop of Winchester, for when Walter became a bishop himself, he chose most of his archdeacons from within his own *familia*.

It seems likely to have been through his connection with Bishop Raleigh, a royal judge as well as a bishop, that Bronescombe first attracted the attention of King Henry III; in 1250 he was sent to Lyons, where the papal court then was, and granted 40 marks for his part in postulating Aymer de Valence, the king's half-brother, to the see of Winchester *de dono regis*.[38] During the next few years he was at least occasionally in the king's employ. In 1251 he received a royal grant of three fat bucks[39] and, a little later, five oaks[40] as timber for some building he must have had in hand. In November he was granted £20 when starting on an errand for the king to the papal court at Perugia.[41] It is not clear whether Bronescombe's business concerned Aymer de Valence or the refusal (to be made in 1252) of the king's brother, Richard, to become king of Sicily. Bronescombe is next known to have been employed by the king in August 1256, when the Constable of Dover was instructed to provide a passage with all speed for him, as he was on the king's errand;[42] his destination is not

---

[31] *C.P.L.* 1 August 1252, p.279.
[32] *C.P.L.* 16 December 1253, p.294; the implication is of a blanket or *ipso facto* excommunication.
[33] *C.P.L.* 9 January 1254, p.294. It may be relevant that the register of John of Pontoise begins (*Registrum Johannis Pontissara, episcopi Wyntonensis AD 1282–1304*, ed. C. Deedes, C & Y, 1915 & 1924, vol. I, p.2f) with a settlement, made in June 1254, over the extent of the archdeacon of Surrey's jurisdiction.
[34] *C.P.L.* 25 February 1254, p.301.
[35] *C.P.L.* 11 February 1256, p.327.
[36] *C.P.L.* 13 July 1257, p.347.
[37] *C.P.L.* 9 June 1257, p.349.
[38] *C.C.R* 1247–51, p.376; *C.L.R.* IV 1251–60, p.27; *C.L.R.* IV 1251–60, p.56.
[39] *C.C.R* 1247–51, p.416.
[40] *C.C.R* 1247–51, p.494.
[41] *C.L.R.* IV 1251–60, p.5.
[42] *C.L.R.* IV 1251–60, pp.316f.

mentioned. He is not again recorded as in the royal service until after his elevation to the episcopate.

Any influence the king may have had on Bronescombe's election as bishop of Exeter is unknown; the register simply tells us that it was uncontested – *concorditer ab omnibus* (3). It is quite likely that the canons wanted an experienced and competent administrator to reclaim the diocese from the state in which the previous bishop, Richard Blund, had left it. It seems significant that there are quite a few entries in, or additions to, the register relating to the doings of Bishop Briwere, but only one document from Bishop Blund's time,[43] and nearly all the other references to him concern the scandal of his deathbed (83). The diocese seems also to have been heavily in debt at his death, and the executors of his will had to be inhibited from the distribution of his legacies until the sum of the debts had been discovered (26).

Naturally, once he was a bishop, Bronescombe continued to be of use to the king. As a feudal magnate, he provided forces for the royal army. Moreover, in June 1258 he was granted a passport until Easter 1259 for a journey to Germany as the king's envoy to Richard of Cornwall, King of the Romans;[44] in February 1259 he was granted 100 marks for his expenses on this journey.[45] In 1262 we find him requested to join the king for a postponed meeting in Paris in the new year.[46] In February 1263, some weeks after Henry's return to England, Bronescombe was appointed, together with Henry of Almaine (the king's nephew), William de Valence (half-brother of the king) and others, as the king's proctor in connection with the late peace,[47] the attempt of the previous October to settle the English constitutional issue by the Provisions of Westminster; he was also sent to treat with the king of France,[48] Louis IX, who was attempting to arbitrate. In July, together with the bishops of Worcester, Coventry, Lincoln and London, who with him had urged their reissue, as one of the king's proctors he confirmed the Statutes of Oxford.[49] In October, the Provisions were still the subject of dispute and Bronescombe was still occupied with negotiations for peace.[50] After the Mise of Amiens in January 1264, which proved unacceptable to the baronial party, his knight service was summoned to assemble with the royalist forces at Oxford,[51] where Henry was soon to be joined by his son Edward; negotiations continued between the king's party and the opposition led by Simon de Montfort, earl of Leicester, but the civil war had begun. Simon de Montfort won the battle of Lewes in May 1264, and both Edward and Henry of Almaine fell into his hands. Henry and Simon turned again to arbitration, but the papal legate to England, from Boulogne, openly condemned the baronial party, and issued

[43] The taxation of Holbeton vicarage, f.1f.
[44] *C.P.R.* 1247–58, p.633.
[45] *C.L.R.* IV 1251–60, pp.452f.
[46] *C.C.R* 1261–64, p.177.
[47] *C.P.R.* 1258–66, p.243; *C.C.R* 1261–64, pp.281 & 283 & 293.
[48] *C.P.R.* 1258–66, p.243, recording letters close to the King and Queen of France on the same business.
[49] *C.P.R.* 1258–66, pp.269–70.
[50] *C.P.R.* 1258–66, p.292.
[51] *C.C.R* 1261–64, p.377.

sentences of excommunication and interdict before being recalled to Italy to become Pope Clement IV.

Through much of this period Bronescombe seems to have been with the king, working for a compromise;[52] he was also one of the bishops who voted a clerical tenth for the defence of the realm against the threatened French invasion (563). He demanded, and was present at, Henry's suppression of the London rioters who had insulted the queen, despoiled Richard of Cornwall, and attacked church property.[53] He was summoned, with all the other bishops, to a meeting of parliament at London in January 1265 to discuss the terms of peace, but his itinerary shows that he could not have attended it;[54] he had earlier sent proctors to the parliament held at St Albans in November 1264 (573). He continued to be occupied in the search for a settlement before[55] and after[56] Simon's defeat and death at the battle of Evesham in August 1265. When Edward decided to fall in with the wishes of the papal legate, Ottobuono,[57] and aim for a settlement, he called a parliament at Kenilworth, which he was besieging. Three bishops, one of whom was Bronescombe, and three barons were appointed to seek peace; they co-opted a further six for drawing up a plan for the restoration of order and for solving the problem of the disinherited. The result was the Dictum of Kenilworth, on which Bronescombe's name appeared first in the list of *dictores*.[58] His negotiating talents were used two years later for the making of peace with Llywelyn.[59]

Bronescombe seems to have been on good terms with Edward; in 1270, with other bishops and barons, he witnessed Edward's mandate to Richard of Cornwall to administer his lands while he was overseas on Crusade, while he, Philip Basset, Roger Mortimer and Robert Burnell[60] were appointed guardians of Edward's lands and other rights.[61] (In 1272 he was one of those who sent a letter on behalf of the prelates of England to John of Toledo, cardinal of Porto (890); unfortunately the subject is not mentioned.) Then he was one of the party who went overseas to meet Edward on his return, after his father's death, from Crusade,[62] and he is said to have baptized Edward's first surviving son, Alfonso, when he was with the new king in Gascony in

---

[52] *C.P.R.* 1258–66, p.335.

[53] *C.C.R* 1261–64, p.402.

[54] *C.C.R* 1264–68, p.85.

[55] *C.P.R.* 1258–66, p.488.

[56] *C.P.R.* 1258–66, p.509.

[57] Ottobuono Fieschi, briefly Pope Adrian V in 1276.

[58] W. Stubbs (ed. revised H.W.C. Davis), *Select Charters and other illustrations of English constitutional History* (Oxford, 1913, 9th ed., repr. with corrections 1946), p.407. Cf. Powicke, *Henry III and the Lord Edward* (Oxford, 1947), pp.532f.

[59] *C.P.R.* 1266–72, p.254.

[60] Basset, justiciar in 1261, and Mortimer, a Marcher lord, had been members of the 1259 council of regency; Burnell was bishop of Bath and Wells, 1275–92 (though he was twice refused Canterbury by the Pope).

[61] P. Chaplais (ed.), *Diplomatic Documents I* (HMSO, 1964), p.296, no.423.

[62] *C.P.R.* 1272–81, p.9; in October his passport was extended until the following Easter – *C.P.R.* 1272–81, p.30.

1273–74.[63] He was also appointed, together with the archbishop of Canterbury and the bishop of Worcester, to hold Amaury de Montfort (Simon's son) in safe-keeping in 1275.[64] He does not seem to have acted in the king's service again – his health was perhaps beginning to fail – although he was a witness to the protest made by Edward (who had wanted the promotion of Robert Burnell) when Robert Kilwardby was provided to Canterbury, that royal rights to the temporalities of vacant sees should not be prejudiced by papal provision.[65]

Through the years Bronescombe made various other appearances in crown records. He received several presents from the king of timber[66] and deer;[67] on one occasion the custodians of the temporalities of the diocese of Winchester were ordered to send him 20 *matrices bremias* and 40 pike from the fish-pond at Taunton.[68] Shortly after Bronescombe's promotion Henry granted him a weekly market at Penryn, an annual fair on the vigil, feast and morrow of St Thomas the Martyr, and free warren – the right to hunt small game and rabbits – on all his his demesne lands in the dioceses of Chichester, Winchester and Exeter.[69] The Patent Rolls of February 1267 give his title to the manor of Clyst Sackville, now Bishop's Clyst, and his freedom from any liability for Ralph de Sackville's debts (specifically to the Jews).[70] In 1269 there was trouble about the woodland, that of others and that belonging to his manor of Faringdon, which bordered the highway between Alton and Alresford; Bronescombe agreed to cut it down and bring the land under cultivation.[71] In 1271 there is a brief record of his having been sued by Roger Bigod, earl of Norfolk, at the previous Sussex eyre;[72] the subject of dispute is not stated, but he held land in that shire.

The archangel Gabriel was his patron saint; he dedicated an altar to St Gabriel at Newenham Abbey.[73] He also, in 1276, dedicated to him his chapel in the manor of Bishop's Clyst,[74] and in 1278 established an annual feast of St Gabriel in Exeter cathedral which was to be celebrated with the same sort of honour in lights and other matters as at the feasts of Christmas and Easter (**1297**). On 4 May 1280 he wrote, excusing himself from attendance at the

---

[63] *C.P.R.* 1272–81, p.120; G. Oliver, *Lives of the Bishops of Exeter* (Exeter, 1861), pp.42f, citing *Angl. Sac.* I, 501.

[64] *C.P.R.* 1272–81, p.253.

[65] *C.C.R* Edward I 1272–79, p.39.

[66] *C.C.R* 1256–59, p.421; 1259–61, p.377; 1261–64, p.65.

[67] *C.C.R* 1256–59, p.225.

[68] *C.C.R* 1259–61, p.355; 'mother' bream probably means fish with a visible or tangible roe.

[69] *Calendar of Charter Rolls* II, 1257–1300 (HMSO, 1906), p.16. 28–30 December does not seem a very promising date for a successful fair.

[70] *C.P.R.* 1266–72, p.34.

[71] *C.P.R.* 1266–72, p.380; *Calendar of Charter Rolls* II 1257– 1300 (HMSO, 1906), p.122; in 1285 the Statute of Winchester was to require clear margins of 200 yards on either side of the king's highway.

[72] *C.C.R* 1268–72, p.540.

[73] On 7 July 1270 – G. Oliver, *Monasticon Dioecesis Exoniensis* (Exeter, 1846), p.357fn.

[74] **O** in Appendix I.

provincial Council to be held in London, and appointing Andrew de Kilkenny his proctor (**1407**). On 22 July 1280 he died.[75]

He was presumably a man of some learning, as he was a graduate. The quittance given to his executors mentions some books among his moveables. These included a psalter, a part of the Pentateuch with gloss, the *Panteon* of Godfrey of Viterbo, a *Liber Decretorum et Decretalium* [sic] with *apparatus*, a *Liber de Animalibus*, an unspecified *Liber Avicennae*, and Vegetius' *De re militari* – a wide range of works.[76] His memory was held in considerable respect and affection in his diocese.[77] At his death he was buried in his cathedral between his chapel of St Gabriel and the Lady Chapel; a hundred or so years later, a canopy was built over his tomb, and the following inscription carved:[78]

> Once the true-hearted father, worthy of all love, Here the first Walter lies in great honour. Here he issued many most praiseworthy statutes, Which here like laws safeguard all things. He founded besides the splendid college Which all folk call Glasney, Following a message granted in his dreams. How many places of worship he built, How many good works he did, How holy a life he led, Only the voice that knows can say. Let Exonians rejoice with boundless praises, Chorus and multitudes, for he was born in this city. If you wish to know more, he founded the feast of Gabriel. Therefore in Heaven may that faithful father rejoice.

4. THE BISHOP'S HOUSEHOLD

Bronescombe, like any other bishop, needed a considerable body of men to minister to his public and private needs.[79] The ideal household of a bishop consisted of intimates and servants, of officials and domestic and outdoor staff. Among the most important, in the thirteenth century, were the official-principal to exercise the deputized jurisdictional and disciplinary powers of the

[75] *C.P.R.* 1272–81, p.394; on 7 August John de Exonia and Henry de Bollegh brought news of his death and received licence to elect his successor.

[76] *Pecham*, I pp.205–07. (*Pecham* I p.202 lists the executors as Sir Roger de Dartford, Sir Reginald le Arceveske, canons of Exeter, Sir Peter de Guldeford, chaplain, Gervase de Crediton MA, Sir Hugh de Plympton and Sir Richard de Grangiis.) Reginald le Arceveske bought the *liber decretorum et decretalium* for 100 shillings. Bronescombe left £2,083 15s 1d gross, after funeral and other necessary expenses, so his efforts to restore the diocese to financial health seem to have been successful.

[77] G. Oliver, *Lives of the Bishops of Exeter* (Exeter, 1861), p.128, says that William of Worcester's *Itinerarium* referred to him as 'Walter the Good'.

[78] Olim sincerus/ pater, omni dignus amore,/ primus Walterus/ magno iacet hic in honore;/ edidit hic plura/ dignissima laude statuta/ que tanquam iura/ servant hic omnia tuta;/ ad hoc collegium/ quod Glasneye plebs vocat omnis/ condidit egregium/ pro voce data sibi somnis./ Quot loca construxit/ pietatis, quot bona fecit,/ quam sanctam duxit/ vitam vox dicere que scit./ Laudibus immensis/ iubilet gens Exoniensis/ et chorus et turbe/ quia natus in hac urbe./ Plus si scire velis,/ festum statuit Gabrielis./ Gaudeat in celis/ igitur pater iste fidelis.

[79] In 1179 the Third Lateran Council, c.74, laid down that, for the purpose of procurations, bishops were not to travel with a household of more than thirty persons.

bishop as ordinary, the chancellor to control the chancery, the registrar to keep the archives and see to the compilation of the register, a notary public to draw up and attest legal documents, and perhaps someone doing the work of official-peculiar (although the office under this name is not known until early in the fourteenth century) to see to the bishop's extra-diocesan jurisdictions. All of these were in charge of their own departments of clerks. The bishop's proctors and commissaries would probably come from the household, although, by the nature of their posts, they were often away from the bishop's side. Then there were his chaplains. The senior members of his domestic staff, the chamberlain and the steward or seneschal, also ranked as *commensales*, those who ate at the bishop's board. Of this rank too were the household knights who, with their contingent of men at arms, formed the bishop's bodyguard.

Bronescombe's officials were, first, Robert de Tyfford,[80] who became archdeacon of Cornwall in 1264 (**538**), then Robert Everard, who was official by September 1263 (**503**)[81] and may still have been so in 1270 (**829**), but after this he fades from the register; his successor seems to have been John de Esse. John had held a position of some importance in the household as early as 1259 (**181**), and he may have been the official-peculiar, for he was recorded in 1262 as paying to Roger de Dartford, the steward, £12 levied on the peculiar jurisdiction of the lord bishop (**426**); three weeks earlier he had paid the arrears of his office and received letters of quittance (**427** – sic). Nearly two years later he was again recorded as rendering his accounts and receiving letters of quittance, although the occasion was not specified (**516**). He was first described as official-principal in 1272, when he was engaged in a conflict of jurisdictions with the earl of Cornwall (**1085**). After August 1274 it appears that he combined the post with the archdeaconry of Cornwall (**985**); he was last referred to as official in 1275 (**1092**) and as archdeacon in 1277 (**1237**).[82] The last official mentioned was Andrew de Kilkenny MA in 1280 (**1395**); he went on to become precentor of the cathedral, Dean of Arches some time after 1282, and then in 1286 dean of Exeter under Bronescombe's successor, Bishop Quivel.[83]

Bronescombe's first chancellor was probably William de Capella, and his second John de Esse. William was very close to the bishop; he accompanied him at least once on his travels abroad.[84] He was twice recorded as receiving charge of Bronescombe's seals (**66**; **116**),[85] he had a box of his own in the cathedral treasury (**194**), and the register tells of his making many unspecified journeys for the bishop (**62–65**; **91**; **277**; **297**; **328**; **334**; **354**; **413**); the fact that these journeys were recorded proves that they were more than mere errands, but all one can assume is that they concerned confidential matters of

---

[80] To be distinguished from the man of the same name who was chancellor of the cathedral.

[81] He was holding the post in August 1264 (**563**).

[82] His death is referred to in *Quivel*, p.326.

[83] *Quivel*, p.360.

[84] *C.P.R.* 1247–58, p.634.

[85] He surrendered the seals in Paris, and received them back a year later after having been at the Curia.

some sort. John succeeded him (whether immediately or not) since he is described as chancellor and official when he was attacked by the earl of Cornwall's men in 1272 (**1085**). No other reference is made to the bishop's chancellor; we know that Bronescombe's predecessor, Bishop Blund, had a chancellor, Walter de Lodeswell, who also held the office of chamberlain (**83**).[86]

The identity of the registrar is obscure. There are two early candidates, Bartholomew de Lardario, who in June and July 1258 received three proctorships written in his own hand (**57**; **59–60**), and just possibly Robert of Poitou, of whom it is recorded that in 1262 a transcript was held in the registry under his seal (**445**). The only other hint even at the existence of a registrar is the '*Hic incepi*' of April 1267, already mentioned at the end of the section on the physical appearance of the MS; could it have been William de Capella, who continued frequently in the bishop's company, at least until 1275?[87] Nor do we hear of any notary-public in the household, though Bishop Blund had had one in Richard de Totnes (**83**). A possibility is Richard de Hydon, who was the only layman not a knight to belong in the upper echelons of the household; he did frequently accompany the bishop.

Other key positions were held by Richard de Grangiis, the chamberlain (**1155**), Peter de Guildford, the bishop's principal chaplain, who seems on one occasion to have been the keeper of the bishop's court rolls (**892**), and Roger de Dartford, the steward (**954**); all three were executors of Bronescombe's will.[88] Others who were very frequently in attendance were Gervase de Crediton (another executor), John Noble, who became archdeacon of Exeter and then dean of the cathedral, Robert de Polamford, William de Ponchardon (who is actually described as 'a clerk of our household' – **1047**), Hugh Splot de Plympton, and John Wiger, the clerk, who must be distinguished from the knight of the same name. The rest of the bishop's intimates seem to have been Henry de Bollegh, first provost of Bronescombe's collegiate foundation at Glasney, Thomas de Buckland, Edward de la Knolle, dean of Wells (who must have been a close personal friend to appear so often outside his diocese and within the household), and Roger de Thoriz, who was, like John Noble, successively archdeacon of Exeter and dean of the cathedral. The remaining men who can fairly be described as members of the household were John de Blagdon, John de Bradley, official of Cornwall and archdeacon of Barnstaple 1267–70, Richard de Braundsworthy, Philip de Cancellis, Philip de Exeter, who was archdeacon of Barnstaple from 1279, Ralph de Hengham, precentor of Exeter and royal justice, Thomas de Hertford, archdeacon of Totnes 1271–75, Robert de Kennford, Walter de Pembroke, archdeacon of Totnes 1264–65, and John of Pontoise, archdeacon of Exeter 1274–80 and later bishop of Winchester.

The thirty men now mentioned held between them fourteen canonries in the collegiate church of Crediton, thirteen in the cathedral, nine at Bosham, two at Probus, and one each at Glasney, Crantock and St Teath. Only five seem not to have held a prebend at all, and of these Philip de Exeter was at

---

[86] Bronescombe himself had been chancellor of the diocese.
[87] He too outlived Bronescombe, dying in 1283: *Quivel*, p.341.
[88] The executors are listed on p.xxi, fn.76; see also *Pecham*, I p.202.

least archdeacon, while Robert de Polamford, like Hugh Splot, Roger de
Dartford and three other lesser members of the household,[89] held the living of
Lawhitton, which was in the bishop's gift, and Bartholomew de Lardario was
rector of Gerrans (also in the bishop's gift), and John de Blagdon was
commended to Ashprington and collated to Paignton; only Robert of Poitou
seems not to have held a benefice in the diocese or in one of the bishop's
peculiars. Of these thirty, moreover, twenty-five were described as MA.

From another point of view, of the fifty-four men who held, however
briefly, prebends in the cathedral during Bronescombe's episcopate, twenty-
nine acted for him in some way or other, whether once only or regularly; of the
others, five were dignitaries, four held their prebends only very briefly, and
five more were certainly non-resident for various reasons.[90] This leaves only
eleven who might have served the bishop directly but apparently did not. The
general impression given is that Bronescombe made some use of the canonries
of his cathedral, but that the rewards or incomes of his household officials were
more likely to be found from Crediton or Bosham, both collegiate houses of
which the prebends were in his gift.

Bronescombe made considerable use of the thirty named men when
appointing commissaries or proctors, but he did, of course, use others. He
seems to have maintained permanent proctors at the papal court, though it is
likely that they were not in his sole employment. Richard de Honiton was
probably there continuously between 1259 and 1266; Luke de Paignton was
there in 1259, perhaps on a permanent basis, for in 1264 he was honoured
with a papal provision to East Antony (**562**). Nicholas de Honiton seems to
have been there 1270–78, together with Richard de Carswell, 1273–78, and
Edmund de Warfield, 1274–78. Others who served the bishop at the Curia
were Robert de Albo Monasterio, Philip de Exeter, Alured son of Milo, Philip
de Cancellis, and John of Pontoise, who was concerned in various cases on
Bronescombe's behalf, as well as on his own business, from 1276 to 1278.
Some of these appointments were generally to look after the bishop's interests,
but others gave specific powers to confer benefices when they should fall
vacant at the Curia (**323**, for example), or to act as executor (**969–70**), or to
deal with Bronescombe's financial affairs (**856**). There were also at the papal
court at various times such intimate members of the household as William de
Capella, who had the privilege of being ordained subdeacon by the pope, and
Bartholomew de Lardario. These two, Richard de Carswell and Philip de
Exeter, along with Robert de Hallelond and Peter de Montagu, were also
appointed the bishop's proctors in his dealings with the Florentines and others
on financial matters.

Bronescombe also had proctors in England. At the Court of Arches, the
forum of Canterbury's metropolitan jurisdiction, were Richard Paz, 1274–76,
and Ralph de la Pole, 1275–78. Roger de Essex (**715**, in December 1268) and
Nicholas de Musele (**1149**)[91] were appointed to represent him in London, and
other appointments were made of William de Capella and Richard de
Kingston. More specifically, Gervase de Crediton was appointed the bishop's

---

89 Richard Paz, Robert de Paignton, R. Rufus.
90 For example, John de Clifford, the Queen's physician.
91 In the matter of the abbot and convent of Ford in February 1276.

proctor to the synod held at London in July 1278, and Andrew de Kilkenny to that at Easter, 1280 (**1289**; **1407**), which pressure of work and failing health prevented Bronescombe from attending. John de Bradley and John Wiger were his proctors to the parliament at St Albans in 1264, from which he pleaded ill health (**573**). General proctorships were issued to Bartholomew de Lardario, William de Essex, Ralph de la Pole and, of course, William de Capella. It is to be remarked that seven of the twelve appointed for England were of the household, but only four of the twelve at the papal court; this suggests the employment of professional lawyers at the Curia.

Similarly, in the appointment of commissaries within the diocese or in the bishop's peculiars, men of the household were frequently, but not exclusively, used. Powers of ordinary were granted – the term vicar-general seems not yet in use – early in the episcopate, when the bishop was away from his diocese, to Robert de Tyfford, Edward de la Knolle, Walter de Pembroke, William de Stanwey and Ralph de Hengham (**46**). Powers of ordinary were also granted to John de Esse (**181**) and Roger de Dartford (**954–55**). In 1274 the bishop wrote from France, after the General Council of Lyons II, to his official and chancellor, telling them that 'because of an order from our superiors we are unable to return, according to our will, to our own affairs', but granting them power to institute (**971**). Robert Everard and Roger de Thoriz often acted for the bishop, while Gervase de Crediton was made commissary-general in 1276 (**1188**), and Thomas de Buckland in 1277 (**1238**). Henry de Bollegh, Thomas de Buckland and John of Pontoise, together with the archdeacon of Cornwall (John de Esse) and his official (John de Bradley), and the dean, precentor and chancellor of the cathedral were all given powers to deal with the conflicts between Bronescombe and the earl of Cornwall, as also was William de Capella (**990**; **1013**; **1024**; **1067**; **1086**). When Bronescombe was papal judge-delegate in the case of Robert fitzWilliam of Bingham and Sybil Oliver, he made Ralph de Merlawe and Richard Paz his commissaries, reserving final judgment to himself (**1123**). In 1277 Richard de Braundsworthy, a canon of the cathedral, and the prior of Clive were made the bishop's commissaries in settling the dispute between the archdeacon of Cornwall and Bodmin Priory (**1237**). In 1278 Henry de Kilkenny, himself a canon of both Exeter and Chichester, was appointed, with the dean of Chichester, to investigate the matter of the sequestered tithes of the collegiate church of Bosham, a peculiar of Exeter lying in the diocese of Chichester (**1279**).

Of the lesser, or less known, members of the household we know of two other chaplains, called Robert and William, who occur as witnesses from time to time; there was another steward, R. Rogers, who received the accounts of John de Esse (**516**); there are two junior chamberlains, Nicholas and William, who are mentioned respectively as being collated to Morchard Bishop and dispensed for bastardy (**35**; **124**).

Some individual servants are mentioned. Bishop Blund had had a baker called Thomas (**83**), and it can be assumed that Bronescombe had a baker too; there was a door-keeper called Robert (**58**); we know of an unnamed forester at Penryn (**1293**); the bailiff of Bronescombe's deer-park at Paignton was called Durandus (**1156**). Another Durandus is described as *serviens* (**454**), as was a certain Hamund to whom the bishop granted some land at Bishop's Tawton (**404**). It is not clear whether these two were servants or tenants by

serjeanty; the latter seems more likely for Durandus, since he is listed as a witness among the household knights.

A last and separate group was that of the household knights. These seem to have consisted of Sir Roger le Arceveske, Sir Ralph de Arundel, Sir Henry de Champernowne, Sir Matthew de Egloshayle, Sir John Wiger – the knight, not the clerk – Sir Alexander de Oxton, Sir John de Weston, and perhaps Sir John de Hydon. They accompanied the bishop partly for show and partly for protection, but in the register their function was chiefly to act as witnesses. And it is among the household, as witnesses and friends, that we are twice given a glimpse of the bishop's daily life. On 15 February 1261, while in London, the bishop admitted William de Capella to Lelant, to which he had been papally provided, 'before six o'clock one morning, in the bishop's chamber, in front of the hearth, in the presence of John Noble, MA, and John Wiger, MA' (289). And on 1 November 1271, while Bronescombe was at his manor of Chidham, 'before dinner, pausing on his way to the table' he received the homage of Sir William Aguilon in the presence of more than fifteen persons of the household (869).

5. DIOCESAN ADMINISTRATION

In February 1258 '*Magister* Walter, archdeacon of Surrey, was elected bishop of Exeter. Wonderful to relate, within a fortnight the election of the said Walter was accepted by the king and confirmed by the archbishop of Canterbury, and he was ordained priest and consecrated bishop, a series of events hitherto unheard of in so short a time'.[92] The register starts with a full, and canonical, description of his election(1–7; 9–12).[93] Then various forms are given, such as the form of inquisition into a church vacant *de facto or de iure*, and then a letter of institution (14 & 15; 18). The primary duty of a diocesan bishop was indeed the filling of benefices, especially those with cure of souls. So the bulk of even this register is taken up with admissions to benefices in their various forms: admissions and confirmations, inductions, inquisitions, institutions, presentations and resignations, and also collations, commendations, custodies, provisions, and rejections – in all, something over eight hundred.

Of the ninety-odd collations, apart from those to the various collegiate establishments, such as the cathedral, Crantock, Crediton, Glasney, Probus and Bosham, about twenty rectories and eight vicarages appear to have been in the bishop's gift. In the case of many of the others, the right of presentation had lapsed, 'in accordance with the decrees of the Council'[94] to the diocesan through the patron's negligence. Sometimes it is not clear whether or not this was the case; in any event, the lapse was usually held to be without prejudice

[92] J. Le Neve, *Fasti Ecclesie Anglicane*, ed. T.D. Hardy (Oxford, 1854), I p.370, n.58, citing *Flores Historiarum*, ed. H.R. Luard (Rolls Series, London, 1890) III, p.248. *Extra* 1.14.9 shows Innocent III permitting the election to the episcopate of a subdeacon.
[93] His profession of obedience to Archbishop Boniface is recorded: *Canterbury Professions*, ed. M. Richter (C & Y vol.67, 1973), p.75, no.198. See also *C.P.R.* 1247–58, p.618, for the release of the temporalities.
[94] Lateran III, c.8; Lateran IV, c.29.

to the future rights of the patron. Other collations took place because the patron had not presented a suitable person or the presentation itself was 'inept', as at Shebbear or Bampton (**434; 1043**), or while the parish was subject to sequestration, as at Dean Prior (**389**), or because there was no valid patron, as at Meavy when Plympton Priory lacked a prior (**507**). Further causes for collation were that the patron was disabled by reason of a conspiracy he had joined against the bishop and clergy, as at St Michael Penkevil (**1010**), or even, as at Talland, that the delay was in some way deliberate, for there the collation was eventually made 'at the special and express wish of the prior and convent of Launceston' (**543**). The bishop had considerable scope for intervention, since all presentations were made to him and subject to his approval.

Commendations were at this period the subject of some concern within the Church; the legate Ottobuono tried to restrict them in 1268,[95] and at the Second Council of Lyons in 1274 it was decreed[96] that not more than one parish at once might be held *in commendam* by one man, and that only for six months at a time. Indeed, Geoffrey de Poolhampton was commended to Buckerell in 1279 specifically 'according to the Gregorian constitution published at the most recent Council of Lyons' (**1357**). In Bronescombe's register there are seventeen cases of a church being held *in commendam*. At Bere Ferrers, Gerrans and Rockbeare it seems that a man was commended for a probationary period until he took Holy Orders or otherwise fitted himself for the cure of souls: Reginald de Ferrars was commended for three months and instituted not more than seven months later (**71 & 84**); Bartholomew de Lardario was commended for fourteen months and instituted in the fifteenth (**105 & 271**); Walter de Farringdon was commended for a year and instituted at the end of it (**408 & 458**). At Lawhitton, where the church was consolidated in 1261 and the rector assigned the vicarage 'to be possessed by perpetual right of commendation' (**319**), and at St Columb Major, where Roger de Dartford was admitted 'under a perpetual right of commendation' (**632**), the use of a commendation was presumably just an administrative convenience; for Roger it may have been in effect his salary as Bronescombe's steward – he was still the incumbent in 1280, but it may be that his title had been challenged, since the original admission was inspected, and repeated because of the poor state of the seal (**1392**). At Ashprington John de Blagdon was commended, presumably for a year, since, after the this lapse of time, he was commended again (**230 & 307**); the next recorded admission – of another man – was made six years later (**658**). At most of the commended churches there is merely the notice of the commendation and then, from two to seven years later, the record of someone else's institution, and sometimes there is not even that. There is one commendation that seems a little out of the ordinary; William de Capella was commended to St Allen in 1261, and this was repeated 'in special form' in 1272 (**428 & 909**). Apart from the case of Geoffrey de Poolhampton, there is only one other commendation made after Bronescombe had returned from the Council; Hugh Splot, a member of the household and a deacon, was commended to Ugborough on the same day in 1274 that he was admitted to

[95] *Councils and Synods* ii, pp.777–79.
[96] Lyons II, c.14.

Exminster (**994–95**), and there is no notice of any later admission under Bronescombe to Ugborough.

Custodies seem to have been ordered more often for a specific purpose. They too were used for limited periods while a man fitted himself for a benefice by proceeding to higher orders or by obtaining a dispensation for illegitimate birth (**215**; **715**; **131**; **237**; **69**; **468**; **1119**; **202**; **87**), or because the cure of souls must not be neglected while a presentee was being examined by the bishop of the diocese from which he came as to his fitness and suitability (**1147**; cf. **1163**). At St Clether the parish needed a curate while its rector was attempting the monastic life (**227** & **283**), and at Redruth and Thorverton the incumbent was senile or chronically ill (**146**; **526**). When a dispute existed concerning a benefice, it might be wiser to have only a temporary incumbent; at Paul and Woolfardisworthy it was over the advowson (**88**; **529**), while, in the bishop's conflict with Tavistock Abbey in 1265, seven parishes and a chapel, as well as various pensions and tithes, were put in the charge of the rector of Monk Okehampton (**595**).[97] Most of the rest of the custodies are without explanation, and at the bishop's pleasure. There are, however, two interesting instances: Richard de Lyme was given charge of the hospital of the Holy Ghost at Totnes, with the task of supervising its building (**868**); at Georgeham, Stephen Haym was refused institution, although canonically presented, and simply given custody because the bishop desired to reward him more richly (**916**).

Rejecting the presentation of Stephen Haym was unusual, but there are other, more conventional cases of rejection. At Rackenford, Michael de la Stone was rejected 'because he was lacking in years and learning', but he was granted a pension from the church (**662**), while at Bampton the presentee was 'not at all suitable' (**1043**). At Kilkhampton, Bronescombe tried to keep out Bogo de Clare, son of the earl of Gloucester, and perhaps the most notorious pluralist in England, despite his various dispensations. The case was, however, appealed to the Court of Arches, and in May 1280 Bogo was receiving a pension of ten marks from the parish (**1124–25**).[98] At Roche the bishop refused to admit Clement de Liskeard, canonically presented and a subdeacon, without giving any reason but, going by the terms on which Clement, who had appealed to Canterbury, was admitted a few months later, it seems likely that Bronescombe had been in doubt about the sufficiency of the one patron by herself (**1329** & **1335**).

In spite of complaints, contemporary and subsequent, about the growing frequency of papal provisions, there are very few in the register. At Thorncombe, on the admission of a vicar in 1260, there was a clause maintaining the papal right to provide (**239**). William de Capella, MA, was admitted to Lelant 'in accordance with the command of the cardinal priest of St Laurence in Lucina and with papal confirmation' (**289**). One G. Wale, MA, papal notary, was provided to Berry Narbor (**387**). (Peter de Vienne, nephew of the archbishop of Tarentaise, was provided with a pension of ten pounds a year at the instance of the archbishop of Canterbury (**444**).) From

---

[97] This is the custody of a sequestration.
[98] *The Rolls and Register of Bishop Oliver Sutton*, ed. R.M.T. Hill, vol. II (Lincoln Record Society, 1950), p.3.

the papal records we know that Bronescombe was asked to provide Walter de
Stokebrock, a poor priest of the diocese, to some benefice with the duty of
residence within the gift of Tywardreath Priory.[99] Luke de Paignton, MA, or
alternatively Walter Curdet, MA, was provided to Antony (**562**). Philip de
Exeter, MA, was provided to Stockleigh Pomeroy 'by the authority of both
legate and bishop' (**631**); there was a legatine provision to Berry Narbor of
Ottobuono de Fieschi, who was presumably a nephew or cousin of the papal
legate (**661**).[100] It is clear from the names of the incumbents that the vast
majority of parishes, in Cornwall and in Devon, were staffed with local men.

Moving to the ordinary admissions to benefices in the diocese of Exeter, in
what orders were the men who were instituted? what sort of income did most
of them enjoy? and what disciplinary measures did the bishop find necessary?

Of the men admitted to vicarages by Bronescombe's collation, all but two
are described as *presbiter* or *capellanus*.[101] The two exceptions are at Breage and
St Merryn, where MA is the only description given. Seventeen of those
collated to rectories were priests, five deacons and fourteen subdeacons;
twenty are termed simply MA, six *clerici*, two *domini*. In this register, to call a
man simply *clericus* does not necessarily mean that he was only in minor
orders; William de Lapford is called clerk and deacon, Clement de Liskeard
clerk and subdeacon (**421**; **1329**), to quote a couple of examples. Taking all
the admissions, apart from those to the cathedral and the collegiate houses, we
find that of the rectors 29% were certainly priests, 35% deacons or
subdeacons, while some 36% are recorded as *clerici*, *magistri*, or *domini*; of the
vicars 88% were certainly priests, 3.5% deacons or subdeacons, and the
orders of 8.5% were unspecified. Of course, like *clericus*, the terms *magister* or
dominus do not preclude Holy Orders. William de Stanway, the dean of Exeter
cathedral, must surely have been a priest, but he is only referred to as MA;
William de St Martin, who was certainly a priest, is on one occasion called
simply *dominus* (**554** & **654**, then **570**). (It may be significant that while the
vicars in Cornwall seem of similar standing to the Devon vicars, a
considerably smaller proportion of the rectors in Cornwall are described as
being in priest's orders or, indeed, as MA or *dominus*.)

The majority then, even of the rectors, who did not necessarily have the
cure of souls, were at least in the subdiaconate; of the four vicars who were
stated not to be priests, three were definitely deacons. They were required by
canon law[102] to proceed to the priesthood within a year of their admission, but
the lack of ordination lists and the casual use of titles makes it impossible to
guess how far this was observed. Only nine men are recorded as having
advanced their orders while holding a benefice, and these promotions were
noted solely when someone changed his living.

Yet Bronescombe was obviously not indifferent to the orders of his clergy.
Some five weeks after his consecration, he sent letters to the four archdeacons

[99] *C.P.L.* 15 July 1264, p.418; 'if his conduct is good'.
[100] No mention is made of papal confirmation.
[101] Since the latter term is generally agreed to mean, in the England of this period, a
man in priest's orders, and there is nothing in the register to challenge this, I shall
hereafter use only the term 'priest'.
[102] Lateran III, c.3.

ordering that 'all rectors and vicars who were not priests should present themselves in order to receive Holy Orders as the cure of souls demands' (23), and likewise any others who might in any way have the cure of souls. A general summons of this kind was issued on four further occasions, but all these were in the two years after his return from the Council of Lyons. The implication seems to be that he was content with traditional English practice.[103]

There are thirty-six occasions when the register records an ordination, but only fifteen of these mention what orders were conferred; of these fifteen, twelve name the ordinands, but some of them only mention one man, others two or three, while the largest number given is nine. Other ordinations are simply said to have taken place, sometimes with the additional information that they were celebrated solemnly or privately or in the bishop's chapel. Twice it is mentioned that the ordination list was kept by the official (1395 & 1397), but this list has not survived. Ordinations took place with fair regularity; in only four of the twenty-two years of the episcopate is none recorded, and there were three in each of 1264, 1265, 1268 and 1270, and five in 1261. Nearly all were at one or other of the canonically appointed times, the Ember Saturdays, Holy Saturday and the Saturday before Passion Sunday, but one was on Corpus Christi, one on Easter Day, and one on the Second Sunday in Lent, the day after Ember Saturday. If the canon concerning the ordination of those admitted to benefices was observed, it seems likely that Bronescombe, or possibly a suffragan (1038),[104] held other ordinations. There are no references to any confirmations, but this sacrament was not viewed with any great solemnity in the thirteenth century, so it could well have passed unremarked, as in other registers of the period.

Letters dimissory, licence to be ordained by some other bishop, are not often recorded. The first was in June 1258, permitting Philip fitzUrse, clerk, to receive acolyte's or subdeacon's orders anywhere in the province of Canterbury (42); it appears to be entered to show the due form. In July 1274, while Bronescombe was still overseas, John of Pontoise was licensed to receive Holy Orders anywhere and, in the following February, to receive priest's orders anywhere (984 & 1054); it was probably his closeness to the bishop and his occasional service to the king that explain the inclusion of these entries. The other seven letters – one man received them twice – were all issued in the autumn of 1279 or the spring of 1280, in the last year of Bronescombe's life. It had probably not been normal policy to enter them in the register, for there must have been many more in view of the bishop's absences abroad. Conversely, there were two occasions when the register records another bishop

---

[103] Perhaps similarly, there is no reference to any diocesan synod, by this time required. (Bishop Briwere seems to have issued synodal statutes for the diocese – *Councils and Synods* i, pp.227–37.) In 1278 an inquiry was to be held in all the archdeaconries into the state of the clergy (1248–50) and it is possible that a synod was held and statutes issued. Bishop Quivel issued statutes in April 1287 – *Councils and Synods* ii, pp.982–1059 – as well as his *Summula*: see *Councils and Synods*, ii pp.1059–77.
[104] The bishop of Leighlin was appointed his suffragan when Bronescombe was going to be away in London during the winter 1274–75. This is the only reference to Bronescombe using a suffragan.

being asked to examine the suitability of a clerk presented to a benefice in the diocese of Exeter (**1163 & 1171; 1372**).

Bronescombe seems to have been careful to verify the dispensations of the clergy who came to him for admission, particularly those for illegitimate birth. This must be linked with the papal mandate to him of January 1268[105] which censured clergy who obtained a dispensation for holding a plurality of benefices without revealing that they had already had to be dispensed from the defect of bastardy, and laid down that such dispensations were invalid. There are twenty-seven dispensations for bastardy in the register,[106] four to sons of priests, seven to sons of deacons or subdeacons, and two to sons of acolytes.[107] One of the dispensations for bastardy was issued to a woman, a nun on her election as prioress of Polsloe (**668**). Seven have a warning that any similar incontinence on the part of the recipient will invalidate the dispensation and lead to deprivation of the benefice.[108] The first such dispensation entered gives the full form. Papal records show that there were others which were not entered in the register. The most interesting case in the register is that of the dispensation issued to the brothers Alan and Walter de Lostwithiel for bastardy and unlicensed ordination, which Bronescombe refused to accept; he sent them back to the papal court where the plenitude of power might be able to make up for the unworthiness of their lives (**966**).[109] There is only one dispensation for non-residence, that licensing William de Haccombe to study canon law in Paris for three years (**383**), but presumably there were others, as more than a quarter of the clerks of any order mentioned in the register were MA, and some will surely have wanted to proceed to a doctorate. There are only three dispensations for plurality, but again the papal records reveal the register to be defective in this respect.[110] Four men received dispensations for having been ordained outside the diocese without licence; almost certainly there were more cases, because other registers show this to have been a common lapse.

A clear example of Bronescombe's care for the spiritual welfare of his flock is the settlement he made for the inhabitants of hamlets on Dartmoor in the parish of Lydford, for whom it was eight miles in fair weather and fifteen in foul to their parish church. Learning that they were too few and poor to support an oratory, he allowed them normally to receive all the sacraments at Widdecombe church, which was considerably nearer. Once a year, however, they were to hear High Mass at Lydford, to which parish they still belonged; the tithes and other offerings were to be distributed between the incumbents of the two parishes (**292**).

---

[105] *C.P.L.* 6 January 1268, p.434.

[106] Eleven of these were issued specifically by papal, three by legatine authority.

[107] It seems possible that there is a trace here that a celibate clergy was not yet completely established in remote Cornwall, for three of the sons of priests, six of the sons of deacons or subdeacons and one son of an acolyte bear Cornish names.

[108] See Lateran IV, c.14.

[109] No more is heard of them.

[110] For example, the dispensation to Stephen Haym – *C.P.L.* 8 February 1259, p.363, or to John of Pontoise, confirming a previous dispensation – *C.P.L.* 24 November 1276, p.451.

The settlement at Lydford shows that Bronescombe, very properly, was concerned with the material needs as well as the spiritual capabilities of his clergy. How far he ensured a decent living for all incumbents it is difficult to tell; the income from most parishes was naturally related to their geographical situation and to the vagaries of the weather. The nearest thing we have to a general guide to the wealth of the churches is the Taxation of Pope Nicholas IV, made in 1291, which lists the sum for which each parish could be farmed, so giving comparative rather than absolute values. The estimates it gives, where directly comparable figures can be found, seem to vary between 12.5% and 75% of the real value, but the majority come close to 60% as regards the vicarages. The total values in the Taxation of Pope Nicholas for the four archdeaconries are: Barnstaple £691 12s 10d; Cornwall £1043 9s 8d; Exeter £885 12s 10d; Totnes £991 17s 3d. Cornwall was the biggest of the archdeaconries, and the figures suggest that the average Cornish incumbent was only about three-quarters as well off as his Devonian equivalent.[111]

The Council of Oxford[112] had laid down that a vicar, or at least a chaplain with reasonable security of tenure, must be installed where the rector was non-resident, and that those men who actually had the cure of souls should receive a living wage; five marks (£3 6s 8d) a year, or the equivalent, was put forward as the minimum, but it is clear that this standard could not always be reached. For example, Fowey and the Cornish Poughill are valued in the Taxation at 'nothing, because of poverty', and the farmable value of Buckland Monachorum was put at only 3s 4d. Including the consolidations made early in the episcopate, there were, at the least, 140 vicarages in the diocese of Exeter in Bronescombe's time. For 100 of these there is a statement or settlement of the vicar's portion of the revenues; a few other entries simply say that the vicar has been, or must be, provided with a competent stipend.

Some of these taxations or apportionments are given in money terms, at least in part; they range from 12 marks (£8) and all the altarage at Torrington (**220**), to 4 marks (£2 13s 4d) and a corrody at Bodmin and Tywardreath (**377** & **746**; **376**), to 1 mark (13s 4d) from the greater tithes, together with the altarage, 8 acres of glebeland, the fish tithes, and a house at Maker (**756**). To illustrate a range of other taxations: at Oakford the vicar was to receive 40s, all the altarage, the glebeland, the *assisum redditum*, a house, garden and two acres; at Staverton the vicar was assigned land worth 25s, the glebeland, the altarage, mortuary dues, and fruit, hay and mill tithes; at Lanreath he had 1 mark, 'because of the vicar's ill-health', and the altarage (**362**; **671**; **755**). Of the vicarages of which the income is given purely in kind, nearly all have the altarage,[113] that is, the offerings customarily paid to their curate by the people through the year, and usually the glebeland (or *sanctuarium*) and various lesser tithes, with, on occasion, a portion of the greater, or wheat, tithe. Other sources of revenue mentioned include the relic oblations at Perranzabuloe and

---

[111] Tithes of fish are specifically mentioned in 12 parishes in the diocese, of which 10 are in Cornwall; this seems the only overt economic distinction linked with geography.
[112] Council of Oxford, 1222, c.21 – *Councils and Synods* i, p.112 – echoing Lateran IV, c.32.
[113] Incidentally, always spelled 'altalagium' instead of the more usual 'altaragium'; could this be an early example of the Bristol dialect?

at Totnes 'the customary offerings made at confession, and one penny from
the offering at Mass on any day on which the collection comes to a penny or
more. The vicar shall also have whatever may be left to him as parish priest in
the wills of the dead, without deduction except for the legacies due to the
mother church' (**738; 212**). At Bishop's Nympton an apportionment had been
made 'by authority of the see of Canterbury', perhaps because Michael de
Lodeford was a clerk for whom the archbishop wished to make special
provision (**552**).

Something like a quarter of all parishes in the diocese appear to have been
appropriated to a particular convent or prebend. This is a high proportion as
early as the thirteenth century, but there is no evidence that this was an abuse.
Bronescombe appropriated eighteen parishes, and for thirteen of them taxed
an adequate vicarage at once, or very soon afterwards; the other five all have
the clause 'saving a competent vicarage' or something similar. When William,
rector of St Martin's, Exeter, was admitted to the vicarage of Colyton, and
William de Frankhill, rector of Butterleigh, to that of Budleigh, they were not
only moving from rectories to vicarages, but almost certainly the vicarages of
appropriated churches at that (**1023; 1276**).[114] The usual reason given for
appropriation was the poverty of the impropriator, and the difficulties of
supplying the needs of travellers, as when Plympton Priory appropriated Dean
Prior (**400–01**); for similarly obvious reasons the dean and chapter were
granted certain parishes in order to maintain chaplains at various altars in the
cathedral, and for Bronescombe's obit (**841 & 1426; 1297**).

Thus parishes were staffed, most frequently by men in Holy Orders, and
provision was made that these men should not suffer undue poverty. Other
problems arose in the natural course of events. Rectories and vicarages were
consolidated or portions amalgamated when it was found that the revenues of
the parish could not support both. Sometimes this was explicit (**255; 811**), at
others it was presumably the reason why the rector was resident and having
the cure of souls (**74; 76**). There were disputes over tithes (e.g. **845**), or over
presentations (**529; 844**);[115] often the original problem is more obscure than
the settlement.

Then too there was an extraordinary spate of dedications carried out in
1259 and again in 1261, with a further group in Lent 1269. Twenty-seven of
the fifty-two named churches or chapels are in Cornwall, two in Somerset, and
the rest in Devon. Usually the notice is simply that the bishop dedicated a
church; at Combeinteignhead he dedicated two altars and a high altar, at
Kentisbeare three altars and a graveyard, and an altar at the chapel of Tregear
(**176; 204; 264**). Of the 1269 dedications the register unfortunately gives no
details, but records only that the bishop dedicated many churches throughout
Devon and Cornwall (**731**). The reason for all these dedications is obscure;
not many of them are likely to have been new churches, though there may
have been an occasional dedication to a new saint. The Council of

---

[114] Colyton was appropriated to the dean and chapter, Budleigh to Polsloe Priory.
What happened at St Merryn is more obscure; John de Withiel resigned the living and
was the following day collated to the vicarage (**93–94**) but a rector seems to have been
collated in 1281 – *Quivel*, p.354.
[115] On each occasion the patron seems to have presented two candidates.

Westminster in 1102, c.17, had prohibited the consecration of churches until all necessities had been provided for them and their priests; on the other hand, the papal legate, Ottobuono, at the Council of London in 1268, c.3, had emphatically told the bishops of the province to remedy such situations.[116] Some may perhaps have been built and never consecrated; in others, there may have been new altars; some may have been being restored after tempest, fire, or collapse had made them unfit for their purpose; re-dedication after bloodshed, or something equally sacrilegious, may explain some others.[117]

This brings us to the question of discipline. Visitations by the archdeacons and reports from the rural deans would be the usual means of making lapses by the clergy known to the bishop.[118] We only hear directly of the visitation of two parishes, Bridestowe (**127**),[119] and Dotton. Dotton was a vicarage appropriated to Dunkeswell Abbey, and the bishop found a scandalous state of affairs, with the church unused, the bells sent away, the font removed (**213**). Halwell was sequestered because the rector was non-resident, and St Cleer because the rector had not advanced his orders nor been resident (**112; 1375**); in 1278 Richard de Clifford was cited before the bishop for holding benefices in plurality without dispensation (**1251**). A certain Theobald, a clerk, was deprived of his prebend at Chulmleigh because he had married (**232**); William Hurward, priest, was solemnly warned about (sexual) incontinence (**801**). At Poundstock the rector, who was excommunicate for various offences and contumacies, was absolved when he swore to obey the mandates of the Church (**417**); in 1263 the rector of St Dominick paid caution money for his future good behaviour after he had intruded into Dittisham (**477**); in 1272 William de Haselbech was excommunicated after his proctor had intruded into Tawstock and 'had used and partly consumed the goods of Oliver de Tracy, MA, which he had found in the church and sanctuary, and because of other offences'(**929**).[120] At Hartland there was a worse case, for Oliver de Dinant's intrusion had been accompanied by bloodshed, and the church had to be reconsecrated (**894**). Somewhat surprisingly, this is one of only two cases recorded in the register of bloodshed in a church;[121] weapons might be flourished, as at Ottery St Mary (**1101**), but threats seem to have been sufficient for the parties on most occasions.

Relatively few examples are to be found of the checking of the laity, apart, that is, from the long series of problems with the earl of Cornwall and his men, to be dealt with below. Certain inhabitants of Exeter had clearly been celebrating rather too rowdily in 1259 (**82** – *scotales*). Rosemund de Heanton was absolved from some unspecified offence in 1262 (**454**). At Okehampton the parishioners confessed that they had tried to cheat their vicar of his

[116] *Councils and Synods* vol. I, AD 871–1204, ed. D. Whitelock, M. Brett & C.N.L. Brooke, ii, p.676; vol. II, ii, pp.750f.
[117] As with **894**, where we are told the church of Hartland was 'reconciled' after the spilling of blood.
[118] The archdeacons themselves might be checked for excessive procurations, as in December 1277 (**1242**).
[119] This entry evidences the existence of a visitation roll.
[120] Cf. *Select Cases from the Ecclesiastical Courts of the Province of Canterbury, c.1200–1301*, ed. N. Adams and C. Donahue (Selden Society, London, 1981), pp.232–36.
[121] The other was at St Allen – **1429**.

mortuary dues and other offerings (**654**) – not an uncommon offence. Henry de Tracy appears to have been guilty of intrusion (**891–92 & 894**), and there was bloodshed at Hartland; at Ottery St Mary certain minions of the devil made an armed assault on the rector to deprive the church of its fruits and its rights (**1101**); Agnes de Cruwys had committed an unspecified fault (**1126 & 1177**). Henry de Pomeroy was guilty of poaching in Bronescombe's deer-park at Paignton; this may be linked with the attack on Cargoll deer-park, for Henry was as much a Cornishman as a Devonian (**1156**).[122] There was a rather serious case of adultery (**1201 & 1239**).[123] More interesting, because tantalisingly elusive, is the offence of the mayor and burgesses of Exeter; whatever they had done, it had been enough to cause the exodus of part of the cathedral chapter. The citizens repented of their evil ways and sought the recall of the dispersed canons (**930**). But overall, the register is reticent about Bronescombe's problems with misconduct in the parishes; for the most part this was the concern of his archdeacons. It is also reticent about Bronesombe's duty as papally appointed *minister Crucis* in the city and diocese of Exeter (**1091**), responsible for arranging the affairs of those who were going on Crusade. Indeed, this is the only reference in the register to the Church's efforts to raise a Crusade, although we know that Bronescombe, like other bishops, had received a letter from the Pope in 1272, urging him to use all his influence to this end.[124]

6. RELIGIOUS HOUSES

There are more than eighty religious houses mentioned in the register, but some fifty are outwith the diocese. Of these latter, thirteen are mentioned only as patrons of priories or parishes within the diocese; four of these came from outside the kingdom, St Serge at Angers, the abbey of Bec, Mont St Michel, and the abbey of Ste Marie at St Pierre-sur-Dives. Two more foreign houses are mentioned: St Martin des Champs, Paris, was warned that, if it took no action, the bishop would provide a prior to Barnstaple (**1053**); Ste Marie le Val negotiated with Merton Priory an exchange of their dependent priories at Caen and Tregony (where Bronescombe was concerned as diocesan), a transaction which brought Tregony from the Benedictine to the Augustinian Rule (**1277**). The other frequent reason for the appearance of houses from outside the diocese is their receipt of *littera predicationis* – licence to preach, meaning to preach in order to raise money. Nine alien houses occur solely in this context – in one case there is a note added 'but let a preacher by no means be admitted' (**235**). Within the diocese, the dean and chapter received this privilege (**122**),[125] as later did Taunton Priory, to complete the building of its church (**1262**).

---

[122] The king appointed judges under a commission of oyer and terminer to investigate both cases – *C.P.R.*, 1272–81, p.120.

[123] See also O.F. Robinson, 'Canon law and marriage', *Juridical Review*, 1984, 22–40.

[124] *C.P.L.* 30 September 1272, p.444.

[125] It was for an indefinite term and presumably for the fabric fund, although there is no readable entry in the Fabric Rolls recording the occasion; v. *The Accounts of the Fabric*

Other matters concerning houses, and religious corporations, outside the diocese covered a wide range of matters. In 1261 there was a composition with Malmesbury Abbey concerning jurisdiction over Pilton Priory (**331**).[126] Kirkstead Abbey deposited a chirograph at Exeter concerning Coningsby church, where Bronescombe had been rector (**244**). Bronescombe and the Priory of the Holy Sepulchre, Warwick, came to an agreement about their adjoining properties in London (**290**).[127] Tandridge Priory was compensated for a pension it had been required to pay to one of Exeter's clergy (**857**). The warden of the Franciscan convent at Oxford was asked to account for the books and other goods left in his care by one of Bronescombe's clerks, who had since died (**1047**). Bronescombe arbitrated a dispute between the hospital of Jerusalem in England and the bishop of Worcester (Godfrey Giffard, formerly a canon of Exeter) over Down Ampney, which the hospital claimed had been appropriated to them by papal licence, while the bishop disputed the validity of their documents (**1226–27**).[128] A record was made of privileges issued by the pope to the Praemonstratensian Order, and of Archbishop Pecham to the University of Oxford (**1284; 1341**).[129] Roger de Thoriz, sometime dean of Exeter, left his fourteen books to the use of the Exeter Franciscans and Dominicans (**1442; F** in Appendix I). A few further entries concern the collegiate church of Bosham, which was sited in the diocese of Chichester, a peculiar of the bishops of Exeter since the eleventh century (**209**). It was visited by the bishop's commissaries in 1259 (**113**); there is a copy of a settlement, made between 1198 and 1215, between the bishops of Chichester and Exeter over the extent of their various jurisdictions (**336**); the abbot and convent of Westminster wrote to Bronescombe about services due for the manor of West Stoke near Bosham (**469**); the canons of Bosham were to present to a private chapel nearby (**931**); there was a dispute about tithes among four of the canons (**1279**). Another collegiate house, but within the diocese, about which there was concern, was Crediton (**352; 744; 926**), which had been the seat of the bishopric until 1050.

Within the diocese, most entries dealing with religious houses were matters of routine. They are predominantly about presentations to parishes, including a number of cases where the right of presentation had lapsed,[130] and consents to the taxation of vicarages. Various entries concern the institutions,

of Exeter Cathedral, 1279–1353, part I 1279–1326, ed. A.M. Erskine (D & C vol. 24, 1981).

[126] The abbey was to provide priors or administrators, while the bishop was to have the right, as ordinary, of visitation.

[127] . . . 'about the agreed division of land between them, and the quitclaim for the gable of the bishop's hall, and the ownership of a certain piece of land 17½ ells long between the corner of the hall and the post of the bishop's wardrobe'.

[128] In 1331 the bishop admitted to the parish at the presentation of the Prior of Clerkenwell and of Brother Leonard, *locum tenens* of the priory of St John of Jerusalem – *Calendar of the Register of Adam de Orleton, Bishop of Worcester 1327–33*, ed. R.M. Haines (Worcestershire Historical Society & Historical MSS Commission, 1979) p.64, no.134.

[129] Cf. *Councils and Synods* ii, pp.851–53.

[130] There was an invalid presentation by Torre Abbey (**434**), and a collation at the special request of Launceston Priory (**543**).

obediences and benedictions, and the resignations and deaths of priors and abbots. Nowhere is there given the full sequence of events which made a new head of a house; indeed, only one licence to elect is recorded. This was at Launceston, where the old prior had resigned, clearly on grounds of age and infirmity, and been granted a pension (**378**). The bishop quashed some uncanonical elections(**109**; **405**),[131] but twice at least he provided the house's chosen man (**282**; **451**). In general, the notice of confirmation of an election, the release of the spiritualities, the admission, the obedience and the benediction of a new abbot or prior seem to be given at random; the register was not systematic in this respect.

Other entries were less routine, but still uncontroversial. Apart from various dedications during the course of Bronescombe's spate of them,[132] there is a copy of the settlement between Plympton Priory and Canonsleigh Priory, Augustinian mother and daughter (**276**), copies of privileges granted by the earl of Cornwall to Launceston Priory (**240–42**), and a licence for a layman to be buried in the hospital of St Laurence, Crediton (**1274**).

Episcopal visitations were a regular part of the maintenance of due discipline in monastic houses as in the parishes; it is in the latter context that we are told there existed a visitation roll (**127**).[133] Bronescombe, however, is recorded in the register as having visited only nine of the twenty-nine abbeys and priories in his diocese; it seems quite likely that the register is defective in this respect – as with dispensations. Furthermore, all the visitations mentioned took place in the first five years of the episcopate, and all but one (**449**)[134] in the first three years; later notices of visitation are to the dean and chapter or to the diocese as a whole (**1128**; **1242**; **1255**).[135] Archbishop Boniface visited, through his clerks, seven religious houses in 1261 (**345–46**; **350**; **355–57**; **360**). At Polsloe Priory Bronescombe laid down certain statutes, but without putting them in writing; Plympton was visited in 1259, since corrections given earlier were then accepted, and again in 1260; at Bodmin Priory he made corrections, which were given in writing (**195**; **196 & 269**; **267**). These were normal relationships.

There were other occasions, but not very many, when Bronescombe was in definite dispute with religious houses; sometimes we have the story in detail, sometimes only flashes. There was trouble at Launceston with a prior who was alleged to be disobedient and grossly inefficient (**129–30**, **135**, **143**, **168**; cf. **378**). Plympton Priory was convicted of a number of intrusions, submitted, and was fined and absolved (**389**, **475**, **488**, **495–96**, **607**). A major conflict was that between the bishop and John Chubbe, abbot of

---

[131] On the second occasion the reasons were not given 'to spare peoples' feelings'!
[132] The Dominican convents at Truro (**142**) and Exeter (**186**); the conventual churches of St Mary, Totnes (**182**) and St Germans (**379**); the various altars at Newenham Abbey in 1270 and 1277 – G. Oliver, *Monasticon Dioecesis Exoniensis* (Exeter, 1846) p.357fn.
[133] At Bridestowe in 1259: 'sicut in rotulo visitationis plenius continetur'.
[134] This was at Pilton Priory, where it is noted he took twenty shillings procuration. The others visited, apart from the ones mentioned below, were St Nicholas' Priory, Exeter, (**125**), Launceston (**262**), Tywardreath (**263**), and St Germans (**268**).
[135] In 1275 there was another notice (**1110**) to the diocese at large – perhaps linked with the Council of Lyons?

Tavistock, whom ironically the bishop had provided by special grace after an uncanonical election (**451**). Chubbe had at least twice before been excommunicated, and absolved only on promising to mend his ways, and various churches depending on the abbey had been sequestered in 1265 (**595**). In 1269 he was deposed for disobedience, repeated contumacy, and mismanagement (**733**). He was alleged, among other enormities, to have seized a monk celebrating divine office, stripped him of his vestments, and to have held him prisoner for some considerable time, also to have smashed through the gates of the abbey, set fire to the cloister and taken by force the chest in which the abbey's archives were kept. From a different point of view, however, we are told that Bronescombe had done the monastery inestimable damage, that the abbot had been grossly plagued by the archdeacon and other ecclesiastical officials, and that Bronescombe acted summarily and without consideration of the evidence.[136] The king took the abbey into his custody after the deposition of its abbot.[137]

In 1272 the simple fact was recorded that the monks of Barnstaple Priory sought absolution and, after swearing to abide by the bishop's settlement, were absolved; the next entry about the Priory was three years later when, because of the failure of St Martin des Champs to present a prior, the bishop was threatening to provide one himself (**893; 1053**). Similarly, in 1274, the prior of Bodmin was to perform a penance, but there is nothing about the circumstances; there was a further dispute between the Priory and the archdeacon of Cornwall over tithes and interference in 1277, and the bishop appointed commissioners to settle the matter (**979; 1237**), but the details are unknown. At Ford, there was rather an obscure altercation, which seems to have had its origins in a dispute over the presentation to the parish of Tawstock;[138] this led to the abbot of Ford, acting under a papal commission, excommunicating Bronescombe. Trouble dragged on from 1275 to 1277 with mutual excommunications, intervention by all the other Cistercian abbots, a settlement brought about by the king, ending with the submission of the abbey, the payment of a large fine (which was mostly remitted under the settlement) and absolution (**1089, 1129, 1175–77, 1198, 1206–07, 1224–25**). In 1279 Buckland Abbey was founded by the Lady Amice, Countess of Devon, with monks from Quarr Abbey, but without a licence from Bronescombe; only intervention by the archbishop of Canterbury[139] and by the queen on their behalf brought about the absolution and acceptance of the new monastery (**1378 & 1409 & 1428**).

---

[136] *Cal.Inq.Misc.* I, p.129, no.385; *C.C.R.* 1268–72, p.101.
[137] *C.P.R.* 1266–72, pp.398f.
[138] See O.F. Robinson, 'Canon law in theory and in practice: insights from a thirteenth century diocese', *22 Index* 1994, 473–80.
[139] *Registrum Epistolarum fratris Johannis Peckham, archiepiscopi Cantuariensis*, ed. C.T. Martin (Rolls Series, 1882), I, p.44.

7. THE DEAN AND CHAPTER

The cathedral chapter was a body of considerable importance in the diocese, if only because its assent was necessary for the ratification of many of the bishop's actions, such as appropriations (e.g., **353** or **393** or **809–10**), or certain grants (e.g., **541**). Again, for example, it assented to and confirmed the compositions, mentioned above, with Warwick Priory and Malmesbury Abbey, two of the attempts at reorganizing the collegiate church of Crediton (**352; 926**), and also the foundation charter of Glasney, as well as the relevant appropriations.[140] The dean acted as the bishop's commissary in quite a number of cases; he was probably often the natural choice. We find him filling vacant benefices, installing canons, and generally acting for the bishop (**46; 475; 510; 679; 829; 954–55; 971**); in particular, the dean was for some time engaged in the clearing up of the outrages committed in Cornwall against the Church by Richard de Seyton and others (**1012–13; 1044–45; 1429**).

The chapter was also one of the greatest patrons in the diocese, and a high proportion of the entries in the register which concern it are records of presentations to livings, some by the dean alone, along with a number of taxations of vicarages. Indeed, on one occasion in 1270 the dean and chapter appeared before Bronescombe and swore to fill the vicarages of the parishes impropriated to them, within a month of any vacancy, with 'suitable persons who may be instituted without any canonical difficulty' (**819**).[141] Three appropriations to the dean and chapter are recorded as being made by Bronescombe: of Upottery, where Bronescombe himself had been patron, which was to support three chaplains praying for the souls of Bishops Briwere and Blund, of himself, of Sir Thomas de Hertford and of all the faithful departed (**841**); of St Breward, for the diocesan feast of St Gabriel on the first Monday in September, and also for the bishop's own soul, those of his two immediate predecessors, of his successors, and of his parents (**1297**):[142] and of Buckerell (again in his own patronage) just two days before his death, to pray for his soul in his new chapel of St Gabriel where he was to be buried (**1426**).

The chapter was visited from time to time. Bronescombe was bound to visit it at the start of his episcopate, but there is no record of this; Archbishop Boniface of Savoy visited it in 1261, immediately after visiting the bishop himself (**343–44**). In fact the first notice of visitation preserved in the register dates from 1275. The bishop issued, through the prior of St Nicholas', Exeter, and the precentor of Crediton, a notice of visitation to the city and diocese, with a particular warning to the dean and chapter to whom he had issued statutes in 1268 (**732**) 'which, so far, they have taken so little care to observe that we forbear to mention their shame' (**1110**). Just over a month later he issued a notice of visitation directly to the dean and chapter (**1128**). This

---

[140] **G** of 1267 in Appendix I.

[141] This may have been connected with the statutes for the chapter which Bronescombe had issued in 1268.

[142] This appropriation ends with the requirement that each dean and canon, as he was so made, should swear to observe this along with all the other ancient and approved customs of the church of Exeter.

presumably led to the issue of a second set of statutes.[143] These were not very different from the earlier ones which had laid down that there should be twenty-four canons and twenty-four vicars choral. Divine office was to be said regularly, and those canons in residence were to attend on pain of forfeiting their day's rations; the dean was to reside, under the same pain; all canons were to be in Holy Orders as laid down by the Council of Lyons; canons and junior clergy were to show respect for their seniors; obits were to be celebrated with due form; the canons were to meet in chapter over any important business; chapter property was not to be alienated or dispersed; in accordance with the Council of Lyons two competent clerks were to be appointed, with two subordinates, to maintain the altars and other furnishings of the cathedral; sowers of discord were to be expelled from the chapter; no canon, vicar or other member of the cathedral body was to appear in the choir in secular dress; the statutes were to be strictly observed under penalty. These statutes were nowhere near as full as the *Ordinale Exoniense*[144] which Bishop Grandisson published fifty years later, nor indeed does he seem to have owed much to them; they do, however, make fairly clear the day to day routine expected of the cathedral body, and they provided a standard by which to check on the actual state of affairs when the bishop visited, as we know he did again in 1278 (**1255**).

A number of miscellaneous matters are of interest. In 1270 a formal settlement was made between the dean and chapter and the archdeacon of Exeter as to the extent of their respective jurisdictions. It was agreed that the dean was to have authority over the cathedral, the church of Heavitree and all the chapter's appropriated churches and manors outside the city and its suburbs, where such authority was customary, while the archdeacon was to have jurisdiction over the city and suburbs, but from the proceeds of this he was to keep a one-pound candle burning in the choir at Mattins and before the high altar at High Mass (**818**). Then, although the procedure is not given in the statutes, there are entries on the election of a new dean in 1274. First the chapter petitioned, through two of the canons, for a licence to elect, which Bronescombe granted (**983**); a month later he wrote to the chapter that the election had lapsed to him through their delay, and inhibited them from proceeding further (**987**); after a further month he collated John Noble as dean (**996**). In 1276 the bishop confirmed the dean and chapter's appointment, with the consent of the precentor, of a succentor and headmaster of the choir school (**1154**). The dean was given notice of the citation of the bishop and representatives of the clergy to Convocation, to be held in London early in 1278 (**1241**). And stitched in at the end of the register[145] is an instrument by which Roger de Thoriz, then archdeacon of Exeter, left the ownership of his library of some fourteen volumes, all theological, to the dean and chapter, although their use was to be for the Franciscan and Dominican houses in Exeter.

[143] Appendix II. Both sets of statutes are preserved in the Dean and Chapter archives – MSS 2101 and 2106.
[144] *Ordinale Exon.* vols. I–III, ed. J.N. Dalton, Henry Bradshaw Society (London, 1909 & 1926), vol. IV, ed. G.H. Doble (London, 1940).
[145] **F** in Appendix I.

The chapter clearly provided a pool of men useful to the bishop, for all his archdeacons were canons of the cathedral, and there is no hint that he was not on anything but good terms with the dean. What does not emerge from the register, apart from the reference to the shameful failure of the chapter to observe their statutes, is a hint of the trouble that was to erupt in the next episcopate. Although – or perhaps because – they had both been members of the chapter together, the next bishop. Peter Quivel, and the next dean, John Pycot, did not recognize each other;[146] moreover, in 1283 the precentor was murdered in the cathedral yard, and there were rumours concerning the complicity of the dean.[147] There had been the scandal of Bishop Blund's deathbed at the start of Bronescombe's episcopate; he may have been strong enough to hold things in order, but not sympathetic enough to prevent factions forming.

8. SECULAR AFFAIRS

Bronescombe, like every other mediaeval bishop, was a secular as well as spiritual lord, with considerable lay responsibilities, and spiritual duties that brought him into close contact with the secular world. Because the functions were so intertwined, the register gives us considerable information on this aspect of his administration. For instance, Bronescombe confirmed the charters of others, or preserved them by having them copied into the register.[148] On the other hand, we learn almost nothing of his ordinary jurisdiction over, for example, wills.[149]

As soon as he had been consecrated, Bronescombe found himself faced with the problem of restoring his diocese to solvency; so bad were its affairs that the pope granted him a faculty to retain for one year the fruits of all the benefices he had held on his promotion in order to help pay off his predecessor's debts.[150] He also incurred numerous debts with various Italian merchants, chiefly Florentine,[151] both in London and through his proctors in France and Italy. In the register itself it is recorded that he borrowed at least 946 marks from the Florentines, and not only at the start of his episcopate, mostly through proctors who were also appointed to the papal Curia. These merchants seem to have been true bankers, providing letters of credit (**324– 25**). In addition, Bronescombe borrowed money from various individuals (**37; 67; 249**). It seems likely that Bronescombe managed to clear his (fairly rich)

---

[146] *Quivel*, p.367f.

[147] *Quivel*, pp.438–50.

[148] For example, the charter (**243**) of Earl Richard, enfranchising the burgesses of Launceston; the priory seems to have been the lord of the old Launceston (**240–42**), so these probably refer to Dunheved, the new Launceston.

[149] Though we do find him dealing with that of Thomas Pincerna, former archdeacon of Totnes (**531**).

[150] *C.P.L.* 4 February 1259, p.363.

[151] Their names include: Agolanti, Baudini, Ricc(h)obaldi, Buonacursi, Rodolphi, Rinaldi, Rambertini, Gherardini, Plebanelli (or Pinvarelli), Uberti and Scoldi. A certain Spina Philippi from Pistoia is the only Italian named who is specifically not from Florence.

diocese of debt, for he left a considerable sum at his death,[152] and we only hear of one Italian loan in the next episcopate.[153]

The expenses a bishop had to bear might indeed exceed his income. He must grant pensions *de camera sua* to worthy clerks of his own or to others recommended to him. There were charities and religious foundations, in particular, his own cathedral,[154] to which a bishop was expected to contribute. There was the cost of maintaining a large household, with its numbers of knights and servants as well as clerks; further, the bishop had a palace in Exeter and a house in London, which must have been sources of expenditure. There were legal expenses at Canterbury and the Curia, and, in Bronescombe's case, arising from the series of disputes with the earls of Cornwall, to which we shall return. And there were, of course, taxes, both clerical and secular. We hear quite often in the royal records of secular demands on him, for example, for his knight service.[155] Bronescombe was required to come to the pope's aid in paying the debts incurred through the Sicilian business,[156] but there is only one reference in the register to direct royal taxes, when a clerical tenth was raised in 1264 to repel a threatened French invasion after the battle of Lewes (**563**).[157]

To provide for all these needs Bronescombe received certain payments both as secular and as spiritual lord, with often no very clear distinction, as with the fines he received for offences condemned in the ecclesiastical courts. We hear too of freewill offerings (**415-16; 426**). He was entitled to a procuration for himself and his household when he visited a religious house. For his support, he held a number of manors; the 1308 rent roll of the diocese of Exeter recorded twelve in Devon and seven or eight in Cornwall.[158] Moreover, he had three manors which had been granted (to Bishop Briwere) along with the collegiate church of Bosham, at Horsley (Surrey), Chidham (Sussex), and Faringdon (Hampshire) (**209**). He was granted various lands, often with the advowson, at Woodcroft, Melhuish Barton, Clyst William, Manaccan (**A**; **D**; **E**; **H**; **I**; **J**; **K**; **L**; **M**; **N**; **188**; **1159**), and also at 'Wolaumpton' (Woolavington?), where his rights as lord and those of his successors were maintained in a royal charter.[159] He seems also to have been lord at Thorney,[160] Penlease,

[152] See p.xxi, fn.76 .
[153] *Quivel*, p.362.
[154] *The Accounts of the Fabric of Exeter Cathedral, 1279-1353*, part I 1279-1326, ed. A.M. Erskine (D & C vol.24, 1981), pp.vii & ix-x.
[155] E.g. *C.C.R.* 1256-59, p.297; *C.C.R.* 1259-61, pp.157 & 193; *C.C.R.* 1261-64, pp.302ff & 377; *C.P.R.* 1258-66, p.536. In July 1277 we are told 2 knight's fees were rated at £40 – *Cal.Fine R.* 1272-1307, p.86. (The service due from the bishop for the years 1210-12 was estimated in the *Red Book of the Exchequer* II, p.556, at 15 knights.)
[156] *C.P.L.* 13 January 1262, p.383.
[157] Bronescombe had to pay a twentieth in 1270 – *C.P.R.* 1266- 72, p.466.
[158] Ashburton, Bishop's Clyst, Bishop's Nympton, Bishop's Tawton, Bishopsteignton, Chudleigh, Crediton, Fluxton in Ottery St Mary, Morchard Bishop, Newport, Paignton and Teignmouth; Cargoll, Berners in Egloshayle, Lawhitton, Pawton in Breock, Penryn (in the town and outside it), St Germans, Tregear in Gerrans.
[159] *Calendar of Charter Rolls* II 1257-1300 (HMSO, 1906), p.19.
[160] *Cal.Inq.Misc.* I, p.415, no.1465.

Brownstone (near Kingswear?), and at Frogmire or Frogmore (in the parish of Sandford?), for at all these places he received homage or made grants of land (**869–72**; **154**; **406**; **407**); he also made grants of wardship three times – twice with marriage, for twenty marks (**455**, **546**, **1425**). On one occasion we know he manumitted a serf, one Peter Dureman (**208**).

The lands held by the bishop sometimes brought him into contact with the king or the king's courts; for instance, an assize of novel disseisin was brought against him by Henry de Tracy over land at Bishop's Tawton, but a settlement was reached between the parties (**272**). The King twice presented to parishes in the diocese as the guardian of a minor (**1050**; **1419**), and he also mediated Bronescombe's disputes with Ford Abbey (**1198**) and the Earl of Cornwall (**1314**; **1414**). The bishop had appealed to the secular arm for aid against obstinate excommunicates such as the Abbot of Ford, William de Ditton and Agnes de Cruwys (**1177**), and Sir John de Alet and the Lady Isabella de Albo Monasterio (**1201**). The queen is mentioned twice, once when her physician, John de Clifford, was admitted to a prebend in Exeter cathedral (**1296**), and later when she appealed to Bronescombe to relax the excommunication he had pronounced against Buckland Abbey, which had been founded without his consent (**1378** & **1409**).

In the register, the most prominent aspect of Bronescombe's involvement with secular affairs concerned his relations with the greatest magnate in the south-west, Richard, earl of Cornwall, brother of Henry III, and King of the Romans or Holy Roman emperor-elect, and with his son Edmund, earl of Cornwall, first cousin of Edward I. Our general information would suggest that Bronescombe and Earl Richard, at least, were probably on easy terms personally, but there was an undoubted conflict of jurisdictions – and pride – among their followers. Some of the incidents were relatively simple to settle. At Bodmin in 1260 William Blund, a clerk, was forced to undergo trial by battle, contrary to canon law; all the participants were excommunicated, and the principals were not absolved until May 1262 (**266** & **439**).[161] In 1268 we learn that Philip Basset and Robert de Estalle, archdeacon of Worcester, as well as Henry of Almaine, son of the earl, (who, on behalf of the judges, agreed that there was a case to answer) negotiated a settlement after Bronescombe had complained of the injuries, losses and damages inflicted on himself and the liberties of the Church, and on the prior, convent and church of Bodmin, by the bailiffs of the earl. Henry admitted the truth of the complaints about the selling, removal, disposal or illegal enjoyment of the goods of the prior and convent, and agreed to the restoration to their proper state of the said bishop and prior and their churches (**703**).

In 1272 Edmund succeeded to his father, and he seems to have had considerably more awkward relations with the bishop. The years 1273, 1274 and 1275 were occupied with the ramifications of a series of disputes which had three main roots: the tearing down of the enclosure round Bronescombe's new deer-park at Cargoll (**924**);[162] the actions of Sir Richard de Seyton, the steward of Cornwall, who 'did not fear unjustly to lay hold of and to brutally to imprison the rector of Little Petherick, the vicar of St Petrock's, Bodmin, and

---

[161] The duel was with a cobbler, not a romantic clash of knights.
[162] *C.P.R.* 1272–81, p.120.

Andrew Gydion, priests, having trumped up against them a false charge of
wrongdoing, to the danger of his soul, the prejudice of ecclesiastical rights,
and the scandal of many' (**990**); and the outrage at St Allen, where the bishop
had been sending experienced men, clerics in priest's orders, peaceably to
admonish the earl's adherents for their attacks on the Church's liberties, but
armed Cornishmen had assaulted the bishop's clerics, even in church.
'Furthermore, they spilt blood in the house of God, inflicted other savage
injuries and put the fear of death into them, foully defiled the sacred vestments
that they wore, cut off the bottom halves of their hoods and the tips of their
caps – in the manner of a tonsure – turned their savage anger even on the
dumb animals, their palfreys and other horses, cut the ears, tails and upper
lips of some of them clean off, others they killed, others mutilated and hacked
them to the bone. To sum up, they committed sacrilege, rapine, and other
enormities, which would take too long to tell, in despite of God, in contempt of
the Church, and to the overthrow of ecclesiastical privilege' (**1429**).

These three incidents, and particularly the last, were the source of a steady
flow of excommunications, interdicts and, in due course, penitent submissions
of the offenders. The trouble seems to have arisen largely because the
respective jurisdictions of the two most influential men in the county were
almost bound to clash; it may also be pertinent that Bronescombe was abroad
in 1273–74.[163] There was a general and growing resentment among secular
lords in England of the claims of the church courts, which was to culminate in
Circumspecte agatis of 1286; there was also more specific local prejudice against
the enclosure of considerable tracts of land for deer-parks – it is interesting,
here and in other dioceses, to note how many highly respectable persons were
convicted of poaching.[164] Their behaviour may have indeed been disgraceful,
but the instigators of these outrages seem to have been persons of rank, and
their assaults had a semi-official character.

Furthermore, the sheriff of Cornwall, and others, were at this period
complaining to the king about Bronescombe's encroachments in matters of
jurisdiction.[165] There was, for example, trouble between the earl and the
bishop, or between their men, over the Tamar ferry at Saltash, on which the
bishop's men claimed free passage.[166] In 1278 there was a settlement – in
Norman French, the only occasion on which Latin is not the language of the
register – concerning the sand-pits at Mylor, from which Bronescombe seems
to have been taking more than his due (**1314**).[167] Contained in this settlement
was the submission of William de Monkton, later to be steward of Cornwall,
who had exceeded his powers.[168] But concord did not come easily in their
Cornish relationship. The bishop did, in fact, live to see a general settlement

[163] *C.P.R.* 1272–81, pp.120 & 123.
[164] It seems to have been regarded with a certain tolerance, rather as smuggling is
nowadays.
[165] *C.P.R.* 1272–81, p.293. Cf. *Registrum Epistolarum fratris Johannis Peckham,
archiepiscopi Cantuariensis*, ed. C.T. Martin (Rolls Series, 1882), I, pp.121f.
[166] *The Caption of Seisin of the Duchy of Cornwall* (1337), ed. P.L. Hull (D & C, 1971),
p.xxiii.
[167] *C.P.R.* 1272–81, p.293.
[168] Bishop Quivel still had trouble with him – *Quivel*, p.394; cf. *Pecham*, II, p.164.

of his differences with the earl of Cornwall,[169] although he still had had to suggest to the earl that the mediators appointed for this purpose meet outside Cornwall to avoid further delay or prejudice (**1324**). In the summer of 1279, Archbishop Pecham was writing to the bishop of Llandaff, asking him to excommunicate those in Cornwall falsely accusing Bronescombe.[170] In 1280 a proctor was appointed to collect the surety of £100 which Earl Edmund was obliged to pay the bishop 'by the ordinance of the most gracious lady, the lady Eleanor, Queen of England, and of the venerable father, the lord bishop of Bath and Wells' (**1414**),[171] and so, reconciled,[172] Bronescombe died some six weeks later.

[169] *C.P.R.* 1272–81, p.406 – of November 1279.
[170] *Registrum Epistolarum fratris Johannis Peckham, archiepiscopi Cantuariensis*, ed. C.T. Martin (Rolls Series, 1882), I, pp.35f.
[171] *C.C.R.* 1279–88, pp.59f.
[172] But Edmund of Cornwall seems not to have been content: *Pecham*, II pp.45f, records the appointment, in June 1282, of the dean, archdeacon and chancellor of St Paul's as judges, vice the archbishop, in the earl's claim against Bronescombe's executors.

REGISTER OF WALTER BRONESCOMBE

[Fo.2]   Registrum domini Walteri Exon' episcopi primi consecrationis sue:
Anno primo.

1   Anno gratie mccl septimo die S. Stephani prothomartiris obiit Ricardus,
Exon' episcopus.

2   Die Martis post Epiphaniam Domini eodem anno facta est convocatio
canonicorum ad tractandum de electione.

3   Anno eodem vii kalendas Martii, scilicet in crastino Cathedre S. Petri,
magister Walterus, archidiaconus Surr', concorditer ab omnibus electus est in
episcopum Exon'.

4   Anno eodem v nonas, scilicet die Dominica in media Quadragesima,
presentata est electio domino regi apud Westm[onasterium]. Et eodem die
idem dominus rex regium consensum adhibuit et litteras suas patentes super
hoc domino .. Cant' direxit.

5   Anno eodem et die eodem presentata fuit domino .. Cant' apud Lamheye
dicta electio, decretum electionis, procuratorium capituli Exon', et littera
domini regis de suo consensu.

6   Anno eodem iv nonas Martii, domino Cant' rei publice et propriis
negotiis apud Westm' occupato, magistri Eustachius de Lenn', Pontius,
rector ecclesie de Lamheye, Rogerus de Cant' et Michael de Bristoll', de
speciali precepto domini .. archiepiscopi in capella de Lamheye electionem
ipsam examinantes, in scriptis eam redegerunt.

7   Anno eodem iii nonas Martii dictus .. archiepiscopus, ut supra occupatus,
prefixit diem crastinum ad pronuntiandum super ipsa electione apud Bixle
iuxta Derteford'.

8   Anno eodem scilicet ii nonas Martii dominus .. archiepiscopus dictam
electionem canonice celebratam confirmavit in ecclesia de Bixle, presente
domino Radulpho, Tarentasien' archiepiscopo, et multis aliis; et litteras suas
patentes super hoc domino regi direxit. Et cito post confirmatam electionem
dominus electus contulit prebendam suam Exon' magistro Laurentio de Clive
et cancellariam Exon' domino Henrico de Wengham, canonico Exon'.

9[1]   Anno et die eisdem concessit dominus pensionem xv marcarum Petro de
. . ., clerico, . . . et habet litteras . . . sex marcas.

---

[1] This entry was interlined; it starts more than half way across the page, and is largely
illegible.

The Register of Lord Walter I, Bishop of Exeter, the first year of his consecration.

1 [BLUND'S DEATH]. 26 Dec 1257. Richard [Blund], bishop of Exeter, died.

2 [ELECTION ARRANGED]. 8'Jan 1258. A meeting of the canons was held to deal with the election [of a successor].

3 [ELECTION]. 23 Feb 1258. Master Walter [Bronescombe], archdeacon of Surrey, was unanimously elected as bishop of Exeter.

4 [ELECTION NOTIFIED TO THE KING]. 3 March 1258. The election was notified to the lord king at Westminster. And on the same day the same lord king gave his royal consent and addressed his letters patent concerning this to the lord [Boniface of Savoy, archbishop] of Canterbury.

5 [ELECTION NOTIFIED TO THE ARCHBISHOP]. 3 March 1258. There were presented to the lord [archbishop] of Canterbury at Lambeth the said election, the decree [recording the] election, the proxy of the chapter of Exeter, and the lord king's letter of his consent.

6 [EXAMINATION OF THE ELECTION]. 4 March 1258. Because the lord [archbishop] of Canterbury was occupied at Westminster with state and private business, Masters Eustace de Lenn, Pontius, rector of Lambeth church, Roger de Canterbury and Michael de Bristol, by special instruction of the lord archbishop, examined the said election in the chapel at Lambeth and reported on it in writing.

7 [DAY APPOINTED]. 5 March 1258. The said archbishop, being occupied as above, appointed the following day for pronouncing on the said election at Bexley by Dartford.

8 [CONFIRMATION OF THE ELECTION]. 6 March 1258. The lord archbishop confirmed, in Bexley church, that the said election was canonically conducted, in the presence of the lord Ralph, archbishop of [Moutiers en] Tarentaise and many others; and he addressed his letters patent concerning this to the lord king. And forthwith after the confirmation of the election, the lord [bishop-]elect collated to his [former] prebend at Exeter Master Laurence de Clive, and Master Henry de Wingham, canon of Exeter, to the chancellorship of Exeter.

9 [PENSION]. 6 March 1258. The lord [Walter] granted a pension of fifteen marks to Peter de . . ., clerk, . . . and he has letters . . . six marks.

10   Anno et die eisdem, presentata domino regi littera domini .. Cant' apud Westm' super facto confirmationis electionis predicte, idem dominus rex, recepto sacramento fidelitatis in forma canonica, possessionem bonorum temporalium domino electo concessit, litteras suas patentes custodi episcopatus super hoc dirigendo.

11   Anno eodem vii idus Martii, hoc est Sabbato quo cantatur Sitientes, idem electus a domino .. archiepiscopo, una cum dominis .. Norwicen' et Coventren' electis, est apud Cant' in presbiterum ordinatus.

12   Anno eodem vi idus Martii, hoc est die Dominica in Passione, idem electus Exon', una cum predictis Coventren' et Norwicen' electis, ab eodem domino .. Cant' est apud Cant' in episcopum Exon' consecratus, presentibus dominis Bathonien' et Salesbirien' episcopis et multis aliis.

13   Anno eodem iii nonas[2] Martii, relato rumore de obitu magistri Laurentii de Clive, dominus Exon' episcopus contulit prebendam Exon' domino Elie de Cumbe apud Derteford' quam prius contulerat eidem magistro Laurentio.

14   INQUISITIO SUPER ECCLESIA DE FACTO VACANTE. Anno et die eisdem apud Derteford' Iacobus de Haveringe, clericus, tulit litteras presentationis domini H. de Boun, filii .. comitis Hereford' et Essex', de se ipso facte ad ecclesiam de Pouderham' de facto vacantem et optinuit litteras inquisitionis in hec verba: W., miseratione divina Exon' episcopus, dilecto filio .. archidiacono Exon' salutem, gratiam et benedictionem. Quia dominus H. de Boun, filius nobilis viri comitis Herefordie et Essex', dilectum in Christo Iacobum de Haveringe, clericum, ad ecclesiam de Pouderham' vacantem et ad eius advocationem spectantem, ut dicit, nobis presentavit, vobis mandamus in virtute obedientie firmiter iniungentes quatinus in pleno capitulo decanatus illius in quo ecclesia ipsa consistit diligentem fieri faciatis inquisitionem an predicta ecclesia vacans sit, quo modo, a [Fo.2v] quo tempore, si sit sine litigio, quis eiusdem verus sit patronus, quanteque sit estimationis, et quid inde inveneritis per litteras vestras patentes harum seriem continentes nobis constare faciatis. Datum apud Derteforde die Mercurii ante Palmas, consecrationis nostre anno primo.

15   INQUISITIO SUPER ECCLESIA DE IURE VACANTE. Anno eodem die Veneris proxima ante Palmas, hoc est viii idus Martii, magister Oliverus de Tracy fecit presentari apud Merton' litteras presentationis domine A., comitisse Devon', de se ipso facte ad ecclesiam de Chepingtauton' de iure vacantem, ut dicit, et obtinuit litteras inquisitionis in hec verba: W. miseratione divina etc., archidiacono Barn' salutem etc. Quia nobilis mulier domina A., comitissa Devon', dilectum in Christo filium magistrum

---

[2] Almost certainly an error for *iii idus*.

10 [RELEASE OF THE TEMPORALITIES]. 6 March 1258. When the lord king had received the letter of the lord [archbishop] of Canterbury concerning the fact that the aforesaid election was confirmed, the same lord king, after he had received the oath of fealty in canonical form, granted the possession of the temporalities to the lord [bishop-]elect, and he addressed his letters patent concerning this to the keeper of the see [William de Axmouth].

11 [ORDINATION OF THE BISHOP-ELECT]. 9 March 1258. The same [bishop-]elect, together with the lords elect of Norwich [Simon Walton] and of Coventry [and Lichfield] [Roger Longspée], was ordained priest at Canterbury by the lord archbishop.

12 [CONSECRATION]. 10 March 1258. The same [bishop-]elect of Exeter, together with the aforesaid [bishops-]elect of Coventry and Norwich, was consecrated as bishop of Exeter by the same lord [archbishop] of Canterbury, at Canterbury, in the presence of the lord bishops of Bath [William Bitton] and of Salisbury [Giles de Bridport] and many others.

13 [COLLATION]. 13 March 1258, Dartford. Having heard news of the death of Master Laurence de Clive, the lord bishop of Exeter collated Sir Elias de Combe to the prebend at Exeter to which he had previously collated Master Laurence.

14 [FORM OF] INQUIRY INTO A CHURCH VACANT DE FACTO. 13 March 1258, Dartford. James de Havering, clerk, brought letters of presentation, made concerning himself to the church of Powderham, vacant *de facto*, by Sir H[enry] de Bohun, son of [Humphrey de Bohun] the earl of Hereford and Essex, and he obtained letters of inquiry in these words: Walter, by divine compassion bishop of Exeter, to our beloved son the archdeacon of Exeter, greeting, grace and benediction. Because Sir Henry de Bohun, son of the noble earl of Hereford and Essex, has presented to us our beloved in Christ James de Havering, clerk, for the church of Powderham, which he alleges to be vacant and its advowson belonging to him, we charge you by your duty of obedience, firmly enjoining on you that, in full chapter of that [rural] deanery in which the said church lies, you cause a diligent inquiry to be made into whether the aforesaid church is vacant, in what way, from what time, if it is free of litigation, who is its true patron, and what its value is. And what you discover about this you are to make known to us by your letters patent, including the content of these [original letters].

15 [FORM OF] INQUIRY INTO A CHURCH VACANT DE IURE. 15 March 1258, Merton. Master Oliver de Tracy has had presented the letters of presentation, made concerning himself to the church of North Tawton, vacant *de iure*, as she alleges, by the lady Amice, countess of Devon, and he obtained letters of inquiry in these words: Walter by divine compassion etc, to the archdeacon of Barnstaple, greeting etc. Because the noble dame, the lady Amice, countess of Devon, has presented to us our beloved son in Christ, Master Oliver de

Oliverum de Tracy ad ecclesiam de Chepingtauton' de iure vacantem et ad eius advocationem spectantem, ut dicit, nobis presentavit, vobis mandamus quatinus in pleno capitulo decanatus illius in quo ecclesia ipsa consistit diligentem fieri faciatis inquisitionem an predicta ecclesia vacans sit, quo modo, a quo tempore, si sit sine litigio, quis eiusdem verus sit patronus, quanteque sit estimationis, et quid inde inveneritis etc., ut supra. Datum apud Merton' die Veneris ante Palmas, anno consecrationis nostre primo.

16 INQUISITIO. Anno eodem die Pasche, hoc est ix kalendas Aprilis, magister Iohannes de la Lane tulit London' litteras presentationis domine A., comitisse Devon', de se ipso facte ad prebendam ecclesie de Tyverton' quam Willelmus de Plimton' in eadem nuper obtinuit de facto vacantem, et habuit litteras inquisitionis directas .. archidiacono Exon' in forma communi, ut supra, de verbo ad verbum cum dato competenti; obtinuit insuper dictus magister I. dictis die et anno litteras domini episcopi .. officiali Exon' directas in summa continentes quod si inquisitio super dicta prebenda plane faceret pro presentato et iure presentantis, tunc magistrum E., decanum Wellen', in ipsius prebende possessionem corporalem induceret nomine dicti magistri I., nomine custodie, usque in proximum adventum domini episcopi ad partes illas cum dato convenienti.

17 HOMAGIUM. Anno eodem in octabis Pasche, hoc est ii kalendas Aprilis, recepit dominus episcopus homagium Roberti de Popham apud Ferndon' de tenemento quod de eo tenet in eadem villa.

18 INSTITUTIO. Anno eodem ii idus Aprilis magister Iohannes de la Lane obtinuit litteras institutionis de prebenda quondam Willelmi de Plimton' in ecclesia de Tiverton' ad presentationem domine Amicie, comitisse Devon', vere patrone, apud Saltcumb' in hec verba: Universis Christi fidelibus presentes litteras inspecturis Walterus miseratione divina Exon' episcopus salutem in Domino. Ad universitatis vestre notitiam tenore presentium volumus pervenire quod nos dilectum in Christo filium magistrum Iohannem de la Lane ad prebendam de Tyverton' vacantem, quam Willelmus de Plimpton' dudum obtinuit in eadem, ad presentationem dilecte filie nobilis mulieris Amicie, comitisse Devon', vere ipsius prebende patrone, divine caritatis intuitu admisimus eundem I. canonicum ecclesie memorate canonice instituentes. In cuius rei testimonium presentes litteras ei duximus concedendas. Datum apud Saltcumb' iii idus Aprilis, consecrationis nostre anno primo et gratie mccl octavo.

19 INTRONIZATIO EPISCOPI. Anno eodem xviii kalendas Maii, die SS Thiburthii et Valeriani, hoc est a die Pasche in tres septimanas, intronizatus est apud Exon' Walterus Exon' episcopus.

20 INQUISITIO. Anno eodem xiv kalendas Maii apud Credieton' obtinuit Galfredus, clericus, litteras inquisitionis .. archidiacono Exon' directas in communi forma super ecclesia de Est Wogwill' de iure vacante ad presentationem Hugonis de Mallestun', patroni ut dicitur.

Tracy, for the church of North Tawton, which she alleges to be vacant *de iure* and its advowson belonging to her, we charge you that, in full chapter of that [rural] deanery in which the said church lies, you cause a diligent inquiry to be made into whether the aforesaid church is vacant, in what way, from what time, if it is free of litigation, who is its true patron, and what its value is. And what you discover about this etc, as above.

16   INQUIRY. 24 March 1258, London. Master John de la Lane brought letters of presentation, made concerning himself to the prebend in the church of Tiverton which William de Plympton lately held in the same, vacant *de facto*, by the lady Amice, countess of Devon; and he had letters of inquiry directed to the archdeacon of Exeter in common form, as above, word for word with the appropriate date. Further, the said Master John, on the said date, obtained letters of the lord bishop directed to the official of Exeter, containing in sum that, if the inquiry concerning the said prebend made plain [the suitability] of the person presented and the right of the person presenting, he should then induct Master Edward [de la Knolle], dean of Wells, into corporal possession of the said prebend in the name of the said Master John, by the title of custody, until the next visit of the bishop to those parts at a suitable date.

17   HOMAGE. 31 March 1258, Faringdon. The lord bishop received the homage of Robert de Popham for the land he held of him in the same village.

18   INSTITUTION. 12 April 1258, Salcombe. Master John de la Lane obtained letters of institution to the prebend, formerly held by William de Plympton, in the church at Tiverton, at the presentation of the lady Amice, countess of Devon, and true patron, in these words: To all Christ's faithful who inspect the present letters Walter, by divine compassion bishop of Exeter, greeting in the Lord. We wish it to be known to all of you by the tenor of these presents that, at the prompting of divine charity, we have admitted our beloved son in Christ John de la Lane to the vacant prebend at Tiverton, which William de Plympton previously obtained in the same church, at the presentation of our beloved daughter, the noble dame Amice, countess of Devon, true patron of the said prebend, canonically instituting the same John as canon of the aforementioned church. In witness whereof we have had the present letters granted to him. Given at Salcombe, 11 April etc.

19   ENTHRONEMENT OF THE BISHOP. 14 April 1258, Exeter. Walter, bishop of Exeter, was enthroned at Exeter.

20   INQUIRY. 18 April 1258, Crediton. Galfredus, clerk, obtained letters of inquiry addressed, in common form, to the archdeacon of Exeter concerning the church of East Ogwell, vacant *de iure*, at the presentation of Hugh de Malston, patron as is alleged.

21   INQUISITIO. Anno eodem xiii kalendas Maii apud Nymeton obtinuit magister Ricardus de Bolevile litteras inquisitionis .. archidiacono Totton' directas in communi forma super ecclesia de Lyu de iure vacante ad presentationem Nicholai de Bolevile, patroni ut dicitur.

22   PREDICATIO. Anno eodem xiii kalendas Maii concessa fuit littera fratribus hospitalis S. Lazari Ierosolimitan' ad querendam elemosinam fidelium Christi in episcopatu Exon'. Datum apud Cheddeleg'.

23   ORDINES. Anno eodem xii kalendas Maii apud Nimetun' exivit littera domini episcopi quatuor archidiaconis episcopatus directa con[Fo.3]tinens in summa quod singuli eorum citent peremptorie omnes rectores et vicarios ecclesiarum sue iurisdictionis qui non sunt presbiteri quod representent se in maiori ecclesia Exon' in vigilia Sancte Trinitatis sacros ordines prout animarum cura requirit recepturi.

24   ORDINES. Anno die et loco predictis exivit littera .. officialis de eodem sub eadem forma de Polton', de Penrin', et de Lanland' decanis directa.

25   SEQUESTRUM. Anno die et loco predictis dominus episcopus sequestravit fructus et proventus ecclesie de Lyu a precedenti vigilia Clausi Pasche perceptos propter resignationem tunc factam Henrici, rectoris ipsius, et officialis demandavit executionem . . . decano de Okempton'.

26   SEQUESTRUM TESTAMENTI. Anno eodem viii kalendas Maii, recepta littera apostolica cuius tenor residet penes W. de Capella, exivit littera episcopi in hec verba: W. miseratione etc. dilectis in Christo filiis .. decano Exon' et coexecutoribus suis testamenti bone memorie R. predecessoris nostri salutem gratiam et benedictionem. Quoniam fidedignorum relatu intelleximus quod per eundem predecessorem nostrum Exon' ecclesia variis et gravibus debitis est onerata et per quasdam inportunas exactiones in brevi faciendas in futurum, ut timemus, oneranda, ac quidam novi creditores nuper ad nos venientes coram nobis vos intendunt convenire, bona ipsius defuncti sequestrantes, vobis mandamus in virtute obedientie firmiter iniungentes quatinus distributioni bonorum defuncti memorati supersedeatis omnino, facientes bona predicta sine dispersione conservari quousque de exitu exactionum predictarum ad indempnitationem ipsius ecclesie discussio plenior habeatur; pro firmo tenentes quod si contra hoc nostrum mandatum ipsa bona distribuere presumpseritis, conquerentibus universis de vobis, auctore Domino, plenum nichilominus exhibebimus iustitie complementum Exonien' ecclesie indempnitati insuper provisuri. Et quod in hiis ratione previa decreverimus statuendum opitulante Domino faciemus inviolabiliter observari. Et qualiter hoc nostrum mandatum proponitis adimplere per litteras vestras patentes harum seriem continentes nobis constare faciatis. Datum apud Cheddeleg' in crastino S. Georgii martiris consecrationis nostre anno primo. Responsio decani: Reverendo patri etc. W. decanus etc. Litteras vestras recepi etc. Mandatum igitur vestrum gratanter acceptantes, vobis bona fide promittimus quod in administratione bonorum ipsius testamenti,

21   INQUIRY. 19 April 1258, Bishop's Nympton. Master Richard de Bolevile obtained letters of inquiry addressed, in common form, to the archdeacon of Totnes concerning the church of North Lew, vacant *de iure*, at the presentation of Nicholas de Bolevile, patron as is alleged.

22   PREACHING. 19 April 1258, Chudleigh. A licence was granted to the brethren of the hospital of St Lazarus, Jerusalem, for seeking alms from Christ's faithful in the diocese of Exeter.

23   ORDINATION. 20 April 1258, Bishop's Nympton. The lord bishop issued a letter, addressed to the four archdeacons of the diocese, containing in sum that each of them cite immediately all the rectors and vicars of the churches in their jurisdiction who are not priests to present themselves in the cathedral church of Exeter on 18 May, to receive holy orders, as the cure of souls requires.

24   ORDINATION. 20 April 1258, Bishop's Nympton. The official issued a letter on the same matter in the same terms, addressed to the [rural] deans of Pawton, Penryn and '*Lanland*'.[a]

25   SEQUESTRATION. 20 April 1258, Bishop's Nympton. The lord bishop sequestrated the fruits and revenues of the church of North Lew received since 30 March, on account of the resignation then made of Henry, its rector, and the official demanded execution from the [rural] dean of Okehampton.

26   SEQUESTRATION OF A WILL. 24 April 1258, Chudleigh. On the receipt of a papal letter, of which the terms are in W. de Capella's keeping, the bishop issued a letter in these words: Walter, by the compassion etc, to our beloved sons in Christ, the dean of Exeter and his co-executors of the will of Richard of blessed memory, our predecessor, greeting, grace and benediction. Because, from the report of trustworthy persons, we have understood that the church of Exeter has been burdened with various and heavy debts by the same predecessor of ours – and is, we fear, to be burdened in future by some troublesome exactions soon to be made – and certain new creditors, lately come to us, intend to sue you in our court, we sequestrate the property of the said deceased, and we charge you, by your duty of obedience, firmly enjoining on you to refrain altogether from distributing the property of the aforementioned deceased, seeing to it that the aforesaid property is conserved without dispersal, until such time as a fuller discussion takes place on the outcome of the aforesaid exactions for indemnifying the said church. You are to be fully aware that if, contrary to this our command, you presume to distribute the said property, then, under God's hand, you shall moreover pay the full amount required by justice to all that lay a complaint against you, and furthermore shall provide for the indemnifying of the church of Exeter. And we shall, with God's help, cause to be observed inviolably that which, for the

[a] Perhaps Landrake? a peculiar of the bishop, as was Penryn, while Pawton was one of his manors and may at that period have been a peculiar too. Or Lezant, also a peculiar?

consilio vestro amodo frui volentes, preter conscientiam vestram consensum et voluntatem de ipso testamento distribuendo, solvendo vel ordinando nichil de cetero attemptabimus set vobis tanquam superiori nostro in premissis humiliter fideliter et devote obediemus. In cuius etc. Datum Exon' die S. Marci evangeliste anno gratie mcclviii.

27   Anno eodem vi kalendas Maii exivit talis littera quatuor archidiaconis directa: W. miseratione etc. dilecto filio .. archidiacono Exon' etc. Cum inter sollicitudines alias ex officii nostri debito precipue teneamur animarum invigilare saluti ut converse ad episcopum pastorem et animarum suarum oves veri Pastoris solatio foveantur ecclesia sponsi sui letetur amplexibus, onusque suum sequatur emolumentum, et cura suo resideat in pastore, commendationes, custodias beneficiorum curam animarum habentium, simpliciter vel ad tempus, quibuscumque personis, quocumque modo preter intitulationem, per predecessores nostros commissas, in quibus dubium non est pro tempore suo et voluntate curam sibi retinuisse specialem, ex nunc auctoritate presentium quamvis ipsis decedentibus evanuerint de iure penitus revocamus. Quocirca vobis mandamus in virtute obedientie firmiter iniungentes quatinus hoc nostrum mandatum in singulis vestri archidiaconatus capitulis et ecclesiis sic commissis publicetis seu publicari faciatis, auctoritate nostra districtius inhibentes ne huiusmodi commendationes seu custodias retinentes nisi per nos prius canonice instituantur, sub quocumque colore ad sacros ordines accedere nec de illis beneficiis que sub sequestro nostro ex nunc retinemus disponere seu intromittere aliquatenus audeant vel presumant sicut canonicam effugere volueritis ultionem. Qualiter vero hoc nostrum mandatum fueritis executi per litteras vestras harum seriem continentes cum expressione beneficiorum et nominibus beneficiatorum huiusmodi citra diem ordinum in proximis iv temporibus celebrandorum aperte et [Fo.3v] distincte nos certificetis. Datum apud Peinton' vi kalendas Maii consecrationis nostre anno primo.

28   PREDICATIO. Anno eodem vii idus Maii apud Polton' admissus est Robertus Peverel, clericus, nuntius ecclesie Bethleemitan' ad querendam elemosinam fidelium Christi in diocesi Exon'.

29   LEGITIMATIO. Anno eodem xvi kalendas Iunii Walterus de Kilmonseo, clericus, obtinuit litteram dispensationis in hac forma: Universis Christi etc.

foregoing reason, we have decreed to be laid down in these matters. And you are to make known to us the manner in which you propose to carry out this our command, by means of your letters patent, including the content of these [original letters].

Reply of the dean: To the reverend father etc, William, dean etc. I have received your letters etc. We therefore, accepting your order with gratitude, promise you faithfully that we, 'in administering the property of the said will, being desirous of enjoying your confidence from now on, will not hereafter attempt anything by distribution, payment or furnishing from the said will, without your awareness, consent and desire, but we will obey you humbly, faithfully and devotedly as our superior in the aforementioned. In witness whereof etc. 25 April 1258, Exeter.

27 [REVOCATION OF CUSTODIES]. 26 April 1258, Paignton. The following letter was issued, addressed to the four archdeacons: Walter, by the compassion etc, to our beloved son the archdeacon of Exeter etc. Since, among the other cares arising from the duty of our office, we are especially bound to watch over the health of souls so that the sheep, having turned to the bishop and pastor of their souls, may be cherished by the solace of the True Shepherd, that the Church may rejoice in the arms of her bridegroom, that the burden may be followed by its reward, and that the cure may rest with its own shepherd; we, by the authority of these presents, from this time forward totally revoke the commendations [and] custodies – even although on our predecessors' deaths they vanished *de iure* – of benefices having the cure of souls that have been granted by our predecessors, whether absolutely or for a period, to whatsoever persons, by whatsoever method save definite entitlement, in which there is no doubt that during their [our predecessors'] time of office and approval they continued to hold for themselves a special care. For which reason we charge you, by your duty of obedience, firmly enjoining on you that you publish or cause to be published this our order in each of the chapters and churches of your archdeaconry (thus committed to you), and by our authority we lay a most stringent inhibition on the holders of commendations and custodies of this kind – unless they have previously been canonically instituted by us – that, as they shall hope to avoid canonical punishment, they shall not dare or presume under any pretext to seek Holy Orders, nor to dispose of, or to any extent intromit with, anything from those benefices which we from now onwards retain under our sequestration. You shall certify to us clearly and precisely the manner in which you have carried out this our command, by means of letters patent, including the content of these [original letters], with a statement of the benefices and the names of those thus beneficed, before the day of the next ordination in the coming Ember Days [15–18 May].

28 PREACHING. 9 May 1258, Pawton. Robert Peverel, clerk, emissary of the church at Bethlehem, was admitted to seek alms from Christ's faithful in the diocese of Exeter.

29 LEGITIMATION. 17 May 1258, Exeter. Walter de Kilmonseo, clerk, obtained a letter of dispensation in these terms: To all Christ's etc, Walter, by

Walterus miseratione divina etc. Mandatum domini pape suscepimus in hec verba: Alexander etc. Cum igitur apostolici mandati tenorem secuti, facta super premissis inquisitione diligenti per fidele testimonium dilecti in Christo filii G., archidiaconi Cornub', in publicam formam redactum invenerimus quod prefatus clericus morum gravitate, vite honestate, et litterarum scientia commendabilis demonstratus ut ad sacros ordines promoveri et in eisdem ministrare, ac beneficium ecclesiasticum etiam si curam habeat animarum obtinere possit dummodo ad ordines quos ipsius cura requirit se faciat statutis temporibus promoveri et personaliter resideat in eodem, defectu natalium predicto non obstante, auctoritate nobis in hac parte commissa, cum ipso dispensamus, presentes litteras in testimonium premissorum eidem concedentes. Datum Exon' etc.

30[3]   CELEBRATIO ORDINUM. Anno eodem xv kalendas Iunii, hoc est in vigilia Sancte Trinitatis, celebravit dominus episcopus solempnes ordines apud Exon'.

31   Anno et die eisdem Radulphus de Hellestun', clericus, obtinuit consimiles litteras apud Exon'.

32   INSTITUTIO ECCLESIE DE LYU. Anno eodem xiii kalendas Iunii apud Exon' magister Ricardus de Bolevile, clericus, ad presentationem domini N. de Bolevile, veri patroni ecclesie de Lyu-Tortoun', ad eandem ecclesiam admissus; litteras institutionis sue obtinuit in forma consueta et similiter litteras inductionis.

33   INSTITUTIO ECCLESIE DE KADELEG'. Anno eodem die et loco Robertus de Horsy, clericus, ad presentationem domine Iohanne Briwer', vere patrone ecclesie de Kadeleg', ad eandem ecclesiam est admissus, et litteras institutionis et inductionis obtinuit in forma consueta.

34   INSTITUTIO PREBENDE S. KARANTOCI. Anno eodem et die xii kalendas Iunii apud Saltcumbe dominus episcopus contulit prebendam ecclesie S. Karantoci que fuit Willelmi de Beybir', capellani, per ipsius Willelmi resignationem vacantem, Stephano Haym, clerico, et W. de Capellam, clericum, nomine suo investivit et litteras institutionis et inductionis concessit in forma consueta.

35   INSTITUTIO ECCLESIE DE MORCESTR' EPISCOPI. Anno eodem xi kalendas Iunii apud Saltcumb' exivit littera institutionis Nicholai, camerarii, in ecclesia de Morcestr' Episcopi ad collationem domini episcopi spectante eo quod idem episcopus eundem N. in subdiaconum ordinavit et in ipsa ecclesia canonice instituit personam.

---

[3] This entry was clearly added, as it is inserted, in smaller writing, at the end of the previous entry.

divine compassion etc. We have received a mandate from the lord Pope in these words: Alexander etc. Since therefore, having followed the tenor of the papal mandate, and having made a diligent inquiry concerning the foregoing through the faithful witness of our beloved son in Christ Geoffrey [de Bisimano], archdeacon of Cornwall, set out in legal form, we have found that the aforesaid clerk, by the seriousness of his morals, the honesty of his life, and his knowledge of letters, is shown to be worthy of commendation, to the end that he may be preferred to Holy Orders and minister in the same, and may be able to obtain an ecclesiastical benefice, even if it involves the cure of souls, provided that he arranges for himself to be promoted, within the appointed times, to those orders which the said cure requires, and shall reside personally in the same, we, by the authority vested in us in this regard, give him a dispensation, notwithstanding the aforesaid defect of birth, granting to the same the present letters in testimony of the aforesaid.

30   CELEBRATION OF ORDERS. 18 May 1258. The lord bishop held a solemn ordination at Exeter.

31   [LEGITIMATION]. 17 May 1258, Exeter. Ralph de Helston, clerk, obtained similar letters.

32   INSTITUTION TO LEW CHURCH. 20 May 1258, Exeter. Master Richard de Bolevile, clerk, at the presentation of Sir N. de Bolevile, true patron of North Lew church, was admitted to the same church; he obtained letters of his institution in customary form, and similarly letters of induction.

33   INSTITUTION TO CADELEIGH CHURCH. 20 May 1258, Exeter. Robert de Horsy, clerk, at the presentation of the Lady Joan Brewer, true patron of Cadeleigh church, was admitted to the same church; and he obtained letters of institution and induction in customary form.

34   INSTITUTION TO A PREBEND AT CRANTOCK. 21 May 1258, Salcombe. The lord bishop collated Stephen Haym, clerk, to the prebend in the church of Crantock which William de Bibury, chaplain, had held, vacant through the resignation of the said William, and [the bishop] invested W. de Capella, clerk, in his name, and he granted letters of institution and induction in customary form.

35   INSTITUTION TO THE CHURCH OF MORCHARD BISHOP. 22 May 1258, Salcombe. A letter was issued to Nicholas, chamberlain, of institution to the church of Morchard Bishop, in the bishop's collation, inasmuch as the same bishop has ordained the same Nicholas into the subdiaconate, and canonically instituted him as parson in the said church.

36   INSTITUTIO ECCLESIE DE MORTEHO. Anno eodem x kalendas Iunii apud Saltcumb' exivit littera institutionis magistri Iohannis de Alleswrthy, dudum presentati ad ecclesiam de Morteho per dominum Henricum de Tracy, tunc custodem terrarum et heredis Radulphi de Bray, bone memore R., quondam Exon' episcopo, in predicta ecclesia eo quod dominus episcopus eundem magistrum I. in subdiaconatum ordinavit et in ipsa ecclesia canonice instituit personam.

37   MUTUUM DOMINI EPISCOPI. Anno et die predictis apud Saltcumb' recepit dominus episcopus mutuo de domino Maugero de S. Albino quinquaginta marcas sterlingorum, solvendas eidem in octabis S. Michaelis proxime venturis; et confecit ei litteras suas obligatorias patentes.

38   INSTITUTIO DE WIMPL'. Anno et die predictis apud Saltcumb' Rogerus de Derteford' ad ecclesiam de Wimple per priorem de Cowik' presentatus vacantem per resignationem Willelmi Pincern, clerici, nuper rectoris ipsius, ad eandem est admissus, salva dicto priori annua pensione debita et consueta ab antiquo, et litteras institutionis et inductionis obtinuit in forma consueta.

39   LEGITTIMATIO SICUT ALIAS FACTA. Anno eodem ix kalendas Iunii apud Saltcumb' Nicholas de Huneton', presbiter, obtinuit litteras dispensationis super defectu natalium quem patitur in hac forma: W. Dei gratia etc. dilecto in Christo filio Nicholai de Hunetun', presbitero, etc. Presentatum a te nobis mandatum apostolicum recepimus in hec verba: Alexander episcopus etc. Volentes igitur a te adimi notam originis quam culpa tuorum intulit genitorum, recepto de te testimonio fidedigno quod non sis paterne incontinentie imitator sed honeste conversationis et vite aliasque tibi merita suffragantur ad dispensationis gratiam obtinendam quod, non obstante defectu natalium quem pateris de soluto genitus et soluta, in susceptis ministrare ordinibus et ecclesiasticum beneficium secundum formam pretax-atam valeas obtinere si tibi aliud canonicum non obsistat, auctoritate nobis commissa tecum misericorditer dispensamus, ita tamen quod si beneficium ecclesiasticum curam etc. assequi etc. ut in bulla. In cuius rei testimonium presentes litteras tibi duximus concedendas. Datum etc.

40   DISPENSATIO ORDINUM. Anno die et loco supradictis idem presbiter litteras dispensationis obtinuit super eo quod ad omnes ordines [Fo.4] sacros se fecit ab alienis episcopis sine sui diocesani licentia promoveri post litteram apostolicam in hec verba: Cum igitur ambitionis huiusmodi notam quam incircumspecte contraxisti per vite meritum et laudabilis fame testimonium studiose abolere dicaris, recepto de te super hoc testimonio fidedigno, et iniuncta tibi penitentia salutari ut susceptorum ordinum executione decetero leteris, auctoritate nobis commissa tecum misericorditer dispensamus. In cuius etc.

36 INSTITUTION TO MORTHOE CHURCH. 23 May 1258, Salcombe. A letter was issued to Master John de Aldsworth, formerly presented to Morthoe church by Sir Henry de Tracy, then guardian of the lands and heir of Ralph de Bray, to Richard of blessed memory, former bishop of Exeter, of institution in the said church, inasmuch as the lord bishop has ordained the same Master John as subdeacon and canonically instituted him as parson in the said church.

37 LOAN TO THE LORD BISHOP. 23 May 1258, Salcombe. The lord bishop received from Sir Mauger de St Aubyn a loan of 50 marks sterling, to be repaid to the same within the octave of next Michaelmas, and [the bishop] drew up for him his letters patent acknowledging the debt.

38 INSTITUTION TO WHIMPLE. 23 May 1258, Salcombe. Roger de Dartford, having been presented by the prior of Cowick to the church of Whimple, vacant by the resignation of its former rector, William Pincern, clerk, was admitted to the same, saving to the said prior the long-established, due and customary annual pension; and he obtained letters of institution and induction in customary form.

39 LEGITIMATION AS OTHERWISE ENACTED. 24 May 1258, Salcombe. Nicholas de Honiton, priest, obtained letters of dispensation concerning the defect of birth under which he labours in these terms: Walter, by God's grace etc, to our beloved son in Christ Nicholas de Honiton, priest, etc. We have received the papal mandate, which you have presented to us, in these words: Alexander bishop etc. Wishing therefore to have the stigma of your birth, which was imposed by the fault of your parents, removed, and having received trustworthy evidence about you that you are not an imitator of your father's incontinence, but are of honest conversation and life, and that in other respects your merits intercede to obtain for you the favour of a dispensation, we, by the authority vested in us, mercifully grant you a dispensation so that you, notwithstanding the defect of birth under which you labour as being born of an unmarried father and mother, may be allowed to minister in the Orders that you have received and to obtain an ecclesiastical benefice in accordance with the terms previously agreed, if no other canonical bar exists; on such terms, however, that if you seek an ecclesiastical benefice [having the] cure [of souls] etc, as in the bull. In testimony whereof we have had granted to you the present letters. Given etc.

40 DISPENSATION OVER ORDINATION. 24 May 1258, Salcombe. The same priest obtained letters of dispensation, following a papal letter, for having had himself promoted to all Holy Orders by other bishops without licence from his own diocesan, in these words: Since therefore you are said to have wiped away zealously the stigma, which you heedlessly contracted, of this sort of ambition by the merit of your life and the testimony of your praiseworthy reputation, after having received trustworthy reports of you concerning this, and after a wholesome penance has been imposed on you, we, by the authority vested in us, mercifully grant you a dispensation, so that you may for the future rejoice in the performance of the Orders you have received. In testimony whereof etc.

41   RESIGNATIO ECCLESIE S. HERMETIS. Anno eodem iv kalendas Iunii Wybertus de Cant' resignavit ecclesiam S. Hermetis in Cornub' apud Clarendon' in manus domini episcopi; et idem episcopus incontinente eam contulit Ricardo de Wy, clerico, et concessit ei cartam institutionis eodem die in communi forma sub dato de Spersholt'.

42   LITTERA DIMISSORIA ORDINUM. Anno eodem nonis Iunii exivit littera dimissoria in hec verba: W. etc. Exon' episcopus Philippo filio Ursi, clerico, salutem. Quia ad ecclesiam de Aurington' vacantem et sine litigio existentem a dilecto in Christo filio Willelmo de Raleg', milite, ipsius ecclesie vero patrono, nobis es canonice presentatus, ut ordinem accolitatus et subdiaconatus a quocumque volueris episcopo Cant' provincie ad titulum ecclesie memorate licite recipere possis de nostra licentia speciali plenam tibi tribuimus potestatem. In cuius etc. Datum etc.

43   PRESENTATIO. Anno eodem viii idus Iunii Odo de Lanladron presentavit magistrum Nicholaum de Tregorrec ad ecclesiam de S. Costantino vacantem, et habuit presentatus litteras inquisitionis in communi forma.

44   PRESENTATIO. Anno eodem viii idus Iunii Baudewinus de Ripar' presentavit Eliam de Herteford', clericum, ad ecclesiam de Walkamton' vacantem etc., et habuit litteras inquisitionis in communi forma.

45   COLLATIO VICARIE DE TINTAGEL. Anno eodem iv nonas Iunii apud Horslegh' exivit littera institutionis Gervasii de Truuer, capellani, in vicaria ecclesie S. Marcelliane de Tintagel, quam dominus episcopus ei contulit auctoritate Concilii Lateranens' quia tanto tempore vacavit quod ipsius collatio ad eum extitit devoluta, et ipsum G. in eadem vicaria instituit et litteras institutionis et inductionis concessit in forma consueta.

46   ORDINATIO EPISCOPATUS EXON', EPISCOPO ABSENTE. Anno eodem xiv kalendas Iulii per quandam litteram patentem episcopi excitata est potestas officialis ordinaria et per eandem litteram data est ei potestas concedendi litteras dimissorias ordinandis. Item per aliam litteram data est potestas eidem conferendi beneficia usque ad valentiam x marcarum. Item per tertiam litteram data est potestas E., decano Wellens', W., archidiacono Barn', et predicto officiali in examinationibus et confirmationibus electionum, admissionibus presentatorum ad beneficia vacantia, institutionibus, et aliis maioribus negotiis ordinariam potestatem tangentibus. Item per quartam litteram data est potestas W., decano Exon', W., archidiacono Barn', in presentia officialis predicti in ecclesia Exon' conferendi dignitates prebendas et beneficia ecclesiastica vacantia ad collationem domini episcopi spectantia seu auctoritate Concilii Lateranen' devoluta; ita quod ex evidenti utilitate et urgenti necessitate alterius absentiam alter compleat. Item per quintam litteram facta est commissio omnium causarum a sede apostolica commissarum vel committendarum .. cantori Exon', .. archidiacono Barn', et .. officiali Exon', et unicuique eorum in solidum usque ad revertionem domini

41 RESIGNATION FROM ST ERVAN. 29 May 1258, Clarendon. Wybertus de Canterbury resigned the church of St Ervan in Cornwall into the hands of the lord bishop; and the same bishop at once collated to it Richard de Wye, clerk, and, on the same day at Sparsholt, granted him a charter of institution in customary form.

42 LETTERS DIMISSORY FOR ORDINATION. 5 June 1258, Sparsholt. Letters dimissory were issued in these words: Walter etc bishop of Exeter, to Philip fitzUrse, clerk, greeting. Because you have been canonically presented to us to the church of Arlington, vacant and not the subject of litigation, by our beloved son in Christ, William de Raleigh, knight, true patron of the said church, by our special leave we give you full power to receive lawfully, to the title of the aforementioned church, the orders of acolyte and subdeacon from whatever bishop you wish in the province of Canterbury. In testimony whereof etc. Given etc.

43 PRESENTATION. 6 June 1258. Odo de Lanladron presented Master Nicholas de Tregorrec to the vacant church of Constantine; and the presentee had letters of inquiry in customary form.

44 PRESENTATION. 6 June 1258. Baldwin de Reviers presented Elias de Hertford, clerk, to the vacant church of Walkhampton, etc; and he had letters of inquiry in customary form.

45 COLLATION OF TINTAGEL VICARAGE. 10 June 1258, Horsley. A letter was issued to Gervase de Truro, chaplain, of institution to the vicarage of the church of St Marcelliana, Tintagel, to which the lord bishop collated him by the authority of the Lateran Council, because it had been vacant for so long that the collation of the said [vicarage] had devolved on [the bishop]; and he instituted the said Gervase in the same vicarage, and granted him letters of institution and induction in customary form.

46 REGULATION OF THE DIOCESE OF EXETER IN THE BISHOP'S ABSENCE. 18 June 1258. By a certain letter patent of the bishop, the official's power as ordinary was activated, and by the same letter he was granted the power of issuing letters dimissory to ordinands. Again, by another letter, the same was empowered to confer benefices up to the value of ten marks. Again, by a third letter, E[dward de la Knolle], dean of Wells, W[alter de Pembroke], archdeacon of Barnstaple, and the aforesaid official were empowered to examine and confirm elections, to admit persons presented to vacant benefices and to institute them, and [to deal with] other major matters of business linked with the power of the ordinary. Again, by a fourth letter, W[illiam de Stanway], dean of Exeter, [and] Walter, archdeacon of Barnstaple, were empowered to confer, in the presence of the aforesaid official in Exeter cathedral, vacant dignities, prebends and ecclesiastical benefices in the collation of the lord bishop or devolved [on him] by the authority of the Lateran Council, on terms that, where there was clear benefit and urgent necessity, either might act in the absence of the other. Again, by a fifth letter, appointment as commissary was given to the precentor of Exeter, the

episcopi in Angliam; ita quod per eius adventum omnes predicte littere evanescant. Et tradite sunt predicte v littere patentes et xiv littere clause domino Thome de Herteford', canonico Exon', ut in adventu reddantur vel de eorum eventu plane respondeatur.

47 PREDICATIO. Anno eodem ix kalendas Iulii admissi sunt nuntii hospitalis S. Thome martiris in Accon' ad querendas elemosinas Christi fidelium in diocese Exon'.

48[4] Eodem die et anno nuntii hospitalis S. Marie de Rocidevall' eodem modo fuerunt admissi etc.

49 MUTUUM. Anno eodem et die recepit dominus episcopus mutuo de Girardo Ricchobaldi xvi marcas et dimidiam, solvendas in festo Assumptionis London', quas solvit pro procuratione magistri Arloti apud Abendon'.

50 Anno et die supradictis apposuit dominus episcopus signum suum in signum et testimonium compulsionis et cohertionis magistri Iohannis de Winton' de xx marcis, solvendis infra quindenam Nativitatis S. Iohannis Baptiste Lond' anno predicto, et non ut obligetur exinde.

51 MUTUUM. Anno et die predictis confessus est dominus episcopus se recepisse centum marcas sterlingorum de predicto Girardo solvendas in festo S. Petri ad Vincula London'.

52 CARTA FEOFEAMENTI. Anno eodem xv kalendas Iulii apud Wite Waltham Radulphus de Fisserton' optinuit cartam domini episcopi in hec verba: Universis sancte matris ecclesie filiis presens scriptum visuris vel audituris W. miseratione divina Exon' episcopus salutem in Domino. Noveritis nos dedisse, concessisse, et hoc scripto nostro confirmasse Radulpho de Fisserton', clerico, pro homagio et servicio suo unum ferlingum et dimidium terre in Fisserton' cum pertinentiis suis in manerio nostro de Tauton', habendum et tenendum sibi et heredibus suis de nobis et successoribus nostris libere quiete et integre iure hereditario in perpetuum, reddendo inde annuatim ipse et heredes sui nobis et successoribus nostris unam marcam argenti ad quatuor anni terminos in predicto manerio constitutos, equis portionibus, pro omni servicio seculari, exactione et demanda. Nos vero et successores nostri [Fo.4v] totam predictam terram cum omnibus pertinentiis suis predicto Radulpho et heredibus suis tenemur warantizare per predictum servicium contra omnes gentes inperpetuum. In cuius rei testimonium huic scripto sigillum nostrum apponi fecimus. Hiis

---

[4] This entry is inset, following directly on the previous entry, so was presumably added somewhat later.

archdeacon of Barnstaple, and the official of Exeter, and to each of them on his own, for all causes committed or to be committed by the papal see, until the return of the lord bishop to England; on terms that, on his arrival, all the aforesaid letters are to cease to have effect. And the aforesaid five letters patent and fourteen letters close were delivered to Sir Thomas de Hertford, canon of Exeter, so that on [the bishop's] arrival they might be returned or a full account given of what resulted from them.

47 PREACHING. 23 June 1258. Emissaries of the hospital of St Thomas the Martyr in Acre were admitted to seek alms from Christ's faithful in the diocese of Exeter.

48 [PREACHING]. 23 June 1258. Emissaries of the hospital of Ste Marie de Roncesvalles were admitted in the same way, etc.

49 LOAN. 23 June 1258. The lord bishop received a loan from Girardo Ricchobaldi of sixteen and a half marks, to be paid at London on the feast of the Assumption [15 August]; which he paid at Abingdon for the procuration of Master Arlotus [the papal nuncio].

50 [LOAN]. 23 June 1258. The lord bishop affixed his seal as a sign and witness of being bound and obliged of Master John de Winchester[b] for 20 marks, to be paid at London within fifteen days of the Nativity of St John the Baptist [24 June] in the aforesaid year, and thereafter he would have no liability.

51 LOAN. 23 June 1258. The lord bishop acknowledged that he had received 100 marks sterling from the aforesaid Girardo to be paid in London on the feast of St Peter ad Vincula [1 August].

52 CHARTER OF ENFEOFFMENT. 17 June 1258, White Waltham. Ralph de Fisherton obtained a charter from the lord bishop in these words: To all the sons of Holy Mother Church who see or hear this present document, Walter, by divine compassion bishop of Exeter, greeting in the Lord. You are to know that we have given, granted and by this document of ours confirmed to Ralph de Fisherton, clerk, in return for his homage and service, one and a half farthings[c] of land, with its appurtenances, at Fisherton in our manor of [Bishop's] Tawton, to have and to hold for him and his heirs from us and our successors, freely, with immunity, in its entirety, by hereditary right in perpetuity, for a rent of one silver mark that he and his heirs [shall pay] annually to us and our successors, on the quarter days established in the aforesaid manor, in equal instalments, for all secular service, tax and claim. We indeed, and our successors, are bound by the aforesaid service to warrant all the aforesaid land with all its appurtenances to the aforesaid Ralph and his

b Master John is in the genitive, but the context strongly suggests that it was the bishop who was indebted.
c According to the OED a farthing of land can be a quarter of a hide, a virgate, or an acre; here, judging from 154, it is a quarter of an acre.

testibus: domino Rogero Baupel', Henrico de Chambernoun', Iohanne de Weston', Willelmo de Fuleford', Rogero le Arcevesk', Thoma de Ernesburg', Philippo de Reveton', Willelmo de Hakkelan', Rogero le Frankelayn, et aliis.

53[5] PENSIO. Anno eodem xi kalendas Iulii Lond': Universis etc. Walterus Dei gratia Exon' episcopus salutem in Domino. Noverit universitas vestra quod nos caritatis intuitu damus et concedimus dilecto nostro Girarducio Mayneti, scolari de Florentia, nepoti dilecti nostri Girardi Ricobaldi, civis et mercatoris Florentini, duas marcas sterlingorum de camera nostra nomine annue pensionis persolvendas dicto Girarducio vel eius procuratori singulis annis in festo S. Michaelis donec eidem uberius duxerimus providendum; salvo quod ad uberiorem provisionem memorato Girarducio faciendam per aliquem compelli contra voluntatem nostram nullatenus valeamus. In cuius rei testimonium presentibus litteris sigillum nostrum duximus apponendum. Datum Lond' die Veneris proxima ante Nativitatem B. Iohannis Baptiste anno gratie mccl octavo.

54 RESIGNATIO. Anno eodem x kalendas Iulii London' Thomas de Windesor', clericus, viva voce et litteratorie resignavit totum ius quod habuit ad ecclesiam S. Melori in Cornub'.

55 INSTITUTIO. Anno et die eisdem ibidem dominus contulit ecclesiam S. Meliori domino Waltero de Fermesham cum honere {sic} viginti marcarum solvendarum annuatim magistro Iohanni de Agnania quoad vixerit, et habuit [litteras] institutionis in forma prescripta.

56 PENSIO. Anno et die eisdem Lond' Thomas de Windesor' optinuit tales litteras: Universis etc. W. Dei gratia etc. Noveritis nos caritatis intuitu concessisse dilecto clerico nostro Thome de Windesor' decem marcas percipiendas singulis annis de camera nostra et successorum nostrorum ad duos anni terminos – unam videlicet medietatem ad festum S. Michaelis et alteram medietatem ad Pascham – quousque eidem Thome vel alicui persone ecclesiastice ydonee quam ad hoc elegerit in competenti beneficio ecclesiastico per nos vel successores nostros provisum fuerit.

57 PROCURATIO. Anno et die eisdem Lond' magister B. de Lardar' recepit unam procurationem generalem in omnibus causis et negotiis domini episcopi, manu sua propria scriptam, cum potestate componendi et transigendi.

58[6] Anno eodem iv nonas Iulii Paris' precepit dominus apponere signum suum in testimonium in transcripto litterarum trium papalium Roberti hostiarii ad curiam Romanam transmissarum.

---

[5] There is a big X through this entry, made, I think, while the register was missing after Stapledon's murder.
[6] This and the next entry were transposed in MS and corrected by a & b.

heirs against all persons in perpetuity. In testimony whereof we have had our seal affixed to this document. Witnessed by: Sir Roger Beaupel, Henry de Champernowne, John de Weston, William de Fulford, Roger le Arcevesk, Thomas de Ernesborough, Philip de Reveton, William de Hakkelane, Roger le Franklin, and others.

53 PENSION. 21 June 1258, London. To all etc, Walter, by God's grace bishop of Exeter, greeting in the Lord. Let all know that we, at the prompting of charity, give and grant to our beloved Girarducius Maynetus, scholar of Florence and nephew of our beloved Girardo Ricobaldi, citizen and merchant of Florence, two marks sterling from our private purse, as an annual pension to be paid to the said Girarducius, or his proctor, each year at Michaelmas (29 September), until we shall have thought fit to provide more generously for him, saving that we are in no way to be constrained by anyone to make a more generous provision against our will for the aforementioned Girarducius. In testimony whereof we have caused our seal to be affixed to the present letters. Dated etc.

54 RESIGNATION. 22 June 1258, London. Thomas de Windsor, clerk, both orally and in writing resigned all the right which he had to the church of Mylor in Cornwall.

55 INSTITUTION. 22 June 1258, London. The lord [bishop] collated Sir Walter de Fermesham to the church of Mylor, with the burden of paying 20 marks a year to Master John de Anagnis, for his life; and he had [letters] of institution in prescribed form.

56 PENSION. 22 June 1258, London. Thomas de Windsor obtained the following letter: To all etc, Walter, by God's grace etc. You are to know that we, at the prompting of charity, have granted to our beloved clerk, Thomas de Windsor, ten marks, to be received annually from the private purse of us and our successors, at two dates in the year – to wit, one half at Michaelmas and the other half at Easter – until provision shall be made by us or our successors of the same Thomas, or any suitable ecclesiastical person whom he chooses for this [purpose], to an adequate ecclesiastical benefice.

57 PROXY. 22 June 1258, London. Master Bartholomew de Lardario received an appointment as proctor-general for all legal and other business of the lord bishop, written in his own hand, with power to settle and compromise.

58 [SEALING]. 4 July 1258, Paris. The lord [bishop] ordered his seal to be affixed, as evidence, on the transcript of the three papal letters of Robert Hostiarius[d] which were to be sent to the Roman curia.

---

[d] Or 'the doorkeeper'.

59   PROCURATIO. Anno eodem viii idus Iulii Paris' liberata fuit quedam procuratio generalis et libera eidem magistro Bartholomeo ad agendum, componendum, transigendum in omnibus causis domini episcopi et etiam ad substituendum alium procuratorem, et est scripta manu eiusdem B.

60   PROCURATIO. Anno eodem vi idus Iulii magister B. recepit Paris' unam procurationem generalem manu sua scriptam in omnibus causis et negotiis domini.

61   Anno eodem xvii kalendas Augusti Paris' exivit littera excitatoria, monitoria et comminatoria pro Iohanne, cissore Paris', directa archidiacono Totton' contra Iohannem, rectorem ecclesie de Widecumb', de xviii marcis quas eidem mutuavit Paris' xii annis elapsis.

62   MUTUUM. Anno eodem ii kalendas Augusti recepit W. de Capella, clericus, Paris', litteras mercatorum Florentinorum ad recipiendum de eorum societate in curia Romana c marcas.

63   MUTUUM. Eodem die ibidem recepit litteras procuratorias domini ad contrahendum mutuum usque ad summam quinquaginta marcarum.

64   MUTUUM. Anno et die eisdem recepit alias litteras procuratorias ad contrahendum mutuum xl marcarum, que postea anno revoluto reddite fuerunt domino Lond' in absentia eiusdem W.

65   PROCURATIO. Anno et die eisdem recepit litteras procuratorias predictus Willelmus ad impetrandum, contradicendum et substituendum in curia Romana.

66   DE SIGILLIS. Anno et die eisdem ibidem reddidit predictus Willelmus sigilla domini episcopi in manus suas Paris', et iter arripuit ad curiam Romanam; et postmodum rediit in vigilia apostolorum Petri et Pauli apud Horsleg' et, revoluto anno, in festo Assumptionis S. Marie recepit totalem sigillorum custodiam.

67   MUTUUM. Anno eodem die Nativitatis B. Marie apud Fermesham' recepit Willelmus de Petresfell', clericus, quandam litteram [Fo.5] obligatoriam de xl marcis quas[7] dominus ab eo recepit mutuo, solvendas in sequenti festo Pasche.

68   OBEDIENTIA. Anno eodem in octabis Nativitatis B. Marie apud Chiddeham abbas de Bello Loco prestitit domino W. episcopo obedientiam pro ecclesia S. Keverane in Cornub' quam habuit in proprios usus,

---

[7] MS has '*quos*'.

59   PROXY. 8 July 1258, Paris. An appointment as proctor-general without restriction, able to raise actions, to settle or to compromise, and also to substitute another proctor, in all causes involving the lord bishop, was delivered to the same Master Bartholomew; and this was written in the same Bartholomew's hand.

60   PROXY. 10 July 1258, Paris. Master Bartholomew received an appointment as proctor-general, written in his own hand, for all legal and other business of the lord [bishop].

61   [ADMONITION]. 16 July 1258, Paris. A letter, arousing, warning and threatening, was issued, addressed to the archdeacon of Totnes on behalf of John, tailor of Paris, against John, rector of Widdecombe church, because of the eighteen marks which he had lent to the same in Paris twelve years previously.

62   LOAN. 31 July 1258, Paris. William de Capella, clerk, received from the Florentine merchants letters to receive 100 marks from their partnership at the Roman curia.

63   LOAN. 31 July 1258, Paris. [William de Capella] received the lord [bishop]'s letters of proxy to contract a loan up to the sum of 50 marks.

64   LOAN. 31 July 1258. [William de Capella] received other letters of appointment as proctor to contract a loan of 40 marks, which afterwards, a year later, were returned to the lord [bishop] in London, in the absence of the same William.

65   PROXY. 31 July 1258. The aforesaid William received letters of proxy to claim, deny, and substitute at the papal curia.

66   THE SEALS. 31 July 1258, Paris. The aforesaid William returned the lord bishop's seals into his hands, and started his journey to the Roman curia; afterwards, he returned on 28 June to Horsley and, a year later, received the full custody of the seals on the feast of the Assumption [15 August].

67   LOAN. 8 September 1258, Felmersham. William de Petersfield, clerk, received a certain promissory letter concerning the 40 marks which the lord [bishop] had borrowed from him, as a loan to be repaid at the following Easter.

68   OBEDIENCE. 15 September 1258, Chidham. The abbot of Beaulieu promised obedience to the lord bishop Walter for the church of St Keverne in Cornwall, which was appropriated to the abbey, in the presence of the abbot of

presentibus abbate de Nateleg', magistris Iohanne Nobili et B. de Lardar', Roberto, capellano, Matheo de Eggloshayl', et aliis.

69   CUSTODIA. Anno eodem die S. Mathei apostoli missa est littera archidiacono Cornub' sub hac forma: W. Dei gratia etc. archidiacono Cornub' etc. Quia Roberto filio Roberti, clerico, custodiam ecclesie S. Wyneri in Cornub' usque ad Natale Domini proximo futurum tradidimus, vobis mandamus quatinus dictum R. in possessionem ipsius ecclesie usque ad dictum tempus inducas corporalem. Datum etc.

70   INSTITUTIO. Anno eodem vii kalendas Octobris exivit talis littera: Omnibus etc. Walterus etc. Noveritis nos magistrum Rogerum de Elleston' ad ecclesiam de la Roche vacantem ad presentationem Ricardi de la Roche, eiusdem ecclesie veri patroni, caritatis intuitu admisisse ac eum in eadem ecclesia rectorem instituisse cum onere residentie personalis. Datum etc.

71   COMMENDATIO. Anno eodem in crastino S. Michaelis Reginaldus de Ferrariis optinuit commendationem ecclesie de Ber' per litteras domini episcopi patentes duraturas usque ad festum Natalis proximo venturum.

72   INHIBITIO. Anno eodem in crastino S. Michaelis inhibuit dominus episcopus per litteras suas patentes executores bone memorie R., Exon' episcopi, predecessoris sui, ne ad distributionem bonorum ipsius procedant donec satisfactum fuerit domino pape et domino regi super debitis dicti regis et decimis eidem regi concessis, videlicet usque ad summam octingentarum marcarum sicut solutionem de proprio evadere voluerint, et tradita fuit littera apud Sarr' magistro Iohanni filio Roberti.

73   INSTITUTIO. Anno eodem in crastino S. Luce evangeliste admissus fuit magister Galfridus de Tauton ad vicariam de Sudbovi vacantem ad presentationem magistri et fratrum hospitalis de Brug' de consensu domini H. de Tracy et habuit litteras domini episcopi predictas; tamen dominus H. optinuit litteras patentes domini episcopi sigillo signatas continentes pro-testationem de iure suo in eadem tempore vacationis.

74   CONSOLIDATIO. Anno et die eisdem consolidata erat vicaria ecclesie de Cheristonton' vacans parsonatui dum rector eiusdem ecclesie residentiam in ea faciat personalem.

75   INSTITUTIO. Anno eodem die Lune proxima post festum Thome apostoli apud Chamerewell' institutus est magister Thomas de Boklond' in sexaginta solidos percipiendos de bonis ecclesie de Wydecumb' per manus rectoris eiusdem secundum quod in carta bone memorie W[illelmi] quondam Exon' episcopi plenius continetur, et habuit litteras.

Netley, Masters John Noble and B. de Lardario, Robert, chaplain, Matthew de Egloshayle, and others.

69 CUSTODY. 21 September 1258. A letter was sent to the archdeacon of Cornwall in these terms: Walter, by the grace of God etc, to the archdeacon of Cornwall etc. Because we have entrusted the custody of the church of Gwinnear in Cornwall to Robert fitzRobert, clerk, until next Christmas, we order you to induct the said Robert to corporal possession of the said church until the said time. Given etc.

70 INSTITUTION. 25 September 1258. The following letter was issued: To all etc Walter etc. You are to know that we, at the prompting of charity, have admitted Master Roger de Elleston to the vacant church of Roche, at the presentation of Richard de la Roche, true patron of the same church, and have instituted him rector in the same church with the duty of residing in person. Given etc.

71 COMMENDATION. 30 September 1258. Reginald de Ferrars was commended to the church of Bere Ferrars by the bishop's letters patent, to have effect until next Christmas.

72 INHIBITION. 30 September 1258. The lord bishop by his letters patent inhibited the executors of Richard of blessed memory, bishop of Exeter and his predecessor,[e] from proceeding with the distribution of his property until satisfaction should be made to the lord pope and the lord king concerning the debts of the said king and the tenths granted to the same king, to wit, up to the sum of 800 marks, as they should wish to avoid payment out of their own property; and the letter was handed over to Master John fitzRobert at Salisbury.

73 INSTITUTION. 19 October 1258. Master Geoffrey de Tawton was admitted to the vacant vicarage of Bovey Tracy, at the presentation of the master and brethren of the hospital at Bridgwater, with the consent of Sir Henry de Tracy; and he had the aforesaid letters of the lord bishop. However, Sir Henry obtained the lord bishop's letters patent, stamped with his seal, containing a declaration of his rights in the same in time of vacancy.

74 CONSOLIDATION. 19 October 1258. The vacant vicarage of Church-stanton church was consolidated with the parsonage, so long as the rector of the same church is residing there in person.

75 INSTITUTION. 23 December 1258, Camberwell. Master Thomas de Buckland was instituted to 60 shillings, payable from the property of the church of Widdecombe in the Moor by the hand of the rector of the same, in accordance with what is more fully contained in the charter of W[illiam] of blessed memory, former bishop of Exeter;[f] and he had letters.

[e] Richard Blund, bishop of Exeter 1245–57.
[f] William Brewer, bishop of Exeter 1224–44.

76 CONSOLIDATIO. In crastino Natalis Domini anno eodem Lond' consolidata fuit vicaria ecclesie S. Hyvonis in Cornub' vacans parsonatui ad instantiam Ricardi de Manneton' rectoris eiusdem dummodo in eadem ecclesia residentiam faciat personalem, reservata domino episcopo taxatione vicarie ecclesie supradicte nisi rector eiusdem resideat ut tenetur.

77 RESIGNATIO. Anno eodem nonas Februarii apud Exon' Radulphus de Turbervill' resignavit prebendam suam de Appeldurham in manus domini episcopi et super hoc dedit litteras.

78 EXCOMMUNICATIO {pro bonis episcopi defuncti[8]}. Anno eodem die Veneris proxima post Purificationem B. Virginis emanavit littera domini episcopi decano et archidiacono Exon' directa quod, competenti monitione premissa, puplice ac sollemniter excommunicari facerent omnes illos qui, preter conscientiam et mandatum venerabilis patris R[icardi] predecessoris sui defuncti, super collationibus beneficiorum et aliis rebus disponendis sub nomine defuncti litteras dictaverunt, scripserunt, consignarunt, consignationi fraudulenter consenserunt, et etiam qui huiusmodi litteris scienter et prudenter usi sunt vel utentur eorumque fauctores; item omnes illos qui bona ipsius episcopi, qualiacumque fuerint, iniuste asportarunt seu asportari procurarunt aut alias abstulerunt, et debent certificare quod et factum est per litteras decani qui executus est mandatum.

[Fo.5v] **79** INSTITUTIO. Consecrationis domini Walteri Exon' episcopi [anno] secundo Dominica xl, hoc est septimo decimo kalendas Aprilis, institutus fuit Willelmus de Stanweye, subdiaconus, in ecclesiam de Clystydon' et habuit litteras.

80 INSTITUTIO. Anno et die eisdem institutus fuit Nicholas Bozun in ecclesiam de Ministre et habuit litteras.

81 CONSIGNATIO. Anno et die eisdem consignata fuit quedam littera super aque ductu de domo Fratrum Predicatorum usque ad curiam domini episcopi in suis adventibus et eo apud Exon' quandocumque commorante, ita quod nullus successorum suorum processu temporis in eodem aque ductu ius sibi possit vendicare.

82 ABSOLUTIO. Anno et die eisdem signata fuerunt duo paria litterarum Fratribus Minoribus et Predicatoribus directarum ad absolvendum omnes illos qui propter communes potationes que scotales vocantur in excommunicationis sententiam inciderunt.

83 Anno eodem die Mercurii proxima ante festum S. Benedicti, hoc est xiv kalendas Aprilis, in capitulo de Buffestr' coram domino episcopo comparuerunt dominus Walterus de Lodewell', presbiter, cancellarius et camerarius bone memorie R[icardi] Exon' episcopi defuncti tempore mortis sue, et

---

[8] Added by a later hand.

76 CONSOLIDATION. 26 December 1258, London. The vacant vicarage of the church of St Ive in Cornwall was consolidated with the parsonage at the request of Richard de Manaton, rector of the same, for as long as he was residing in person in the same church; the assessment of the vicarage of the aforesaid church was reserved to the lord bishop, if the rector does not, as he is obliged, reside.

77 RESIGNATION. 5 February 1259, Exeter. Ralph de Turberville resigned his prebend of Appledram [in Bosham] into the lord bishop's hands, and gave [him] letters concerning this.

78 EXCOMMUNICATION. 7 February 1259. The lord bishop sent out a letter addressed to the dean and the archdeacon of Exeter: that, after adequate warning had been given, they should see to the public and solemn excommunication of all those who, contrary to the knowledge and command of the venerable father Richard, his deceased predecessor, dictated letters in the name of the deceased for the collation of benefices and the disposition of other matters, wrote them, sealed them [and] gave fraudulent assent to the sealing, and also those who knowingly and purposely have made or will make use of such letters, and their accomplices; also all those who unlawfully carried off, or engineered the carrying off, or otherwise abstracted, the goods of the said bishop, of whatever kind they might be. And they must certify that this had been done by letters from the dean, who put the order into effect.

79 INSTITUTION. 16 March 1259, the second year after the consecration of the lord Walter, bishop of Exeter. William de Stanway, subdeacon, was instituted to the church of Clyst Hydon; and he had letters.

80 INSTITUTION. 16 March 1259. Nicholas Bozun was instituted to the church of Manaccan; and he had letters.

81 GRANT UNDER SEAL. 16 March 1259. A certain letter was sealed concerning the water supply from the house of the Dominican friars to the palace of the lord bishop at his visits and whenever he is staying in Exeter, on terms that none of his successors should, by the passage of time, be able to claim a right in the same water supply for himself.

82 ABSOLUTION. 16 March 1259. Two pairs of letters were sealed, addressed to the Franciscan and the Dominican friars, for the absolution of all those who had fallen under sentence of excommunication on account of the communal drinking-bouts known as 'scot-ales'.

83 [CONFESSION AND ABSOLUTION]. 19 March 1259, Buckfast Abbey. In chapter at Buckfast there appeared before the lord bishop Sir Walter de Loddiswell, priest, chancellor and chamberlain to Richard of blessed memory, late bishop of Exeter, at the time of his death, and Master Richard de Totnes,

magister Ricardus de Totton', clericus et notarius eiusdem, penitentia ducti ad cor redeuntes, sponte iurati in presentia domini episcopi, dompni {sic} abbatis Buffestrie, Willelmi de Pontestok', monachi, magistrorum Iohannis Nobilis, Bartholomei de Lardar', et aliorum, confitebantur quod, anno Domini mccl septimo, vocati intraverunt cameram episcopi de nocte et invenerunt quosdam de familia congregatos, clericos et laicos, qui eis denuntiaverunt episcopum esse in debili statu et quod tractarent de bonis episcopi disponendis, beneficiis conferendis, et super hiis litteris conficiendis et consignandis et, data fide a singulis de illo facto nunquam revelando, consenserunt omnes, beneficia assignarunt, litteras scripserunt et consignarunt. Rogati si episcopus tunc mortuus esset vel vivus in lecto, dicunt quod nescierunt set postea nec vivum nec loquentem viderunt eum. Rogati qui fuerint presentes, dicunt quod magistri Iohannes filius Roberti, tunc officialis, Gervasius de Cridton', Thomas de Mollond', et ipsi duo predicti, Henricus, capellanus, Henricus de Cristinestowe, Thomas, panetarius, Reginaldus filius predicti Thome, Willelmus de Fuleford', Caynoc, camerarius. Dicunt etiam quod magistri Iohannes et Gervasius litteras dictaverunt, Thomas de Mollond' et magister Ricardus predictus scripserunt, Henricus capellanus signavit. Dicunt etiam quod multe littere postquam sciverunt episcopum mortuum scripte fuerunt et signate. Hec et alia humiliter et devote confitentes, beneficium absolutionis in forma ecclesie optinuerunt. Indicta quoque purgatione canonica dicto Waltero quod nichil de bonis dicti episcopi post eius obitum asportavit, distraxit seu alienavit sicut fama laborabat, et dicto Ricardo ab officio et beneficio usque ad peractam penitentiam remanentem suspenso, eo quod ordines postea suscepit et falsum testimonium perhibuit famamque suam denigravit. Dictus Walterus postmodum in crastino Pasche in capella domini apud Exon' puplice ac sollempniter se purgavit, et dictus Ricardus penitentiam suam peregit; et sic uterque beneficium absolutionis optinuit.

84 CONTROVERSIA: ORDINATIO: INSTITUTIO. In crastino Clausi Pasche, hoc est vii idus Aprilis,[9] apud Exon' cum mota esset controversia inter Reginaldum de Ferrar', rectorem ecclesie de Ber', ut dicebat, et Rogerum de Valletorta, ipsius ecclesie vicarium, partes de plano supposuerunt se ordinationi domini episcopi qui sic inter partes ordinavit easdem quod, eodem Reginaldo ipsius ecclesie remanente rectore, dictus Rogerus percipiet annuatim per manus Reginaldi x marcas de bonis ipsius ecclesie et, cedente vel decedente eorum altero, cedentis vel decedentis portio accrescat superstiti, et predictus Reginaldus litteras habuit super hoc institutionis.

85 INSTITUTIO. In crastino [Clausi] Pasche apud Exon' admissus fuit Robertus de Winton', presbiter, ad ecclesiam de la Meth' vacantem ad presentationem prioris de Cowik' et gratiam domini episcopi et habuit litteras; solvit tamen pensionem.

[9] This would be 7 April, but 21 April – in accordance with the feast – is probably more reliable.

clerk and notary to the same. Returning to their senses under the influence of repentance, they took oath of their own free will, in the presence of the lord bishop, of the lord abbot of Buckfast, of William de Poundstock, monk, of Masters John Noble, Bartholomew de Lardario, and others, and they confessed that, in the year of the Lord 1257, on being summoned, they entered the bishop's room by night where they found various members of the household gathered together, both clerks and laymen. These told them that the bishop was in a failing condition, and that they were engaged in disposing of the bishop's property, conferring benefices and drawing up and sealing letters on these matters; after each of them had given his word that he would never reveal the deed, they all reached agreement, assigned benefices, wrote and sealed letters. On being asked whether the bishop was then dead or still alive in his bed, they say that they did not know, but that they did not afterwards see him either living or speaking. On being asked who were present, they say: Masters John fitzRobert, at that time the official, Gervase de Crediton, Thomas de Molland, the two of themselves, Henry, chaplain, Henry de Christow, Thomas, pantler, Reginald son of the aforesaid Thomas, William de Fulford, Caynoc, a chamberlain. They say also that Masters John and Gervase dictated the letters, that Thomas de Molland and the aforesaid Master Richard wrote them, and that Henry, the chaplain, sealed them. They say also that many letters were written and sealed after they knew the bishop was dead. After humbly and devoutly confessing these and other things, they obtained the benefit of absolution in the Church's form. And canonical penance was imposed on the said Walter, because he did not carry off, dispose of or alienate any of the goods of the said bishop after his death, as rumour alleged; while the said Richard was suspended from office and benefice until the completion of the rest of his penance, for he subsequently took orders and gave false testimony, blackening his reputation. Later the said Walter publicly and solemnly purged himself in the bishop's chapel at Exeter, on the morrow of Easter [14 April 1259], and the said Richard completed his penance; and thus each obtained the gift of absolution.

84 DISPUTE: ORDINANCE: INSTITUTION. 21 April 1259, Exeter. After a dispute had arisen between Reginald de Ferrars, rector of Bere Ferrars, as he alleged, and Roger de Valletorta, vicar of the same church, the parties submitted themselves entirely to the ordinance of the lord bishop, who made a ordinance between the same parties as follows: while the same Reginald should remain rector of that church, the said Roger shall receive annually by the hand of Reginald ten marks from the property of that church and, on the resignation or decease of either of them, the share of the departed or deceased should accrue to the survivor, and the aforesaid Reginald had letters of institution concerning this matter.

85 INSTITUTION. 14 April 1259, Exeter. Robert de Winton, priest, was admitted to the vacant church of Meeth, at the presentation of the prior of Cowick and through the bishop's grace, and he had letters; however, he pays a pension.

86 INSTITUTIO. In crastino Clausi Pasche apud Cerde admissus fuit
magister Robertus Heverard ad ecclesiam de Uplym' vacantem que per
lapsum temporis devoluta fuit ad collationem domini episcopi, et habuit
litteras institutionis in forma communi.

87 CUSTODIA. Die apostolorum Philippi et Iacobi London' commissa fuit
custodia ecclesie de Wdeleg' Philippo de Boell', clerico, usque ad festum
Nativitatis B. Iohannis Baptiste, ita quod nisi infra predictum tempus fuerit in
subdiaconum ordinatus nihil iuris in ipsa ecclesia ratione ipsius custodie possit
vendicare.

88 CUSTODIA. Die Inventionis Sancte Crucis London' commissa fuit
custodia ecclesie S. Paulini in Cornub' Rogero de S. Con[Fo.6]stantino
duratura usque ad festum S. Michaelis proximo venturum, ita tamen quod
annuatim solvat Iohanni Haym, clerico, sexaginta solidos ad certos anni
terminos.

89 INSTITUTIO. In crastino Inventionis Sancte Crucis apud Horsleg'
admissus fuit Warinus de Dyrile, presbiter, ad vicariam ecclesie de Tethe
vacantem ad presentationem prioris de Bodmyn' et habuit litteras
institutionis.

90 INSTITUTIO. In vigilia Assentionis ibidem ad presentationem domini
Egidii de Clyfford' et uxoris sue admissus fuit dominus H. de Bracton ad
ecclesiam de Cumb' in Tynhide vacantem et habuit litteras institutionis; cavit
tamen domino de indempnitate contra presentatos alios.[10]

91 In vigilia apostolorum Petri et Pauli anno eodem rediit W. de Capella de
curia Romana apud Horsleg'.

92 ABSOLUTIO. Vi nonas Iulii apud Horsleg' cum constaret domino
episcopo quod Radulphus de Turbervill' culpabilis non erat de fraudulentis
consignationibus factis nomine bone memorie R. episcopi post obitum ipsius,
pronuntiavit eum immunem et absolutum; et de hoc habuit litteras patentes.

93 RESIGNATIO. Anno et die eisdem ibidem magister Iohannes de Withiel
resignavit [ecclesiam] S. Marine in Cornub' in manus domini episcopi.

94 INSTITUTIO. V nonas Iulii ibidem dominus episcopus contulit vicariam
S. Marine magistro Iohanni de Withiel, ordinans in forma subscripta:
Universis etc. Noverit universitas vestra nos divine caritatis intuitu contulisse
magistro Iohanni de Withiel vicariam S. Marine in Cornub' vacantem cum
omnibus ad eam spectantibus perpetuo possidendam, ordinantes et volentes
quod de omnibus proventibus, redditibus et obventionibus, maioribus et
minoribus, ecclesie memorate idem magister I. ordinet et disponat pro libito
sue voluntatis; salvis tamen de bonis predicte ecclesie viginti marcis annuis

---

[10] A space of more than half an inch was then left, but not filled in, except for a
paragraph mark.

86 INSTITUTION. 21 April 1259, Chard. Master Robert Everard was admitted to the vacant church of Uplyme, which had fallen to the bishop's collation through lapse of time, and he had letters of institution in common form.

87 CUSTODY. 1 May 1259, London. The custody of the church of Woodleigh was committed to Philip de Boell, clerk, until 24 June, on terms that, unless he was ordained subdeacon within the aforesaid time, he could claim no right in the said church by reason of the said custody.

88 CUSTODY. 3 May 1259, London. Roger de St Constantine was given custody of the church of Paul, to continue until next Michaelmas [29 September], on condition that that he pay 60 shillings annually to John Haym, clerk, at fixed dates in the year.

89 INSTITUTION. 4 May 1259, Horsley. Warren de Dyrile, priest, was admitted to the vacant vicarage of the church of St Teath, at the presentation of the prior of Bodmin; and he had letters of institution.

90 INSTITUTION. 21 May 1259, Horsley. At the presentation of Sir Giles de Clifford and his wife, Sir H. de Bracton was admitted to the vacant church of Combinteignhead; and he had letters of institution. However, he gave security to the lord [bishop] for indemnifying him in case of other presentees.

91 [RETURN]. 28 June 1259, Horsley. W. de Capella returned from the Roman Curia.

92 ABSOLUTION. 2 July 1259, Horsley. The lord bishop, being satisfied that Ralph de Turberville was not guilty of the fraudulent grants under seal made in the name of bishop Richard of blessed memory after his death, pronounced him guiltless and absolved; and he had letters patent on this matter.

93 RESIGNATION. 2 July 1259, Horsley. Master John de Withiel resigned St Merryn into the hands of the lord bishop.

94 INSTITUTION. 3 July 1259, Horsley. The lord bishop collated Master John de Withiel to the vicarage of St Merryn, ordaining in the following terms: To all, etc. Let all know that we, at the prompting of divine charity, have collated Master John de Withiel to the vacant vicarage of St Merryn in Cornwall with all that relates to it, to be possessed in perpetuity, ordaining and desiring that the same Master J[ohn] shall order and dispose of all the proceeds, revenues and occasional offerings, greater and lesser, of the aforementioned church according to his own free will, reserving, however, from the property of the aforesaid church 20 marks a year to be paid to Peter

Petro de Tarentesia, clerico, in festo S. Michaelis et Resurrectionis Dominice, equis portionibus, per manus magistri Iohannis in maiori ecclesia S. Petri Exon' solvendis; ita tamen quod, cedente vel decedente eorum altero, cedentis vel decedentis portio superstiti cum integritate accrescat.

95 INSTITUTIO. Eodem die ibidem contulit dominus episcopus dicto Petro de Tarentesya parsonatum viginti marcarum percipiendarum annuatim, in forma supra proximo scripta, cum onere residentie personalis si contingat eum totam ecclesiam assequi post obitum vel cessionem dicti Iohannis, et habuit litteras.

96 INSTITUTIO. Iv nonas Iulii contulit dominus episcopus Radulpho de Turberevill' prebendam de Apeldurham in ecclesia de Bosham vacantem per resignationem eiusdem Radulphi factam Exon' nonis Februarii proximo preteritis, et habuit litteras institutionis.

97 INSTITUTIO. Anno eodem die Mercurii proxima post Translationem B. Thome martiris ad presentationem Ricardi filii Bartholomei de Poltimor' admissus est Iohannes Blundel ad ecclesiam de Poltimor' vacantem et habuit inde litteras.

98 COLLATIO. Die Iovis sequente apud Westmonasterium contulit dominus episcopus Waltero de Merton, presbitero, prebendam quam habuit dominus Henricus de Wingham' in ecclesia Exon' vacantem per confirmationem eiusdem H. in ecclesia London'.

99 COLLATIO. Eodem die apud Bedefunt' contulit titulo commendationis[11] dominus episcopus magistro R. de Tyfford' cancellariam Exon' per confirmationem eiusdem clerici vacantem.

100 INSTITUTIO. Die Veneris sequente apud Eyppeham' ad presentationem illustris regis Alamannie admisit dominus episcopus magistrum Arnold', eiusdem domini regis protonotharium, ad decanatum ecclesie Berriane in Cornub' et eum instituit et habuit inde litteras.

101 INSTITUTIO. Eodem die ibidem dominus episcopus instituit Rogerum de S. Constantino in ecclesiam S. Paulini secundum tenorem ordinationis facte inter ipsum et Iohannem Haym, clericum, et habuit inde litteras.

102 PREDICATIO. Die Sabbati sequente apud Bedefunt' concessa fuit littera predicationis ecclesie Meneven' usque ad annum duratura.

---

[11] These two words were inserted above the line in the MS.

de Tarentaise,[g] clerk, at Michaelmas and Easter in equal instalments by the hand of Master John in the cathedral church of St Peter, Exeter; however, on the resignation or decease of either of them the share of the departed or deceased should accrue in its entirety to the survivor.

95 INSTITUTION. 3 July 1259, Horsley. The lord bishop collated the said Peter de Tarentaise to a parsonage of 20 marks, to be received each year in the terms described immediately above, with the duty of residing in person if it should happen that he gain the whole church on the death or resignation of the said John; and he had letters.

96 INSTITUTION. 4 July 1259, Horsley. The lord bishop collated Ralph de Turberville to the prebend of Appledram in the church of Bosham, vacant by the resignation of the same Ralph made at Exeter on the previous 5 February; and he had letters of institution.

97 INSTITUTION. 9 July 1259. At the presentation of Richard fitzBartholomew of Poltimore, John Blundel was admitted to the vacant church of Poltimore; and he had letters thereon.

98 COLLATION. 10 July 1259, Westminster. The lord bishop collated Walter de Merton,[h] priest, to the prebend at Exeter which Sir Henry de Wengham had held, vacant through the confirmation of the same Henry as bishop of London.

99 COLLATION. 10 July 1259, Bedfont. The lord bishop collated, by right of commendation, Master Robert de Tyfford to the chancellorship of Exeter, vacant through the confirmation of the same clerk [as bishop of London].

100 INSTITUTION. 11 July 1259, Epsom. At the presentation of the illustrious king of the Germans,[i] the lord bishop admitted Master Arnold, protonotary of the same lord king, to the deanery of St Buryan in Cornwall, and instituted him; and he had letters thereon.

101 INSTITUTION. 11 July 1259, Epsom. The lord bishop instituted Roger de St Constantine to the church of Paul, in accordance with the ordinance made between him and John Haym, clerk; and he had letters thereon.

102 PREACHING. 12 July 1259, Bedfont. Licence to preach, valid for a year, was granted to the [cathedral] church of St David's.

g Also known as Peter de Vienne.
h Later Chancellor of England, bishop of Rochester 1274–77, and founder of Merton College.
i I.e. Emperor elect, and he was also elected king of the Romans in 1257; this is Richard of Cornwall, brother of Henry III.

103   CONFESSIO. Eodem die ibidem confessus est Michaelis de Legh', clericus, se scripsisse quasdam litteras post obitum episcopi Ricardi et earum [Fo.6v] consignationi interfuit, unde, iniuncta sibi penitentia salutari, dominus eum absolvit in forma ecclesie.

104   PREDICATIO. Anno eodem die Veneris proxima ante festum S. Margarete concessa fuit apud Horsleg' littera predicationis priori et fratribus et hospitali Lond' per annum duratura.

105   COMMENDATIO ECCLESIE S. GERENDI. Anno eodem et die apud Duntesfaude commendavit dominus episcopus ecclesiam S. Gerendi in Cornub' usque ad festum S. Michaelis proximo futurum et ab eodem festo usque ad annum futurum magistro Bartholomeo de Lardar'.

106   INSTITUTIO VICARIE DE CRISTINESTOWE. Anno eodem in festo S. Petri ad Vincula admissus fuit ad presentationem prioris de Cowik' Willelmus de Golclive, capellanus, ad vicariam ecclesie de Cristinestowe et habuit litteras.

107   INSTITUTIO. Anno eodem die Dominica proxima sequente admissus fuit Elyas de Herteford', clericus, ad presentationem Baldwini de Ripar', comitis Devon', ad ecclesiam de Walkamton et habuit litteras institutionis.

108   INSTITUTIO. Die Lune sequente admissus est et institutus Iohannes dictus Noreys, presbiter, ad vicariam ecclesie S. Austoli in Cornub' et habuit litteras institutionis.

109   PROVISIO DE ABBATE TAVISTOCHIE. Die S. Laurentii apud Chiddeham' propter inanitatem electionis iterate facte in ecclesia Tavistok' de abbate futuro, cum tum primus quam secundus diversis temporibus electus electioni de se facte expresse renuntiasset, providit dominus episcopus de abbate futuro, videlicet de Philippo Trencheful', monacho Winton', et optinuit litteras domino regi directas in hec verba: Excellentissimo domino etc. W. eadem gratia etc. salutem in Eo Qui dat salutem regibus et post triumphum coronam. Excellentie vestre notum facimus quod, vacante abbatia Tavistoch', nostre diocesis, et potestate providendi monasterio viduato de pastore ydoneo ad nos secundum statuta canonum devoluta, de dilecto nobis in Christo fratre Philippo Trencheful', monacho S. Suthini Winton', viro utique sicut a fidedignis recepimus provido et discreto ac in temporalibus ac spiritualibus circumspecto, eidem monasterio auctoritate pontificali duximus providendum, dominationi vestre supplicantes quatinus quod vestrum est quoad administrationem temporalium in hac parte circa eum vestra dignetur exequi celsitudo. Tunc presentes fuerunt multi de canonicis Cicestrensibus et alii plurimi in aula de Chiddeham ante horam prandii.

103 CONFESSION. 12 July 1259, Bedfont. Michael de Leigh, clerk, confessed that he had written certain letters after the death of bishop Richard, and was present at their sealing; for which, after imposing on him a salutary penance, the bishop absolved him in the Church's form.

104 PREACHING. 18 July 1259, Horsley. Licence to preach throughout the year was granted to the prior and brothers and the hospital at London.

105 COMMENDATION TO THE CHURCH OF GERRANS. 18 July 1259, Dunsfold. The lord bishop commended Master Bartholomew de Lardario to the church of Gerrans in Cornwall until the next Michaelmas, and for up to a year following the same feast.

106 INSTITUTION TO THE VICARAGE OF CHRISTOW. 1 August 1259. William de Golclive, chaplain, at the presentation of the prior of Cowick, was admitted to the vicarage of Christow church; and he had letters.

107 INSTITUTION. 3 August 1259. Elias de Hertford, clerk, at the presentation of Baldwin de Reviers, earl of Devon, was admitted to the church of Walkhampton; and he had letters of institution.

108 INSTITUTION. 4 August 1259. John called Noreys, priest, was admitted and instituted to the vicarage of St Austell church; and he had letters of institution.

109 PROVISION OF AN ABBOT TO TAVISTOCK. 10 August 1259, Chidham. Because of the invalidity of the repeated election of the next abbot made in the church of Tavistock – since both the first and the second persons elected (on the separate occasions) had expressly renounced their election – the lord bishop provided the next abbot, to wit, Philip Trenchful, monk of Winchester. He obtained letters addressed to the lord king in these words: To the most excellent lord,etc, Walter, by the same grace etc, greeting in Him Who gives health to kings and, after their triumph, a crown. We make known to Your Excellency that, since the abbey of Tavistock in our diocese was vacant, and the power of providing to the monastery, which had been deprived of a suitable shepherd, had devolved on us in accordance with the canon law, we have thought fit to provide to the same monastery, by pontifical authority, our beloved brother in Christ Philip Trenchful, monk of St Swithun's, Winchester, undoubtedly a provident and discreet man, as we have been informed by trustworthy persons, and circumspect in both temporal and spiritual matters. We beseech Your Majesty that Your Highness will deign to carry out your part in respect of him as regards the administration of the temporalities in this place. There were present at the time many canons of Chichester and very many other persons, in the hall at Chidham, before the hour of dinner.

110[12]   Postea in crastino Assumptionis apud Ferndon' idem clericus [sic] receptus a domino rege optinuit litteras ad priorem et conventum Tavistoch' in spiritualibus in forma consimili, verbis tamen competenter mutatis.

111   RESIGNATIO. Eodem die ibidem resignavit Willelmus de Beibir' prebendam quam habuit in ecclesia de Bosham in manus domini episcopi presentibus eisdem.

112   PERMISSIO. Eodem die ibidem concessit dominus episcopus eidem Willelmo de Beibir', presbitero, quod habeat ecclesiam de Halgwell' ex pristina collatione, quam dudum habuit sequestratam quia non resedit, dummodo ex tunc in ea residentiam faceret personalem.

113   VISITATIO. Anno eodem die S. Laurentii facta fuit sollempnis visitatio in ecclesia de Bosham per magistrum B. de Lardario et W. de Capellam, et sunt ibidem decrete certe correctiones infra certum tempus faciende. Item vocati sunt quidam ex canonicis in crastino S. Michaelis apud Exon' quia non satisfecerunt de portione Willelmi de Beibir', nuper eorum concanonici, et super contemptu sicut per litteras apparet.

114   DILATIO. Anno eodem in vigilia Assumptionis apud Ferndon' representavit se Willelmus de Spekecot' coram domino cum iure suo quod dicebat se habere in ecclesia de Beleston', et accepit responsum sicuti in rotulo continetur.

115   COLLATIO. Anno eodem die Assumptionis apud Ferndon' contulit dominus episcopus Roberto de Keneteford', presbitero, prebendam que fuit Willelmi de Beibir' in ecclesia de Bosham cum onere residendi et habuit litteras.

116   CUSTODIA SIGNI. Anno eodem in crastino Assumptionis commisit dominus episcopus W. de Capella totalem custodiam sigillorum.

117   PROCURATIO. Anno eodem die Lune sequenti proximo fecit magister Arnoldus, decanus S. Berriane, W. de Capella pro[Fo.7]curatorem suum in omnibus ipsum contingentibus apud Maydenhuthe.

118   INDULGENTIA. Anno eodem in vigilia S. Bartholomei apud Honeton' concessit dominus episcopus litteram indulgentie xx dierum visitantibus oratorium B. Edmundi in ecclesia de Cruc constructum in utroque festo et vigiliis eiusdem confessoris.

---

[12] There is a paragraph sign in the margin, but the text follows straight on.

110 [LETTERS CONCERNING THE SPIRITUALITIES]. 16 August 1259, Faringdon. Later, the same clerk, having been approved by the lord king, obtained letters to the prior and convent of Tavistock concerning the spiritualities, in similar terms, but with appropriate changes in wording.

111 RESIGNATION. 10 August 1259, Chidham. William de Bibury resigned the prebend which he held in the church of Bosham into the hands of the of the lord bishop, in the presence of the same people.

112 PERMISSION. 10 August 1259, Chidham. The lord bishop granted to the same William de Bibury, priest, that he might hold, in virtue of his original collation, the church of Halwell,ʲ which had for long been sequestrated because of his failure to reside, on condition that from then on he reside in person there.

113 VISITATION. 10 August 1259. A solemn visitation of the church of Bosham was made by Master B. de Lardario and W. de Capella, and certain corrections were decreed there, to be put into effect within a specified time. Also, certain of the canons were summoned to appear at Exeter on 30 September because they had failed to give satisfaction concerning the portion of William de Bibury, recently their fellow canon, and for contempt, as appears from the letters.

114 POSTPONEMENT. 14 August 1259, Faringdon. William de Speccot presented himself before the bishop with the claim which he alleged he had to the church of Belstone; he accepted the decision, as it is recorded in the roll.ᵏ

115 COLLATION. 15 August 1259, Faringdon. The lord bishop collated Robert de Kennford, priest, to the prebend which had been William de Bibury's in the church at Bosham, with the duty of residing; and he had letters.

116 CUSTODY OF THE SEAL. 16 August 1259. The lord bishop committed to W. de Capella the complete custody of the seals.

117 PROXY. 18 August 1259, Maidenhead. Master Arnold, dean of St Buryan, made W. de Capella his proctor in all matters affecting him.

118 INDULGENCE. 23 August 1259, Honiton. The lord bishop granted a letter of 20 days' indulgence to those visiting the oratory of the Blessed Edmund built in the church of Cruc',ˡ on either feast (and its vigil) of the same confessor.ᵐ

ʲ Halwell in Coleridge Hundred? or Halwill in Black Torrington Hundred? Hingeston-Randolph gives the former on p.99 and the latter on p.143.
ᵏ Perhaps the bishop's Court Roll.
ˡ Crooke Burnell, in the parish of North Tawton, was a manor at this period; it seems the most likely site.
ᵐ 9 June (his translation) and 16 November.

119   INSTITUTIO. Anno eodem die Decollationis B. Iohannis Baptiste apud Exon' ad presentationem procuratoris abbatis et conventus de Valle S. Marie in Norm' admissus fuit Vincentius, capellanus, ad ecclesiam de Clistwik' vacantem per resignationem magistri Iohannis de Brimcot et habuit litteras.

120   PROCURATIO AD CURIAM ROMANAM. Eodem die missa fuit procuratio ad contradicenda et impetranda mandata domini pape Ricardo de Hunaton' et Roberto de Albo Monasterio sub alternatione per mercatores Florentin'.

121   LEGITIMATIO. Anno eodem Reginaldus Cornub' optinuit litteras legitimationis a domino episcopo apud Exon' in crastino eiusdem festi.

122   PREDICATIO PERPETUA. Die Dominica in vigilia S. Egidii exivit littera predicationis apud Exon' pro ecclesia Exon' sine temporis prefinitione. Eodem die venit littera fratris Velasci apud Cridton' ad dominum.

123   CONFIRMATIO. Anno eodem die S. Egidii optinuit Radulphus Turberevill' litteras confirmationis super v marcas quas habuit de bonis ecclesie de Morbath'.

124   LEGITIMATIO. Eodem die optinuit Willelmus, camerarius, litteras legitimationis per apostolicam litteram in forma communi.

125   VISITATIO. Die Martis in crastino S. Egidii visitavit dominus prioratum S. Nicholai Exon'.

126   INSTITUTIO VICARIE. Die Mercurii proxima sequente, hoc est iii nonas Septembris, ad presentationem abbatis et conventus de Torre admissus fuit Symon de S. Laudo, presbiter, ad vicariam ecclesie de Hanok' vacantem et de novo taxatam et habuit litteras in hac forma: Universis etc. Ad universitatis vestre notitiam tenore presentium volumus pervenire quod nos, ad presentationem dilectorum filiorum abbatis et conventus de Torre, qui ecclesiam de Hanok' in proprios usus optinent pleno iure collatam, Symonem de S. Laudo, presbiterum, ad vacantem ipsius ecclesie vicariam divine caritatis intuitu admisimus et ipsum in ea vicaria canonice instituimus; ordinantes quod, solis garbarum decimis dictis abbati et conventui nomine rectorie reservatis, vicaria ipsa in domibus, terra sanctuarii et omnibus minoribus decimis et obventionibus quibuscumque consistat in perpetuum, reservata nobis assignandi acram vel dimidiam terre ipsius sanctuarii predictis religiosis ad construendum in ea domum pro decimis suis recolligendis si voluerint et hoc ecclesie videremus expedire potestate. In cuius etc. Datum apud Cridton' iii nonas Septembris anno secundo.

119   INSTITUTION. 29 August 1259, Exeter. At the presentation of the proctor of the abbot and convent of Ste Marie le Val in Normandy, Vincent, chaplain, was admitted to the church of Clyst St George, vacant by the resignation of Master John de Brimcot; and he had letters.

120   PROXY TO THE ROMAN CURIA. 29 August 1259. A proxy for opposing and requesting papal mandates was sent, through the agency of the Florentine merchants, to Richard de Honiton and Robert de Albo Monasterio, as alternates.

121   LEGITIMATION. 30 August 1259, Exeter. Reginald Cornish obtained letters of legitimation from the lord bishop.

122   PREACHING IN PERPETUITY. 31 August 1259, Exeter. A licence to preach, with no time limit, was issued on behalf of the cathedral church of Exeter. The same day a letter from Brother Velascus to the bishop arrived at Crediton.

123   CONFIRMATION. 1 September 1259. Ralph Turberville obtained letters of confirmation concerning the five marks which he had from the property of Morebath church.

124   LEGITIMATION. 1 September 1259. William, chamberlain, obtained letters of legitimation through a papal letter, in common form.

125   VISITATION. 2 September 1259. The lord bishop visited the priory of St Nicholas, Exeter.

126   INSTITUTION TO A VICARAGE. 3 September 1259, Crediton. At the presentation of the abbot and convent of Torre, Simon de Sancto Laudo, priest, was admitted to the vacant vicarage of Hennock church, which was assessed afresh, and he had letters in these terms: To all etc. We wish it to be known to all of you by the tenor of these presents that, at the presentation of our beloved sons the abbot and convent of Torre, who possess as appropriated the church of Hennock, collated with full right, we, at the prompting of divine charity, have admitted Simon de Sancto Laudo, priest, to the vacant vicarage of the said church, and we have instituted him in that vicarage according to the canons. And we have laid down that only the garb tithes[n] are reserved for the said abbot and convent, as rector, and that the vicarage itself shall consist in perpetuity of the buildings, the sanctuary land[o] and all the lesser tithes, and occasional offerings of whatever kind, reserving to ourselves the power of assigning an acre or a half-acre of the same sanctuary land for the aforesaid religious to erect on it a building for the gathering in of their tithes, if they shall so wish, and should we see this to be in the interest of the church. In testimony whereof etc. Dated [as above].

[n] The tithes of wheat (or other grain), literally their sheaves, also described as the greater tithes.
[o] Also known as glebe-land, but this term is common for the diocese of Exeter.

127   VISITATIO. Die Martis post festum Exaltationis Sancte Crucis facta fuit visitatio in ecclesia de Brigde=destow' {sic} sicut in rotulo visitationis plenius continetur.

128   INSTITUTIO. Die Mercurii ibidem admissus fuit Alfredus de Hamme, presbiter, ad vicariam ecclesie de Merton' ad presentationem eiusdem ecclesie rectoris, salva domino episcopo suppletione vicarie quantum deest de competenti, et habuit litteras introductionis nomine institutionis.

129   EXCOMMUNICATIO. Eodem die propter inobedientiam et manifestam offensam excommunicavit dominus episcopus priorem Lancevaton' in scriptis.

130   PUBLICATIO SENTENTIE. Anno eodem die Iovis in crastino fecit dictam sententiam puplicari in capitulo de Lancevaton' per priores de Bodmin' et Tywordraith'.

131   CUSTODIA. Anno eodem die Iovis predicta commisit dominus episcopus custodiam ecclesie de Brigidestowe vacantis magistro Thome de Radeleg' nomine magistri Nicholai de Plimpton' ad presentationem prioris et conventus de Plimpton' et habuit litteras introductionis nomine custodie durature usque ad Pasche futurum proxime, ita quod ex tunc non possit sibi ius vendicare in eadem nisi interim veniat facturus quod iustitia suadebit.

132   INSTITUTIO. Die Iovis eodem admissus fuit Nicholas le Bon, presbiter, ad presentationem magistri Hervei, rectoris ecclesie S. Felicitatis, ad infra taxate ecclesie vicariam apud Lawitteton' et habuit litteras in hec verba: Universis presentes litteras inspecturis Walterus etc. Ad universitatis vestre notitiam volumus pervenire quod nos, ad presentationem dilecti filii magistri [Fo.7v] Hervei, rectoris ecclesie S. Felicitatis, accedente ad hoc assensu et consensu nobilis mulieris Margerie de Connerton', eiusdem ecclesie vere patrone, dilectum filium Nicholaum dictum le Bon, presbiterum, ad ipsius ecclesie vicariam divine caritatis intuitu admisimus et ipsum in eadem canonice instituimus vicarium; ordinantes ex officio nostro quod omnes obventiones altalagii matricis ecclesie et cappelle {sic} de Connerton', solis garbarum decimis dumtaxat exceptis, terram sanctuarii que ad quinque acras estimatur, item decimas garbarum de Ruvier', de Penpol, de Nantereu, de Trethinegy idem vicarius percipiat nomine vicarie annuatim, onera ordinaria debita et consueta totaliter agnoscendo. In cuius rei testimonium presentes litteras ei duximus concedendas. Datum apud Lawitteton' die Iovis proxima post festum Exaltationis Sancte Crucis, consecrationis nostre anno secundo.

133   LEGITIMATIO. Eodem die apud Lawitteton' optinuit Rad[ulphus] Pippard, subdiaconus, legitimationem secundum formam mandati apostolici in communi forma.

127 VISITATION. 16 September 1259. A visitation was made of the church of Bridestowe, as is contained more fully in the Visitation Roll.

128 INSTITUTION. 17 September 1259, Bridestowe/Crediton?. Alfred de Hamme, priest, was admitted to the vicarage of Merton church, at the presentation of the rector of the same church. The bishop reserved [the right] to supplement the vicarage with whatever was necessary for an adequate living; and he had letters of induction on account of the institution.

129 EXCOMMUNICATION. 17 September 1259. The lord bishop in writing excommunicated the prior of Launceston for disobedience and manifest offence.

130 PUBLICATION OF SENTENCE. 18 September 1259. [The bishop] had the said sentence [of excommunication] published in chapter at Launceston by the priors of Bodmin and Tywardreath.

131 CUSTODY. 18 September 1259. The lord bishop committed the custody of the vacant church of Bridestowe to Master Thomas de Radley, in the name of Master Nicholas de Plympton, at the presentation of the prior and convent of Plympton; and he had letters of induction on account of the custody valid until the next Easter (14 April 1260), on terms that thenceforward he could not claim for himself a right in the same, unless meanwhile he should have come to do what justice shall urge.P

132 INSTITUTION. 18 September 1259, Lawhitton. Nicholas le Bon, priest, at the presentation of Master Harvey, rector of the church of Phillack, was admitted to the vicarage, which was assessed as below, and he had letters in these words: To all who inspect the present letters, Walter, etc. We wish it to be known to all of you that, at the presentation of our beloved son Master Harvey, rector of the church of Phillack, and with assent and consent being given to this ,by the noble dame Margery de Connerton, true patron of the same church, we, at the prompting of divine charity, have admitted our beloved son Nicholas called le Bon, priest, to the vicarage of the said church and have instituted him vicar in the same according to the canons. And by virtue of our office we have laid down that the same vicar shall receive annually, on account of the vicarage, all the occasional offerings of the altarage of the mother church and chapel of Connerton – at least excepting only the garb tithes – the sanctuary land which is reckoned at five acres, also the garb tithes of '*Ruvier*', '*Penpol*', Nanterrow and Trethingey, while he must bear in their totality the ordinary, due and customary burdens. In testimony whereof we have thought fit to grant him the present letters. Dated [as above], in the second year of our consecration.

133 LEGITIMATION. 18 September 1259, Lawhitton. Ralph Pippard, subdeacon, obtained legitimation according to the terms of a papal mandate, in common form.

P Be ordained? reside?

134   ORDINES. Anno eodem in vigilia S. Mathei apostoli celebravit dominus episcopus ordines privatos apud Bodmyn'.

135   ABSOLUTIO. Eodem die Robertus, prior de Lancevaton', humiliter cum instantia petens beneficium absolutionis pre foribus ecclesie de Bodmyn', prestito iuramento solempni de parendo mandatis ecclesie, optinuit beneficium absolutionis, et optinuit diem ad suscipiendum mandatum ecclesie ab illo die in viii dies, ubicumque tunc fuerit episcopus; quo die datus fuit sibi dies (apud Treguni).[13]

136   INSTITUTIO. Eodem die apud Polt' optinuit Michaelis de Legh', subdiaconus, institutionem in ecclesie de Gidelegh' ad presentationem Willelmi Probi, patroni eiusdem, et habuit litteras.

137   TAXATIO VICARIE. Anno eodem die Martis proxima post festum S. Mathei apostoli apud Polton' premissa inquisitione per decanum et capitulum loci facta, taxavit dominus episcopus vicariam ecclesie S. Merteriane de Tynthagel de consensu procuratoris monialium Fontis Ebraudi et concessit litteras institutionis Gervasio, vicario ipsius ecclesie, in hec verba: Universis etc. Noverit universitas vestra quod nos, attendentes quod vicaria ecclesie S. Merteriane de Tynthagel tanto tempore vacavit quod ipsius collatio per negligentiam abbatisse et conventus monasterii Fontis Ebraudi ad nos hac vice secundum statuta concilii generalis sit devoluta, eam dilecto filio Gervasio de Truueru, presbitero, divine caritatis intuitu contulimus et ipsum in eadem canonice vicarium instituimus, iuribus et dignitate Exon' ecclesie semper salvis; ordinantes, de expresso consensu procuratoris monialium predictarum, illustre rege Romanorum Ricardo semper augusto ipsius ecclesie patrono suum ad hoc impertiente consensum, quod vicarius predictus in proventibus ipsius ecclesie omnes obventiones altalagii, solis garbarum decimis dumtaxat exceptis, totam terram sanctuarii excepta dimidia acra terre, cum manso que dicitur Trebliswen, item decimas garbarum de Trewarvene et de Bothcyni nomine vicarie percipiat annuatim et ipsius ecclesie onera debita et consueta totaliter agnoscat. In cuius etc. Datum etc.

138   DEDICATIO. Anno eodem die Mercurii post festum S. Mathei apostoli dedicavit dominus episcopus ecclesiam S. Brioci de Lansant.

139   DEDICATIO. Anno eodem die Veneris proxima sequente dedicavit dominus episcopus ecclesiam S. Niweline.

140   DEDICATIO. Anno eodem die Sabbati sequente dedicavit dominus episcopus ecclesiam de Keynwen iuxta Truueru.

141   DEDICATIO. Anno eodem die Dominica in vigilia S. Michaelis dedicavit dominus episcopus capellam S. Marie de Truueru.

---

[13] The whole phrase from 'quo die' was squeezed in later, and the last two words were added in the margin, where they are doubtfully legible.

134 ORDINATION. 20 September 1259, Bodmin. The lord bishop celebrated private orders.

135 ABSOLUTION. 20 September 1259. Robert, prior of Launceston, humbly and earnestly sought the benefit of absolution before the doors of Bodmin church, having taken a solemn oath to obey the commands of the church; he obtained the benefit of absolution, and he obtained a date for undertaking the Church's command a week hence, wherever the bishop might then be, on which day a date was given him (at Tregony).

136 INSTITUTION. 20 September 1259, Pawton. Michael de Leigh, subdeacon, obtained institution to the church of Gidleigh, at the presentation of William Probus, the patron; and he had letters.

137 ASSESSMENT OF A VICARAGE. 23 September 1259, Pawton. Following an inquiry, made by the dean and chapter of the place, the lord bishop assessed the vicarage of Tintagel church, with the consent of the proctor of the nuns of Fontevrault, and he granted letters of institution to Gervase, vicar of the said church, in these words: To all, etc. Let all know that, mindful that the vicarage of Tintagel church has been vacant for so long that the collation to the same has, through the negligence of the abbess and convent of Fontevrault, devolved on us on this account according to the statutes of the General Council,[q] we have, at the prompting of divine charity, collated to it our beloved son Gervase de Truro, priest, and have instituted him vicar in the same in accordance with the canons, always without prejudice to the rights and dignity of the church of Exeter. And we have laid down, with the express consent of the proctor of the aforesaid nuns, and with the agreement communicated by the illustrious king of the Romans, the ever-imperial Richard, patron of the said church, that the aforesaid vicar shall receive annually, on account of the vicarage, from the income of the same church all the occasional offerings of the altarage – at least excepting only the garb tithes – and all the sanctuary land (except for half an acre of land with the dwelling called Trebliswen), and also the garb tithes from Trewarven and Bossiney, and he is to bear in their totality the due and customary burdens of the said church. In testimony whereof etc. Dated etc.

138 DEDICATION. 24 September 1259. The lord bishop dedicated the church of St Breock.

139 DEDICATION. 26 September 1259. The lord bishop dedicated the church of [East] Newlyn.

140 DEDICATION. 27 September 1259. The lord bishop dedicated the church of Kenwyn.

141 DEDICATION. 28 September 1259. The lord bishop dedicated the chapel[r] of St Mary's, Truro.

q Lateran III c.8 or IV Lateran c.29.
r Later the parish church.

142 DEDICATIO. Anno eodem die S. Michaelis dedicavit dominus episcopus ecclesiam Fratrum Predicatorum de Truueru.

143 Anno eodem in crastino S. Michaelis apud Treguni comparuit prior de Lanst' et supposuit se gratie domini episcopi et confessus est se velle suscipere et servare mandatum ecclesie et incepit dominus precipere prout testatur littera.

144 DEDICATIO. Die Veneris sequente dedicavit dominus episcopus ecclesiam S. Antonii in Roslande.

145 DEDICATIO. Die Dominica in crastino S. Francisci dedicavit dominus episcopus capellam S. Michaelis de Karihaes.

[Fo.8] **146** CUSTODIA. Anno eodem die Dominica in crastino S. Francisci apud Tregaer commisit dominus episcopus custodiam magistri Iohannis de Lanladherun' valetudinarii et ecclesie sue de Ridruth' magistro Iohanni de Bradeleg', officiali Cornub', dum modo persone et ecclesie provideat et defectus suppleat secundum vires facultatum ecclesie.

147 DEDICATIO. Anno eodem in vigilia S. Dionisii dominus episcopus dedicavit ecclesiam de Lammorek.

148[14] IN FORMA PAUPERUM. Eodem die Ricardus dictus Longus, clericus, de Churchton' exhibuit litteras in forma pauperum apud Bodrigan impetratas Anagnia sibi data v kalendas Aprilis pontificatus Alexandri anno v.

149 DEDICATIO. Anno eodem die S. Dionisii dominus episcopus dedicavit ecclesiam S. Austoli.

150 DEDICATIO. Anno eodem die Sabbati proxima post festum S. Dionisii dominus episcopus dedicavit capellam S. Marie de Loo.

151 COLLATIO PREBENDE. Anno eodem et die apud S. Germanum dominus episcopus contulit prebendam Mathei de Bisimano in ecclesia Exon' magistro I. Nobili, presentibus Thome de Herteford', W. de Capella et Roberto de Wisleg', presbitero, sive vacet de iure sive de facto sive utroque modo.[15]

152 COLLATIO PENSIONIS. Anno eodem die Dominica proxima post festum S. Dionisii apud S. Germanum contulit dominus episcopus magistro Willelmo de Capella quinque marcas annuas de abbate et conventu Tavistok' percipiendas; et habebit cartam eorum.

---

[14] This entry was inserted in smaller letters between 147 and 149, for which the marginal headings had clearly been written in advance.
[15] The last phrase was added in smaller letters.

142   DEDICATION. 29 September 1259. The lord bishop dedicated the church of the Dominicans at Truro.

143   [SUBMISSION]. 30 September 1259, Tregony. The prior of Launceston appeared and submitted himself to the bishop's mercy, and he professed himself willing to receive and observe the command of the Church; and the bishop began to give instructions, as is testified in the letter.

144   DEDICATION. 3 October 1259. The lord bishop dedicated the church of St Anthony in Roseland.

145   DEDICATION. 5 October 1259. The lord bishop dedicated the chapel of St Michael Caerhays.

146   CUSTODY. 30 September 1259, Tregony. The lord bishop committed to Master John de Bradley, official of Cornwall, the custody of Master John de Lanladherun, who is sick, and his church of Redruth, on condition that he make provision for the parson and the church and make good what they lack as far as the church's means allow.

147   DEDICATION. 8 October 1259. The lord bishop dedicated the church of Mevagissey.

148   'FORMA PAUPERUM'. 8 October 1259, Bodrigan. Richard called Long, clerk, of Churchton, showed letters *in forma pauperum* which he had obtained for himself at Anagni on 28 March 1259.

149   DEDICATION. 9 October 1259. The lord bishop dedicated the church of St Austell.

150   DEDICATION. 11 October 1259. The lord bishop dedicated the chapel of St Mary at [East] Looe.

151   COLLATION OF A PREBEND. 11 October 1259, St Germans. The lord bishop collated Master J. Noble to the prebend in Exeter cathedral which had been Matthew de Bisimano's, in the presence of Thomas de Hertford, W. de Capella and Robert de Wisley, priest, whether it be vacant *de iure* or *de facto*, or both.

152   COLLATION OF A PENSION. 12 October 1259, St Germans. The lord bishop collated Master William de Capella to five marks a year, to be paid by the abbot and convent of Tavistock; and he will have a charter from them.

153 PROFESSIO TAVISTOK'. Anno et die predictis ibidem frater Philippus electus in abbatem Tavistok' per dominum episcopum est benedictus et fecit professionem suam in hec verba: Ego, frater Philippus, electus abbas ecclesie de Tavistok', promitto tibi, pater domine Waltere, Exonien' episcope, tuisque successoribus canonice intronizandis, et sancte Exonien' ecclesie fidem et canonicam per omnia subiectionem. Et habuit litteras installationis ad archidiaconum Totton' [directas].

154 CARTA. Anno et die predictis ibidem exivit talis littera: Omnibus Christi fidelibus has litteras visuris vel audituris, Walterus miseratione divina Exonien' episcopus, salutem in Domino. Noverit universitas vestra nos recepisse homagium Philippi de Penles de tribus dimidiis acris terre et de uno ferlingo terre cum pertinentiis suis, scilicet de illa dimidia acra terre quam Willelmus de Tremuer eidem Philippo vendidit in Bodelek', et de alia dimidia acra terre quam habuit de Luca de Penles in excambium in villa de Penles, et de tribus ferlengis terre quos emit de Vincentio de Trevansun in villa de Trevansun, et de omnibus aliis terris suis de quibus predictus Philippus antecessoribus nostris rationabile fecit homagium, et concessisse pro nobis et successoribus nostris dicto Philippo et heredibus suis quod quieti sint de omnibus predictis terris pro uno relevio et pro una secta. Et tenetur dictus Philippus et heredes sui solvere nobis et successoribus nostris singulis annis xviii denarios de auxilio de predictis tribus dimidiis acris terre et de uno ferlingo terre, sine incremento, et rationabile auxilium de alia terra sua propria, prout facere consuevit et pares sui faciunt. Et concessit predictus Philippus pro se et heredibus suis quod non poterit dare, alienare neque vendere predictas terras sine licencia vel consensu predicti Walteri, domini sui, Exon' episcopi. Et si predictas terras dare, alienare vel vendere voluerint, quod predictus Walterus et successores sui propinquiores sint quam aliqui alii, dummodo tantum dare voluerint quantum alius. In cuius rei testimonium huic scripto sigillum nostrum apposuimus, hiis testibus: domino Radulpho de Arundel, domino Radulpho de Tynten', Iohanne de Husting', Petro de Tregludno, magistro Odone de Tregontros, et aliis. Datum apud S. Germanum die Dominica ante festum S. Michaelis in Monte Tumba, anno gratie Domini mcclix.

155 DEDICATIO. Anno eodem die Lune post festum S. Dionisii dominus episcopus dedicavit ecclesiam de Sheviok'.

156 DEDICATIO. Anno eodem die Martis sequente dominus episcopus dedicavit ecclesiam de Aunton'.

157 DEDICATIO. Anno eodem die Mercurii sequente dominus episcopus dedicavit ecclesiam de Ramme.

158 DEDICATIO. Anno eodem die Iovis sequente dominus episcopus dedicavit ecclesiam de Pileton'.

153 PROFESSION [OF OBEDIENCE] FOR TAVISTOCK. 12 October 1259, St Germans. Brother Philip, abbot-elect of Tavistock, was blessed by the lord bishop and made his profession in these words: 'I, brother Philip, abbot-elect of the church of Tavistock, promise to you father, lord Walter, bishop of Exeter, and to your canonically enthroned successors, and to the holy church of Exeter my loyalty and canonical subjection in all matters.' And he had letters of installation [addressed] to the archdeacon of Totnes.

154 CHARTER. 12 October 1259, St Germans. The following letter was issued: To all Christ's faithful who see or hear these letters, Walter, by divine compassion bishop of Exeter, greeting in the Lord. Let all know that we have received the homage of Philip de Perlees for three half acres of land and one farthing of land, with their appurtenances, namely, that half acre of land in Bodellick which William de Tremuer sold to the same Philip, and another half acre in the vill of Perlees which he had by exchange from Luke de Perlees, and the three-quarters of an acre of land in the vill of Trevanson which he bought from Vincent de Trevanson, and all his other lands, for which the aforesaid Philip has done homage in due form to our ancestors; and [let all know] that, on behalf of ourselves and our successors, we have granted the said Philip and his heirs that they should have quiet possession of all the aforesaid lands in return for one relief and one suit of court. And the said Philip and his heirs are bound to pay each year to us and our successors 18 pence as an aid for the aforesaid three half acres of land and one farthing of land, without any increase, and also a reasonable aid for the other land of his holding, as he has been accustomed to do and as his peers do. And the aforesaid Philip, on behalf of himself and his heirs, undertook that he shall have no power to give, alienate or sell the aforesaid lands without the leave or agreement of the aforesaid Walter, his lord, the bishop of Exeter. And if he or his heirs should wish to give, alienate or sell the aforesaid lands, the said Walter and his successors are to have a more immediate [right to acquire] than any other persons, provided only that they shall be willing to pay as much as any other. In testimony whereof we have affixed our seal to this document. Witnesses: Sir Ralph de Arundel, Sir Ralph de Tynten, John de Husting, Peter de Tregludno, Master Odo de Tregontros, and others. Dated [as above].[s]

155 DEDICATION. 13 October 1259. The lord bishop dedicated the church of Sheviock.

156 DEDICATION. 14 October 1259. The lord bishop dedicated the church of Antony.

157 DEDICATION. 15 October 1259. The lord bishop dedicated the church of Rame.

158 DEDICATION. 16 October 1259. The lord bishop dedicated the church of Pillaton.

[s] But using a Cornish feast.

[Fo.8v] **159** DEDICATIO. Anno eodem die Veneris [sequente] dedicavit dominus episcopus ecclesiam S. Melani in Estwevelsir'.

160 DEDICATIO. Anno eodem die S. Luce evangeliste dominus episcopus dedicavit ecclesiam de Bothflumet.

161 DEDICATIO. Anno eodem die Lune sequente dominus episcopus dedicavit ecclesiam S. Dominice.

162 DEDICATIO. Anno eodem die Mercurii sequente dominus episcopus dedicavit ecclesiam de North Piderwine.

163 DEDICATIO. Anno eodem die Iovis sequente dominus episcopus dedicavit ecclesiam S. Clederi.

164 DEDICATIO. Anno eodem die Veneris sequente dominus dedicavit ecclesiam de Kelly.

165 DEDICATIO. Anno eodem die Sabbati sequente dominus episcopus dedicavit ecclesiam S. Stephani de Lanstaveton' superiore.

166 COMMENDATIO. Anno eodem iii kalendas Novembris apud Cheddeleg', propter exilitatem ecclesie de Pouderham et capelle S. Edmundi super Pontem Exe, commendavit dominus episcopus Iohanni de Ponte, presbitero, dictam capellam S. Edmundi usque ad festum S. Michaelis proximo venturum.

167 INSTITUTIO. Anno eodem kalendis Novembris, hoc est die Omnium Sanctorum, apud Cheddeleg' admisit dominus episcopus magistrum W. de Walesby per magistrum Radulphum de Stanford', procuratorem suum ad hoc specialiter constitutum, ad portionem ecclesie de Axeministr' annexam prebende de Grendale ad presentationem archiepiscopi, decani et capituli Ebor', salva ordinatione vicarie in ipsa ecclesia; et idem procurator optinuit litteram introductionis et iuravit obedientiam nomine domini sui: presentibus Radulpho, precentore, Roberto, cancellario Exon', W., archidiacono Barnestap', Thoma de Herteford', canonico Exon', magistris B. de Lardar', I. de Blakedoun, W. de Capella, I. de Esse, R. de Polamford', et aliis.

168 CARTA. Anno eodem iv nonas Novembris exivit littera domini episcopi in hec verba: Universis presentes litteras inspecturis Walterus miseratione divina Exon' episcopus salutem in Domino sempiternam. Noverit universitas vestra quod, cum bona temporalia prioratus Lanstavet' per incuriam et negligentiam Roberti, dudum prioris ipsius ecclesie, ut de dilapidatione taceamus, adeo sint collapsa quod ipsorum ordinatio ad nos est devoluta, ac dicti loci prior et conventus, nostro minime requisito consensu, de Lankinhorn' et S. Genesii ecclesias magistro Ade de Midelton', clerico, recepta ab ipso premanibus magna pecunie quantitate, ad terminum quinque

159 DEDICATION. 17 October 1259. The lord bishop dedicated the church of St Mellion.

160 DEDICATION. 18 October 1259. The lord bishop dedicated the church of Botus Fleming.

161 DEDICATION. 20 October 1259. The lord bishop dedicated the church of St Dominick.

162 DEDICATION. 22 October 1259. The lord bishop dedicated the church of North Petherwin.

163 DEDICATION. 23 October 1259. The lord bishop dedicated the church of St Clether.

164 DEDICATION. 24 October 1259. The bishop dedicated the church of Kelly.

165 DEDICATION. 25 October 1259. The lord bishop dedicated the church of St Stephen at Launceston.

166 COMMENDATION. 30 October 1259, Chudleigh. Because of the poverty of the church of Powderham and of the chapel of St Edmund's on the Bridge, Exeter, the lord bishop commended John de Ponte,[t] priest, to the said chapel of St Edmund until the next Michaelmas.

167 INSTITUTION. 1 November 1259, Chudleigh. The lord bishop admitted Master W. de Walesby, through Master Ralph de Stanford, his proctor for this particular purpose, to the portion of the church of Axminster annexed to the prebend of Grindale [in York Minster], at the presentation of the archbishop, dean and chapter of York, saving the establishment of a vicarage in the said church; and the same proctor obtained a letter of introduction and swore obedience in the name of his principal, in the presence of Ralph, precentor, Robert [de Tyfford], chancellor of Exeter, W., archdeacon of Barnstaple, Thomas de Hertford, canon of Exeter, Masters B. de Lardario, J. de Blakedoun, W. de Capella, J. de Esse, R. de Polamford, and others.

168 CHARTER. 2 November 1259, Chudleigh. A letter of the lord bishop was issued in these words: To all who inspect the present letters, Walter, by divine compassion bishop of Exeter, eternal greeting in the Lord. Let all know that since, through the lack of care and the negligence of Robert, former prior of the said church, the temporal property of the priory of Launceston has fallen into such a state – we say nothing of the waste – that the ordering of the same has devolved upon us; and since the prior and convent of the said place, without any approach to us for consent, have handed over the churches of Linkinhorne and St Gennys to Master Adam de Middleton, clerk, to farm for

[t] Presumably rector (or vicar) of Powderham.

annorum tradiderint ad firmam; idemque clericus eas aliquando tenuerit nec
de soluta pecunie ipsius quantitate septuaginta novem marcas ad hoc
receperit; nos, volentes ipsius ecclesie utilitati prospicere et magistri predicti
indemnitati precavere, recepta ab ipso primitus libera et spontanea ipsarum
firmarum resignatione, tam nostro quam ipsius ecclesie de Lanst' nomine,
ecclesiam S. Genesii ad terminum quatuor annorum proximo sequentium in
forma infra scripta concedimus ad firmam eo usque possidendam; videlicet
decimas garbarum ipsius ecclesie S. Genesii – excepta decima de Treworgy,
que specialiter ad conventum pertinet – ita tamen quod, si infra predictos
quatuor annos dictum clericum beneficium ecclesiasticum assequi contingat,
recepto a predictis canonicis quod sibi defuerit de predictis septuaginta novem
marcis, scilicet pro quolibet anno viginti marcis, dictam firmam libere et sine
contradictione resignabit. Quod quidem bona fide coram nobis promisit. In
cuius rei testimonium presentibus litteris sigillum nostrum apponi fecimus.
Datum apud Chuddel' iv nonas Novembris consecrationis nostre anno ii.

169   INSTITUTIO. Anno eodem iii kalendas[16] Novembris admisit dominus
episcopus magistrum Thomam de Radeleg', procuratorem magistri Nicholai
de Plimton', ad ecclesiam de Brigidestowe, set non habuit litteras donec
reddat procuratorium.

170   CARTA: INDULGENTIA: REDDITUS. Anno eodem iii nonas Novembris
apud Cheddeleg' obtinuit Thomas de Ponte cartam domini episcopi de
protectione persone et rerum ut reficiat pontes et calceas per episcopatum
Exon'; et habuit litteras indulgentie x dierum, et dat annuatim i libram piperis
in festo S. Michaelis.

171   CUSTODIA. Anno eodem et die ibidem commisit dominus episcopus
Roberto, presbitero, de Bitedon', custodiam sequestri sui in ecclesia de
Bitedon' usque ad Pascham, et hoc demandavit archidiacono Barn' nisi
interim ei aliud demandaverit, et hoc fecit sub expectatione gestus nuper
rectoris eiusdem ecclesie.

172   OBLIGATIO XL MARCARUM. Anno eodem die Omnium Sanctorum
exivit littera patens sub magno signo domini Willelmo, presbitero, pro xl
marcis solvendis in festo Purificationis B. Virginis.

[Fo.9]   **173**   TAXATIO VICARIE. Anno eodem ii nonas Novembris apud
Cheddeleg' optinuit Warinus, vicarius S. Tetthe {sic}, litteras taxationis vicarie
predicte ad presentationem prioris et conventus Bodmyn', consentientibus
ipsius ecclesie portionariis, continentes quod percipiat omnes obventiones
altalagii et terram sanctuarii, et onera archidiaconalia et episcopalia agnoscat,
sine aliqua diminutione vel augmento usque ad annum in forma communi.

---

[16] Presumably an error for *nonas*.

a period of five years, after receiving a large sum of money from him in advance; and the same clerk has held them for some time and has not recovered the money paid out for this, amounting to 79 marks; we, wishing to look to the benefit of the said church, and to take security against loss to the aforesaid Master [Adam], having first received from him the free and voluntary resignation of the said farms, as much in our name as in that of the said church of Launceston, we have granted to him the possession of the church of St Gennys in farm for the next four years in the terms given below: namely, [that he should take] the garb tithes of the same church of St Gennys – with the exception of the tithe from Treworgie, which belongs especially to the convent – on condition that, if within the aforesaid four years the said clerk should happen to gain an ecclesiastical benefice, he should resign the said farm freely and without argument, after having received from the aforesaid canons the amount by which he is short of the aforesaid 79 marks, calculated at 20 marks a year. This indeed he promised in good faith before us. In testimony whereof we have had our seal affixed to the present letters.

169 INSTITUTION. 3 November 1259. The lord bishop admitted Master Thomas de Radley, proctor of Master Nicholas de Plympton, to the church of Bridestowe, but he did not have letters until he should surrender the proxy.

170 CHARTER: INDULGENCE: RENT. 3 November 1259, Chudleigh. Thomas de Ponte obtained a charter from the lord bishop for the protection of his person and property in order that he might repair bridges and causeways throughout the diocese of Exeter; and he had letters of indulgence of ten days, and he gives a pound of pepper annually at the feast of Michaelmas.

171 CUSTODY. 3 November 1259, Chudleigh. The lord bishop gave Robert, priest, of Bittadon, custody of his sequestrated property in the church of Bittadon until Easter, and he gave notice of this to the archdeacon of Barnstaple, unless he should be notified otherwise in the meantime; and he did this in the expectation of action from[u] the man who was recently rector of the same church.

172 BOND FOR 40 MARKS. 1 November 1259. A letter patent was issued under the bishop's great seal to William, priest, for 40 marks, payable on 2 February 1260.

173 ASSESSMENT OF A VICARAGE. 4 November 1259, Chudleigh. Warinus, vicar of St Teath, obtained letters for the assessment of the aforesaid vicarage, at the presentation of the prior and convent of Bodmin and with the consent of those holding portions in the said church; their content was that he should take all the occasional offerings of the altarage and the sanctuary land, and should bear the archidiaconal and episcopal charges, without any diminution or increase for the period of a year, in common form.

---

[u] Or just possibly 'in expectation of the burial of'.

174 DEDICATIO. Anno eodem die S. Leonardi dominus episcopus dedicavit ecclesiam de Cheddeleg'.

175 DEDICATIO. Anno eodem die Sabbati post festum S. Leonardi dedicavit dominus episcopus ecclesiam de Brideford'.

176 DEDICATIO. Anno eodem in vigilia S. Martini dedicavit dominus episcopus duo altaria et unum superaltare in ecclesia de Cumb' in Tynhide.

177 EXONERATIO. Anno eodem die S. Martini apud Peynton' obtinuit Radulphus de Trublevile a domino episcopo absolutionem a prestatione xx marcarum quas solvere debuit Iohanni de Anagnia pro prebenda de Boseham' que ad hoc onerata fuit, et habuit litteras.

178 EXONERATIO. Anno et die eisdem ibidem obtinuit Henricus de S. Cristina consimiles litteras super eadem, et habuit litteras.

179 COLLATIO: INSTITUTIO AXEMINSTR'. Anno eodem vi idus Novembris dominus episcopus contulit vicariam ecclesie de Axeminstr' que tanto tempore vacavit quod etc. Waltero de Aulescumb', presbitero, et habuit litteras institutionis in hec verba: Universis presentes litteras inspecturis Walterus miseratione divina Exon' episcopus etc. Ad universitatis vestre notitiam tenore presentium volumus pervenire quod nos, periculis animarum precavere et earundem saluti prospicere cupientes, vicariam ecclesie de Axeminstr' que tanto tempore vacavit quod ipsius collatio per negligentiam .. decani et capituli seu canonicorum Eboracen' ecclesie – quorum prebendis ecclesia ipsa annexa esse dicitur – secundum statuta Lateranen' Concilii ad nos sit devoluta, dilecto filio Waltero de Aulescumb', presbitero, divine caritatis intuitu contulimus, et ipsum in eadem canonice vicarium instituimus, salvis canonicis predictis dumtaxat xxiv marcis annuis per manus eiusdem vicarii de bonis ecclesie supradicte iuxta predecessorum nostrorum ordinationem annuatim London' percipiendis, nisi canonicis ipsis et Eborac' ecclesie ex privilegio sedis apostolice vel alio iure speciali amplius debeatur. In cuius etc. Datum apud Cheddeleg' etc.

180 PROCURATIO. Anno eodem die S. Machuti exivit littera procuratoria ad impetrandum in curia magistro Luce de Peincton' et Ricardo de Honeton' directa apud Peincton'.

181 ORDINATIO. Anno et die eisdem ibidem exivit littera ordinationis inter magistrum Thomam de Cnolle et David, vicarium de Teington', in hec verba: W. etc. magistro I. de Esse etc. Orta dudum inter magistrum Thomam de la Cnoll' qui possessioni ecclesie de Teington' incumbit ex parte una et David, presbiterum, ipsius ecclesie vicarium ex altera super decimis fabarum et pisorum ipsius ecclesie quas idem vicarius ad se pertinere dicebat, coram .. decano Sar' auctoritate apostolica materia questionis, et partibus ipsis bonum pacis affectantibus ac ordinationi nostre sponte totaliter et absolute se supponentibus nos, partium quieti prospicere cupientes, in negotio ipso taliter

174 DEDICATION. 6 November 1259. The lord bishop dedicated the church of Chudleigh.

175 DEDICATION. 8 November 1259. The lord bishop dedicated the church of Bridford.

176 DEDICATION. 10 November 1259. The lord bishop dedicated two altars and a portable altar in the church of Combeinteignhead.

177 QUITTANCE. 11 November 1259, Paignton. Ralph de Turberville obtained from the lord bishop a discharge from the payment of 20 marks which he owed to John de Anagni on account of the prebend at Bosham which was thus burdened; and he had letters.

178 QUITTANCE. 11 November 1259, Paignton. Henry de St Cristina obtained similar letters concerning the same matter; and he had letters.

179 COLLATION: INSTITUTION TO AXMINSTER. 8 November 1259, Chudleigh. The lord bishop collated Walter de Awliscombe, priest, to the vicarage of Axminster church which had been vacant for so long that etc, and he had letters of institution in these words: To all who inspect the present letters, Walter, by divine compassion bishop of Exeter, etc. We wish it to be known to all of you by the tenor of these presents that, desiring to take security against the dangers to souls and to look to their salvation, at the prompting of divine charity, we have collated our beloved son, Walter de Awliscombe, priest, to the vicarage of Axminster church, which has been vacant for so long through the negligence of the dean and chapter or canons of York – to whose prebends the said church is alleged to be annexed – that its collation has devolved on us in accordance with the canons of the Lateran Council, and we have canonically instituted the said [Walter] vicar in the same, saving to the aforesaid canons exactly 24 marks a year, payable annually in London through the hands of the same vicar from the property of the aforesaid church, according to the ordinance of our predecessors, unless more be due to the said canons and the church of York by reason of a papal privilege or some other special right. In witness whereof etc. Given at Chudleigh etc.

180 PROXY. 15 November 1259, Paignton. A letter was issued, addressed to Master Luke de Paignton and Richard de Honiton, appointing them proctors to raise actions in the papal court.

181 ORDINANCE. 15 November 1259, Paignton. A letter was issued on the ordinance between Master Thomas de la Knolle and David, vicar of Bishopsteignton, in these words: Walter, etc, to Master J. de Esse etc. A matter of dispute was formerly raised before .., dean of Salisbury, acting under papal authority, between Master Thomas de la Knolle, the incumbent of Bishopsteignton church on the one part, and David, priest, vicar of the said church on the other part, concerning the tithes of beans and peas of the said church which, the same vicar alleged, belonged to him; the parties themselves, out of love for the good of peace, are of their own accord submitting

ducimus ordinandum: videlicet quod, ipsius vicarie taxatione in omnibus aliis sui capitulis rata manente, decimas fabarum et pisorum ex curtilagiis quocumque modo excultis seu colendis que extiterunt tempore quo magister Constantinus de Mildehale vicariam taxavit eandem provenientes idem vicarius pure et simpliciter cum integritate percipiat; fabarum vero et pisorum decimas ex agricultura in campis provenientes quocumque modo excolantur idem Thomas simpliciter et absolute percipiat, huiusmodi quoque fabarum et pisorum decimas ex ortis post idem tempus ad curtilagium redactis provenientes ordinationi nostre sub pleniori deliberatione faciende reservamus. Quocirca tibi mandamus quatinus ordinationem ipsam a partibus ipsis per te vel per alium inviolabiliter facias observari, et attemptata in contrarium a quocumque revocare non omittas, contradictores et rebelles per censuras ecclesiasticas apostolica ratione compescendo. Datum etc. scilicet in crastino S. Martini apud Peyncton'.

182 DEDICATIO. Anno eodem die S. Hugonis dominus episcopus dedicavit ecclesiam S. Marie, Totton', scilicet ecclesiam conventualem.

183 DEDICATIO. Anno eodem in crastino S. Edmundi martiris dominus episcopus dedicavit ecclesiam de Trisme.

[Fo.9v] **184** DEDICATIO. Anno eodem in vigilia S. Clementis dominus episcopus dedicavit ecclesiam de Aiscumbe.

185 DEDICATIO. Anno eodem in vigilia S. Katerine dominus episcopus dedicavit ecclesiam de Pouderham.

186 DEDICATIO. Anno eodem in crastino S. Katerine dominus episcopus dedicavit ecclesiam Fratrum Predicatorum, Exon'.

187 RESIGNATIO. Anno et die eisdem ibidem in camera domini episcopi hora tertia Stephanus Haym renuntiavit appellationi et citationi quam fecit Warino, rectori ecclesie de Wer', super ipsa ecclesia coram officiali Cant', in presentia domini episcopi, magistri R. de Teford', domini Thome de Hertford', magistrorum Iohannis Nobilis, Iohannis Wiger, Bartholomei de Lardario, Ricardi de Hallesworth' et Willelmi de Capella.

188 LITTERA EPISCOPI. Anno et die eisdem ibidem exivit talis littera: Omnibus etc. Walterus Exon' episcopus etc. Noverit universitas vestra quod, qualemcumque cartam habuerimus de Willelmo Probo de Giddel' de dono terre de Clist Wilme et de eiusdem warantizatione, damus et concedimus pro nobis et heredibus nostris vel assignatis quod dictus Willelmus vel heredes sui ad warantizationem dicte carte et terre in nullo casu teneatur noviter, licet carta quedam super hac inter nos confecta de warantizatione expressam fecerit mentionem. In cuius etc. Datum etc. ut supra.

themselves voluntarily, totally and absolutely to our ordinance. We, desiring to look to the peace of the parties, think fit to lay down as follows in the said affair: to wit, that while the assessment of the said vicarage shall remain fixed in all other of its headings, the same vicar should take, unconditionally and completely in their entirety, the tithes of beans and peas yielded from the curtilages (in whatever manner cultivated or to be cultivated) which existed at the time when Master Constantine de Mildenhall assessed the same vicarage; the same Thomas, however, shall take, completely and absolutely, the tithes of beans and peas yielded by the tilling of the ground in the fields (in whatever manner they are cultivated). We reserve for our own decision, to be made after fuller consideration, the category of tithes of beans and peas yielded from the gardens which have since that time been incorporated into the curtilage. Wherefore we order you that you see to it, yourself or through some other, that the said ordinance is inviolably observed by the said parties, and that you do not fail to check attempts by any person to the contrary, by curbing objectors and rebels with the Church's censures by apostolic procedure. Given etc, namely on 12 November at Paignton.

182 DEDICATION. 17 November 1259. The lord bishop dedicated the church of St Mary, Totnes, namely the conventual church.

183 DEDICATION. 21 November 1259. The lord bishop dedicated the church of Trusham.

184 DEDICATION. 22 November 1259. The lord bishop dedicated the church of Ashcombe.

185 DEDICATION. 24 November 1259. The lord bishop dedicated the church of Powderham.

186 DEDICATION. 26 November 1259. The lord bishop dedicated the church of the Dominicans at Exeter.

187 RESIGNATION. 26 November 1259, Exeter. In the lord bishop's chamber, at the third hour, Stephen Haym revoked the appeal and summons which he had lodged before the Official of Canterbury against Warinus, rector of the church of Weare Gifford, concerning the said church, in the presence of the lord bishop, Master R. de Tefford, Sir Thomas de Hertford, Masters John Noble, John Wyger, Bartholomew de Lardario, Richard de Holsworthy and William de Capella.

188 LETTER OF THE BISHOP. 26 November 1259, Exeter. The following letter was issued: To all etc, Walter, bishop of Exeter, etc. Let all know that whatsoever charter we have from William Prus of Gidleigh, concerning the gift of land at Clyst William and the warranty of the same, we give and do grant for ourselves and our heirs or assigns that the said William, or his heirs, is not bound in any circumstances to warrant afresh the said charter and land, although a certain charter drawn up between us on this matter makes express mention of a warranty. In witness whereof etc. Given etc, as above.

189   DEPOSITUM. Anno eodem iv kalendas Decembris posita est littera magistri R. de S. Gorono in thesaur' Exon'.

190   LITTERA DE S. GORONO. Anno eodem et die ibidem exivit talis littera sub signo domini: Universis etc. W. miseratione etc. Cum dilectus filius magister Ricardus de S. Gorono, de Linton' de Toriton' et de Aueton' ecclesiarum rector, litteras dispensationis domini Innocentii pape iv sub dato Lugduni v kalendas Maii pontificatus eiusdem anno vii obtentu venerabilis patris domini W. Bathonien' et Wellen' episcopi impetratas exhiberet coram nobis, nec credere possumus eundem magistrum sub obtentu tanti domini pecuniam propter hoc exsolvisse cum in hoc conscientiam suam canonice pignorare se offerret cum effectu, nos eum quoad illum articulum absolvimus et absolutum pronuntiamus; volentes ad ipsius magistri curam exonerandam quod in ecclesia de Toriton' competens ordinetur vicaria, et quod idem magister ecclesiam suam vicarium non habentem cum de peregrinatione sua redierit curet et visitet ut tenetur. In ceteris vero articulis quos ei exposuimus in nostro registro contentis nostram et suam infra annum purgabit conscientiam; alioquin ex tunc in hiis ordinabimus prout anime sue et nostre saluti videbimus expedire. Dispensationem quoque legati Ottonis super ipsius magistri natalium defectu impetratam quam inspeximus bonam et legitimam esse pronuntiamus et pronuntiando declaramus. In cuius rei testimonium presentes litteras eidem magistro duximus concedendas. Datum Exon' iv kalendas Decembris consecrationis nostre anno secundo.

191   PRESENTATIO. Eodem die ibidem incontinenti idem magister R. presentavit Humfre, capellanum suum, de Aueton', ad vicariam ecclesie de Toriton' taxandam. Presentibus archidiacono, Thome de Herteford', magistris I. Nobile, B. de Lardario, W. de Capella, in quorum presentia priora acta sunt. Item magistro R. de Tefford'.

192   INSTITUTIO. Anno eodem iv kalendas Decembris admissus fuit et institutus Ricardus de Motbiri, presbiter, ad vicariam de Birie taxatam in altalagio et domibus iuxta ecclesiam et reservata domino potestate augendi vel minuendi usque ad festum S. Michaelis; et hoc ad presentationem procuratoris abbatis et conventus B. Marie in Valle in Norm'.

193   QUIETA CLAMANTIA. Anno et die eisdem ibidem obtinuit magister R. de Tefford' litteras domini episcopi de quieta clamantia de omni extraordinaria collecta et recepta, excepta collecta Quinquagesime, de episcopatu Exon'.

189 DEPOSIT. 28 November 1259. A letter of Master R. de St Gorran was deposited in the treasury at Exeter.

190 LETTER CONCERNING ST GORRAN. 28 November 1259, Exeter. The following letter was issued under the bishop's seal: To all etc, Walter, by the compassion etc. Since our beloved son, Master Richard de St Gorran, rector of the churches of Lynton, Torrington and Aveton Giffard,[v] has shown before us his letters of dispensation which were petitioned, under the patronage of the venerable father, lord William,[w] bishop of Bath and Wells, from Pope Innocent IV and given at Lyons on 27 April in the seventh year of his pontificate,[x] and we cannot believe that the same Master [Richard] under the patronage of such a bishop should have paid out money for this purpose, since he effectively offered that he would canonically pledge his conscience in this matter, we absolve him and pronounce him absolved on that head; while we wish that an adequate vicarage be established in Torrington church to discharge the cure [of souls incumbent on] the said Master [Richard], and that the same Master, when he returns from his travels, should – not having a vicar – care for his church and visit it as he is bound to do. But as regards the other heads contained in our register which we have set out for him, he is to purge our conscience and his own within the year; otherwise we shall hereafter lay down in these matters what seems to us expedient for his soul and our salvation. We also pronounce, and in pronouncing declare, that the dispensation, which we have inspected, petitioned from the papal legate Otto concerning the said Master [Richard's] defect of birth, is valid and of legal force. In witness whereof we have thought fit to grant the present letters to the same Master [Richard]. Given at Exeter on 28 November in the second year of our consecration.

191 PRESENTATION. 28 November 1259, Exeter. The same Master Richard at once presented Humphrey, his chaplain, of Aveton, to the vicarage – to be assessed – of Torrington church. There were present the archdeacon [of Barnstaple?], Thomas de Hertford, Masters J. Noble, B. de Lardario, W. de Capella, who all witnessed the previous transactions. Also Master R. de Tefford.

192 INSTITUTION. 28 November 1259. Richard de Modbury, priest, was admitted and instituted to the vicarage of Berry Pomeroy, which was assessed [as consisting] of the altarage and the buildings adjoining the church, and the bishop reserved until Michaelmas the power to increase or diminish [the assessment]; this was at the presentation of the proctor of the abbey and convent of Ste Marie le Val in Normandy.

193 QUITCLAIM. 28 November 1259, Exeter. Master R. de Tefford obtained from the lord bishop letters of quittance in respect of all extraordinary collections and receipts from the diocese of Exeter, except for the Quinquagesima collection.

[v] Or Blackawton?
[w] William Button, 1248–64.
[x] 1250.

194 DEPOSITUM. Eodem die ibidem posuit W. de Capella litteras Radulphi de Trublevile et Henrici in thesauro S. Petri Exon' in coffro suo proprio.

195 VISITATIO. Anno eodem die Veneris post festum S. Katerine, hoc est iv kalendas Decembris, visitavit dominus episcopus priorissam et conventum de Polslo et statuit quedam sine scriptis.

196 CORRECTIO. Anno eodem die S. Andree apud Hambir' admisit Brictius, canonicus Plimpt', nomine prioris et conventus, correctiones prius traditas in visitatione ibidem celebrata.

197 INSTITUTIO. Anno eodem in crastino S. Andree ibidem ad presentationem I. de Regny, veri patroni ecclesie de Eggenesford', [Fo.10] admisit dominus episcopus Willelmum de Wemmewrth', presbiterum, ad ecclesiam ipsam vacantem per resignationem W. de Bisimano et eum instituit, et habuit litteras in forma communi.

198 DEDICATIO. Anno eodem die Mercurii post festum S. Andree apostoli dominus episcopus dedicavit ecclesiam de Hambiriton'.

199 DEDICATIO. Anno eodem die Iovis post festum S. Andree dominus episcopus dedicavit ecclesiam de S. Marie Otery.

200 DEDICATIO. Anno eodem in vigilia S. Nicholai dominus episcopus dedicavit ecclesiam Veteris Dunekewill'.

201 INSTITUTIO. Anno eodem die S. Nicholai apud Hambiri Coffin dominus episcopus, ad presentationem Radulphi de Doddesc', admisit magistrum Ricardum de Alleswrth' ad ecclesiam de Legh' Guobol' et eum instituit in eadem cum onere residendi, et habuit litteras inductionis sed non institutionis.

202 CUSTODIA. Anno et die eisdem ibidem ad presentationem Rogeri de Sanford', militis, commisit dominus episcopus Gregorio de S. Melano, clerico, custodiam ecclesie de Sokebroc vacantis usque ad proximum venturum festum S. Iohanni Baptiste in Nativitate, et habuit litteras inductionis.

203 DEDICATIO. Anno eodem in crastino S. Nicholai dominus episcopus dedicavit ecclesiam de Sildenne.

204 DEDICATIO. Anno eodem in crastino Conceptionis S. Marie dominus episcopus dedicavit iii altaria in ecclesia de Kentelesber' et cimiterium.

205 DEDICATIO. Anno eodem die Mercurii post festum S. Nicholai dominus episcopus dedicavit ecclesiam de Sanford Peverel'.

206 COLLATIO. Anno eodem die S. Thome martiris contulit dominus episcopus Rogero de Derteford', clerico, prebendam que fuit magistri Iohannis Wiger in ecclesia Crideton'.

194 DEPOSIT. 28 November 1259, Exeter. W[illiam] de Capella deposited letters of Ralph de Turberville, and of Henry, in his own private chest in the treasury of St Peter's at Exeter.

195 VISITATION. 28 November 1259. The lord bishop visited the prioress and convent of Polsloe, and decreed certain things without putting them in writing.

196 CORRECTION. 30 November 1259, Broadhembury. Brictius, canon of Plympton, in the name of the prior and convent, acknowledged the corrections previously delivered at the visitation held there.

197 INSTITUTION. 1 December 1259, Broadhembury. At the presentation of J. de Regny, true patron of Eggesford church, the lord bishop admitted and instituted William de Wembworthy, priest, to the said church, vacant by the resignation of W. de Bisimano; and he had letters in common form.

198 DEDICATION. 3 December 1259. The lord bishop dedicated the church of Broadhembury.

199 DEDICATION. 4 December 1259. The lord bishop dedicated the church of Ottery St Mary.

200 DEDICATION. 5 December 1259. The lord bishop dedicated the church of Dunkeswell.

201 INSTITUTION. 6 December 1259, Payhembury. At the presentation of Ralph de Doddiscombe, the lord bishop admitted Master Richard de Aldsworth to Doddiscombesleigh church and instituted him in the same with the duty of residing; and he had letters of induction but not of institution.

202 CUSTODY. 6 December 1259, Payhembury. At the presentation of Roger de Sanford, knight, the lord bishop gave Gregory de S Melano, clerk, custody of the vacant church of Shobrooke until 24 June 1260; and he had letters of induction.

203 DEDICATION. 7 December 1259. The lord bishop dedicated the church of Sheldon.

204 DEDICATION. 9 December 1259. The lord bishop dedicated three altars in the church of Kentisbeare, and the graveyard.

205 DEDICATION. 10 December 1259. The lord bishop dedicated the church of Sampford Peverel.

206 COLLATION. 29 December 1259. The lord bishop collated Roger de Dartford, clerk, to the prebend which had been Master John Wyger's in the church of Crediton.

207   PREDICATIO. Die S. Iohannis apostoli et evangeliste dominus episcopus concessit ministro et fratribus et captivis Sancte Trinitatis litteras predicationis usque ad annum cum indulgentia xv dierum.

208   MANUMISSIO. Anno eodem die Circumcisionis Domini signata fuit talis littera magistro Iohanni de Plympton', scilicet sub hac forma: Universis Christi fidelibus presentes litteras inspecturis Walterus, miseratione divina Exon' episcopus, salutem eternam in Domino. Ad universitatis vestre notitiam volumus pervenire quod nos manumisimus et quietum clamavimus magistro Iohanni de Plimpton' Petrum Dureman cum tota sequela sua et catallis ab omni servitute, nativitate et servili conditione pro nobis et successoribus nostris inperpetuum; ita quod nobis vel successoribus predictis in prefato Petro, sequela eius vel catallis aliquid iuris, subiectionis vel servitutis non liceat decetero vendicare. Concessimus etiam prefato Petro pro nobis et successoribus nostris quod libere possit ire et redire per terram nostram absque calumpnia nostra vel successorum nostrorum vel alius {sic}, ubicumque voluerit, sine omni calengia cum sequela sua et catallis suis morari. Quod ne processu temporis alicui vertatur in dubium presentes litteras ei duximus concedendas. Datum apud Lawitteton' die S. Thome martiris anno gratie mccl nono et consecrationis nostre anno secundo.

209   CARTA REGIS DE CAPELLARIA DE BOSEHAM'.[17] Henricus, Dei gratia etc., archiepiscopis, episcopis, abbatibus, prioribus, comitibus, baronibus, iusticiariis, vicecomitibus, prepositis, ministris et omnibus aliis ballivis et fidelibus suis salutem. Sciatis nos concessisse et hac carta nostra confirmasse pro nobis et heredibus nostris venerabili in Christo patri Willelmo, Exonien' episcopo, capellariam de Bosham cum manerio de Chiddeham in comitatu Suthsex', et cum manerio de Ferndon' in comitatu Suthampton', et cum manerio de Horsleg' in comitatu Sutreye, cum omnibus [Fo.10v] terris, decimis, feoudis, serviciis, advocationibus ecclesiarum, collationibus prebendarum et omnibus aliis pertinentiis suis, et cum omnibus libertatibus et liberis consuetudinibus ad eandem capellariam et maneria predicta spectantibus; habenda et tenenda de nobis et heredibus nostris ipsi episcopo et successoribus suis imperpetuum, adeo libere et quiete et pacifice ut aliquis eadem unquam melius et liberius tenuit. Quare volumus et firmiter precipimus pro nobis et heredibus nostris quod idem episcopus et successores sui inperpetuum habeant et teneant predictam capellariam de Bosham cum manerio de Chiddeham in comitatu Suthsexie, et cum manerio de Ferndon' in comitatu de Suthampton', et cum manerio de Horsleg' in comitatu de Sutrreye, cum omnibus terris, decimis, feoudis, serviciis, advocationibus ecclesiarum, collationibus prebendarum et omnibus aliis pertinentiis suis, et cum omnibus libertatibus et liberis consuetudinibus ad eandem capellariam et maneria predicta pertinentibus; adeo libere, quiete, pacifice ut aliquis eam unquam melius et liberius tenuit, sicut predictum est. Hiis testibus: venerabili in Christo patre W[altero], Ebor' archiepiscopo, R. comiti Pictav' et

---

[17] This entry seems to have been written in by the registrar as part of the normal flow of the register.

207 PREACHING. 27 December 1259. The lord bishop granted the master and brethren of the Holy Trinity, and the captives, licence to preach for a year, with an indulgence of fifteen days.

208 MANUMISSION. 1 January 1260. The following letter was sealed for Master John de Plympton, namely in these terms: To all Christ's faithful who inspect the present letters Walter, by divine compassion bishop of Exeter, eternal greeting in the Lord. We wish it to be known to all of you that we have manumitted, and quitclaimed to Master John de Plympton, Peter Dureman with all his brood and chattels from all service, neifty and servile status, on behalf of ourselves and our successors in perpetuity. On terms that it shall not be lawful hereafter for us or our aforesaid successors to claim any right, obedience or service from the aforesaid Peter, his household or chattels. On behalf of ourselves and our successors we have also granted to the aforesaid Peter that he may be able freely to go and return through our land without challenge from us or our successors or anyone [and], with his brood and his chattels, to remain without dispute wheresoever he should wish. In order that this matter should not come to be doubted by anyone with the passage of time, we have thought fit to grant him the present letters. Given at Lawhitton on 29 December in the year of grace 1259 and in the second year of our consecration.

209 ROYAL CHARTER CONCERNING BOSHAM CHAPEL. 26 November 1243. Henry, by the grace of God etc, to the archbishops, bishops, abbots, priors, earls, barons, justices, sheriffs, provosts, minor officials and all other bailiffs and faithful subjects, greeting. You should know that on behalf of ourselves and our heirs we have granted and by this charter of ours confirmed to the venerable father in Christ William,[y] bishop of Exeter, the chapel of Bosham with the manor of Chidham in the county of Sussex, the manor of Faringdon in the county of Hampshire and the manor of Horsley in the county of Surrey, with all the lands, tithes, fees, services, advowsons of churches, collations to prebends and all other of their appurtenances, and with all the liberties and free customs relating to the same chapel and the aforesaid manors; for the said bishop and his successors to have and to hold from us and our heirs in perpetuity, as freely, with such immunity, and as peacefully as anyone has ever held the same on the best terms and the most free. Wherefore we wish and, with authority, order, on behalf of ourselves and our heirs, that the same bishop and his successors are to have and to hold in perpetuity the aforesaid chapel of Bosham with the manor of Chidham in the county of Sussex, the manor of Faringdon in the county of Hampshire and the manor of Horsley in the county of Surrey, with all the lands, tithes, fees, services, advowsons of churches, collations to prebends and all other of their appurtenances, and with all the liberties and free customs pertaining to the same chapel and the aforesaid manors, as freely, with such immunity, and as peacefully as anyone has ever held it on the best terms and the most free, as was said above. Witnessed by the venerable father in Christ Walter,[z] archbishop of York, our

y William Brewer, 1224–44.
z Walter de Gray, 1215–55.

Cornub' fratre nostro, Symone de Monteforti comiti Leycestr', H. de Boun comiti Estsexie et Herfordie, Willelmo de Cantilupo, Bertramo de Cryol, Iohanne filio Galfridi, Radulpho filio Nicholai, Galfrido Dispens', Paulino Peyner, Herberto filio Mathei, Iohanne de Plesset', Waltero de Lutton', et aliis. Datum per manus venerabilis patris R., Cicestr' episcopi, cancellarii nostri, apud Westm' vicesimo sexto die Novembris anno regni nostri vicesimo octavo.

210   Anno eodem die SS Fabiani et Sebastiani consolidavit dominus episcopus portionem magistri Iohannis de Cridewill' quam habuit in ecclesia de Hascumb' portioni domini Henrici de Hascumb', presbiteri, eiusdem ecclesie rectoris.

211   ORDINATIO ECCLESIE S. PAULINI. Omnibus sancte matris ecclesie filiis presens scriptum visuris vel intellecturis Walterus, Dei gratia Exon' ecclesie minister humilis, salutem in Domino sempiternam. Noveritis quod cum inter Rogerum de S. Constantino et Iohannem Haym, clericos, super ecclesia B. Pauli in Cornub', que ad advocationem domini .. illustris regis Alemannie spectare dinoscitur, controversie materia orta fuisset; tandem eisdem iuri quod se in dicta ecclesia vel ad ecclesiam ipsam habere asserebant vel habebant de mera et spontanea voluntate sua pure et absolute renuntiantibus et ordinationi nostre totaliter se subponentibus, quam ordinationem sacramento corporaliter prestito se servaturos promiserunt, nos, divina invocata gratia, de consensu prefati illustris regis dicte ecclesie veri patroni, in forma subscripta ordinavimus et ordinamus; videlicet quod dictus Rogerus dictam ecclesiam cum suis pertinentiis et cum cura animarum habeat, et dicto Iohanni Haym sexaginta solidos singulis annis in festis B. Michaelis et Pasche pro rata de bonis dicte ecclesie, sub pena unius marce nobis quotiens commissa {sic} fuerit solvende, persolvat. Ita quidem quod alterutro eorum cedente vel decedente dicta ecclesia cum pertinentiis suis superstiti remaneat. Predictus vero Rogerus oneribus ordinariis et consuetis ad dictam ecclesiam spectantibus veluti eiusdem rector respondebit. In cuius rei testimonium presentem cartam fieri fecimus patentem. Datum London' in crastino [SS] Philippi et Iacobi consecrationis nostre anno secundo.

212   ORDINATIO VICARIE TOTTON'. Anno eodem iii kalendas Februarii apud Peincton' ordinavit dominus episcopus sic: Universis etc., Walterus etc. Orta dudum inter dilectos filios Nicholaum priorem et conventum ex parte una et Walterum, perpetuum vicarium ecclesie Totton', ex altera super

brother Richard, count of Poitou and earl of Cornwall, Simon de Montfort, earl of Leicester, H[umphrey] de Bohun, earl of Essex and Hereford, William de Cantilupe,[a] Bertram de Crioil,[b] John fitzGeoffrey,[c] Ralph fitzNicholas, Geoffrey Dispenser,[d] Paulinus Peyner,[e] Herbert fizMatthew, John de Plessis,[f] Walter de Lutton, and others. Given by the hand of the venerable father Ralph, bishop of Chichester,[g] our chancellor, at Westminster on 26 November in the 28th year of our reign.

210 [CONSOLIDATION]. 20 January 1260. The lord bishop consolidated the portion which Master John de Cridewill has held in the church of Haccombe with the portion of Sir Henry de Haccombe, priest, rector of the same church.

211 ORDINANCE FOR THE CHURCH OF PAUL. 2 May 1259, London. To all the sons of holy mother church who see or learn of this present document, Walter, by the grace of God humble servant of the church of Exeter, eternal greeting in the Lord. You are to know that since a matter of dispute had arisen between Roger de Constantine and John Haym, clerks, over the church of Paul in Cornwall, of which the advowson is known to belong to the lord [Richard], the illustrious king of the Germans, at length the same parties renounced the right which they were claiming to have, or [actually] did have, in or relating to the said church with pure and free will, unconditionally and absolutely, and submitted themselves completely to our ordinance; taking a corporal oath, they promised that would observe this ordinance. We, after invoking the divine grace, and with the consent of the aforementioned illustrious king, true patron of the said church, have laid down and do lay down in the following terms: to wit, that the said Roger should have the said church with all its appurtenances and with the cure of souls, and that he should pay the said John Haym 60 shillings each year, at the feasts of Michaelmas and Easter, in proportionate shares, from the property of the said church, under penalty of one mark payable to us as often as [the payment] should be omitted. In terms indeed that on the departure or decease of either of them the said church with its appurtenances should accrue to the survivor. Moreover the aforesaid Roger, as its rector, shall be responsible for all the ordinary and customary charges due from the said church. In testimony whereof we have had this present charter made patent. Given etc.

212 ORDINANCE FOR THE VICARAGE OF TOTNES. 30 January 1260, Paignton. The lord bishop ordained as follows: To all etc, Walter etc. A matter of dispute formerly arose between our beloved sons Nicholas, the prior, and the convent, on the one part and Walter, perpetual vicar of the church of

[a] At one time steward of the king's household and keeper of the Great Seal, and bishop of Worcester 1237–66.
[b] Warden of the Cinque Ports and castellan of Dover.
[c] A royal counsellor, one-time sheriff of Yorkshire.
[d] A royal clerk and member of the king's council.
[e] Is this Paulinus Piper, a royal counsellor?
[f] Earl of Warwick 1247–63.
[g] Ralph Neville, bishop 1222–44.

portionibus vicarie predicte materia questionis, tandem, filio pacis interveniente, partibus ipsis in presentia nostra constitutis promittentibusque ac
iurantibus sacramento in Verbo Dei corporaliter prestito stare ordinationi
nostre et se subponentibus voluntati nostre in omnibus, nos, quiete
tranquillitate et utilitate partium predictarum consideratis, cuiuslibet contentionis tollende causa inter partes easdem taliter ordinamus, videlicet quod
predictus Walterus ipsius ecclesie, sicut prius, vicarius existat et ipsi ecclesie et
parochianis eiusdem honeste et honorifice in omnibus serviciis ad vicariam
ecclesie predicte spectantibus deserviat. Et pro omnibus obventionibus et
proventibus quos de ecclesia B. Marie priore et conventu predictis, nomine
vicarie, percipere consuevit [Fo.11] et quos, suo perpetuo, eisdem priori et
conventui remisit et quietos clamavit, de predictis priore et conventu per
manum eiusdem prioris vel eius assignati in predicta ecclesia B. Marie decem
marcas sterlingorum percipiat annuatim, quas predictos priorem et conventum ei solvere et reddere teneri volumus terminis infra scriptis, scilicet
infra quindenam Resurrectionis Dominice v marcas et infra quindenam festi
S. Michaelis mense Septembris v marcas. Item habeat idem vicarius
consuetas obventiones ratione confessionum provenientes et unum denarium
missalem tantum quolibet die quo aliquid oblationis usque ad unum denarium
vel amplius evenerit. Habeat quoque idem vicarius quicquid sibi ex
testamentis deficientium ratione parochie sue legatum sibi fuerit, sine qualibet
diminutione, salvis legatis ad matricem ecclesiam spectantibus. Omnes vero
obventiones alias et proventus ipsius ecclesie undecumque provenientes dicti
prior et conventus, absque omni impedimento, contradictione et reclamatione
predicti vicarii et suorum, cum integritate percipiant annuatim. Et ne presens
nostra ordinatio in recidive contentionis scrupulum relabatur, ordinamus,
statuimus et partibus ipsis sub debito prestiti sacramenti precipimus ut
ordinationem nostram diligenter et fideliter attendant et observent et
nullatenus contraveniant sub pena xl solidorum, quam totiens commissam
intelligi et nobis solvi volumus a parte contra hanc nostram ordinationem
veniente quotiens contra eam expresse fuerit attemptatum seu eam non
observari contigerit. In cuius rei testimonium presentibus litteris, penes
utramque partem divisim remanentibus, sigillum nostrum apponi fecimus.
Datum apud Peyncton' iii kalendas Februarii consecrationis nostre anno
secundo.

213   ORDINATIO ECCLESIE DE DODDETON'. Anno eodem die S. Agathe
virginis apud Exon' ordinavit dominus episcopus sic: Universis etc. Walterus
Exon' episcopus etc. Cum ecclesia S. David de Doddeton', olim parrochialis,
dum adhuc parrochia ipsa secularibus coleretur ab incolis, dilectis filiis ..
abbati et conventui Dunekewill' per bone memorie Willelmum episcopum,
predecessorem nostrum, in proprios usus collata esse diceretur et concessa, et
nos parrochiam nostram – sicut ex officii nostri debito tenemur – visitantes,
inveniremus quod predicti monachi, ipsius parrochie incolis eiectis, fundum
ipsum ad propriam redegerunt culturam, divinum cultum in ecclesia ipsa
subtraxerunt, campanas dimiserunt, et fontes regenerationis populi Christiani

Totnes, on the other, over the apportionment of the aforesaid vicarage; at length, by the intervention of the Son of Peace, the parties themselves met in our presence and they promised and, taking a corporal oath in the Word of God, swore that they would keep our ordinance and submit themselves to our will in all matters. We [therefore], having considered the peace, tranquillity and benefit of the aforesaid parties, and for the sake of removing any kind of contention between the same parties, lay down as follows: to wit, that the aforesaid Walter should remain vicar of that church, as before, and should serve the said church and the parishioners of the same, decently and honourably, in all the duties relating to the vicarage of the aforesaid church. And in exchange for all the occasional offerings and the proceeds which he has been accustomed to take, on account of the vicarage, from the church of St Mary [and] from the aforesaid prior and convent and which, all his life long, he has waived and quitclaimed to the same prior and convent, he shall receive annually from the aforesaid prior and convent, by the hand of the same prior, or his assign, in the aforesaid church of St Mary ten marks sterling; we wish the aforesaid prior and convent to be bound to pay and to render to him these [ten marks] at the dates written below, namely five marks within a fortnight of Easter and five marks within a fortnight of the feast of St Michael in September. Further, the same vicar is to have all the customary occasional offerings made on account of confessions, and one mass-penny only on any day on which there happens to be an offering amounting to one penny or more. The same vicar is also to have whatever shall be bequeathed to him in respect of his parish in the wills of the dying, without any deduction, save for legacies relating to the mother church. The said prior and convent shall receive in their entirety each year all the other occasional offerings and proceeds of the said church, from whatever source, without any hindrance, objection and counter-claim from the aforesaid vicar and his own men. And in order that our present ordinance should not sink back into a recurrent bone of contention, we lay down, decree and order that the parties themselves, under the bond of the oath they have taken, should diligently and faithfully take notice of and observe our ordinance, and that they should in no wise contravene it, under penalty of 40 shillings as often as this is found to have been committed, which we wish to be paid to us by the party acting against this our ordinance as often as it shall happen that this ordinance is expressly disputed, or that it is not observed. In witness whereof we have had our seal affixed to the present letters, [copies of which] are to remain with each party separately. Given etc.

213 ORDINANCE FOR THE CHURCH OF DOTTON. 5 February 1260, Exeter. The lord bishop ordained as follows: To all etc, Walter, bishop of Exeter, etc. Since the former parish church of St David at Dotton, while the said parish was still tended by resident secular priests, was alleged to have been collated and granted by bishop William of blessed memory, our predecessor, to his beloved sons the abbot and convent of Dunkeswell as appropriated to their use; and since, on visiting our parish, as we are bound to do by the duty of our office, we found that the aforesaid monks, having ejected the inhabitants of the said parish, had brought the said estate under their own cultivation, withdrawn divine worship from the said church, taken down the bells, and

eiecerunt, locum ipsum prophanando, monachos ipsos ad presentiam nostram
fecimus evocari super premissis responsuros. Sane abbate et conventu
predictis in presentia nostra constitutis, et ex officii nostri debito an super
huiusmodi iniuriis, quas se commisisse fatebantur, competenter satisfacere
vellent requisitis, finaliter responderunt se monitis nostris et mandatis velle
obedire, ordinationi nostre et gratie se de plano super hiis supponentes,
eamque observare et nullo umquam tempore contra venire bona fide
promittentes. Cum igitur ecclesie nostre Exon' iura conservare et subditorum
nostrorum animarum saluti providere ac singulorum utilitatibus prospicere
teneamur, volentes facta predecessorum nostrorum canonica observare sicut a
successoribus nostra cupimus observari, de consilio et assensu dilectorum
filiorum .. decani et capituli nostri Exon, in negotio ipso taliter duximus
ordinandum: videlicet, quod ecclesia ipsa ad insignia matricis ecclesie sicut
olim fuit restituta et sub debita honestate conservata, monachi ipsi in eadem
ecclesia per unum de monachis suis vel per secularem presbiterum singulis
diebus faciant divina celebrari, et omnes proventus et redditus ipsius ecclesie
pleno iure percipiant tanquam suos, et siquid onus ordinarium de predicta
ecclesia Exon' ecclesie debeatur vel reddi consueverit, solvant annuatim; ita
tamen quod si terram ipsius parrochie vel maiorem eius partem ad dominium
vel culturam secularium personarum devenire contingat, [Fo.11v] per
ydoneum presbiterum secularem nobis et successoribus nostris presentandum
in quem cura animarum canonice transferri valeat eidem ecclesie deserviatur.
Statuentes insuper quod, si monachi ipsi contra hanc nostram ordinationem
non observando eam duxerint veniendum, si, moniti competenter, non
satisfecerint, iure quod in eadem ecclesia habere se dicunt perpetuo cadant. In
cuius rei testimonium etc. Datum Exon' die S. Agathe virginis anno mcclix et
consecrationis nostre anno ii.

214 COMMENDATIO. Anno eodem in crastino S. Agathe virginis apud
Exon' ad presentationem Rogeri de Trelosk, veri patroni ecclesie de
Northindle vacantis, commendavit dominus episcopus ecclesiam ipsam
Radulpho de Ilstinton', cantori Exon', ita quod in cantaria sua predicta per
huiusmodi commendationem non preiudicetur eidem. Eodem die ibidem in
capella S. Fidis idem cantor resignavit ecclesiam de Lawitteton'.

215 CUSTODIA INSTITUTIO. Anno, die et loco eisdem ad presentationem
Dionisie, quondam uxoris Rogeri de Reygni, vere patrone ecclesie de Esse
Reygni vacantis, commisit dominus episcopus custodiam ipsius ecclesie
magistro Alexandro de la Cnoll' usque ad quindenam Pasche. Postea,[18] ii
nonas Iulii apud Horsleg' anno tertio, dominus episcopus instituit eum, et
habuit litteras quia tunc exhibuit legitimationem suam.

[18] This second sentence, in perhaps a different hand and squeezed in, was clearly
added later.

thrown out the fonts wherein Christ's people are reborn, profaning the said place, we have had the said monks summoned to our presence to answer for the foregoing matters. When the aforesaid abbot and convent had indeed assembled in our presence and, according to the duty of our office, been interrogated as to their willingness to make adequate amends for offences of that kind – which they admitted they had committed – they replied finally that they were willing to obey our warnings and commands, submitting themselves under summary procedure to our ordinance and grace concerning these matters, and promising in good faith that they would observe and never at any time disobey them. Since, therefore, we are bound to preserve the rights of our church of Exeter, and to see to the salvation of the souls of the members of our flock and to have an eye to the benefit of each, wishing to observe the canonical acts of our predecessors, just as we desire ours to be observed by our successors, with the advice and consent of our beloved sons our dean and chapter of Exeter, we have thought fit to ordain as follows in this affair: to wit, that the said church should have returned to it the outward signs of a mother church, as it was formerly, and be maintained with due decency, and that the said monks shall have divine worship celebrated every day in the same church by one of their own monks or by a secular priest. They shall take as their own, with full title, all the proceeds and revenues of the said church, and if any ordinary burden is owed or has customarily been paid from the aforesaid church to the church of Exeter, they shall pay it annually; on such terms, however, that if it should happen that the land of the said parish, or the greater part of it, should come into the lordship or cultivation of secular persons, the same church is to be served by a suitable secular priest, to be presented to us and our successors, to whom the cure of souls may validly be transferred in accordance with the canons. We decree, furthermore, that if the said monks should think fit to disobey this our ordinance by not observing it, and if they should not make amends after being suitably warned, they shall lose in perpetuity the rights which they allege they have in the same church. In testimony whereof etc. Given etc.

214 COMMENDATION 6 February 1260, Exeter. At the presentation of Roger de Trelosk, true patron of the vacant church of North Hill, the lord bishop commended Ralph de Ilsington, precentor of Exeter, to the said church, on terms that there be no prejudice to the same as to his precentorship by a commendation of this kind. On the same day in the same place, in the chapel of St Faith, the same precentor resigned the church of Lawhitton.

215 CUSTODY: INSTITUTION. 6 February 1260, Exeter. At the presentation of Denise, formerly wife of Roger de Regny, true patroness of the vacant church of Ashreigney, the lord bishop gave Master Alexander de la Knolle custody of the said church until a fortnight after Easter. Subsequently, on 6 July 1260, at Horsley, the lord bishop instituted him; and he had letters, because he then showed his [letters of] legitimation.

216 CUSTODIA. Anno et die eisdem apud Brankescumb' contulit dominus episcopus custodiam ecclesie de Lawitteton' vacantis Roberto de Wisleg', presbitero, usque ad sue beneplacitum voluntatis.

217 INSTITUTIO. Anno, die et loco predictis ad presentationem et plenam voluntatem prioris et conventus de Berliz, verorum patronorum ecclesie de Marineleg', dominus episcopus admisit magistrum Robertum de Polamesford' ad ecclesiam ipsam vacantem et ipsum instituit in eadem.

218 PREDICATIO. Anno eodem die Sabbati post festum S. Agathe virginis apud Lodres dominus episcopus admisit fratres et nuntios hospitalis de Alto Passu ad querendum et colligendum elemosinas Christi fidelium in episcopatu Exon' absque convocatione et voce predicationis, et habuerunt litteras.

219 ORDINATIO [VICARIE]. Anno et loco eisdem die Dominica in Sexagesima inter magistrum R. Evrard, rectorem ecclesie de Uplim, et Ricardum de Sireburn', presbiterum, quondam ipsius ecclesie vicarium, ordinavit dominus episcopus sic: Universis etc. Walterus Exon' episcopus etc. Noverit universitas vestra quod, cum inter dilectos filios magistrum Robertum Euuerard', rectorem, et Ricardum de Syreburn', presbiterum, qui se gerebat pro vicario ecclesie de Uplym, nostre diocesis, super vicaria eiusdem ecclesie orta esset materia contentionis, tandem – predictis magistro Roberto et Ricardo se et totum ius quod habebant seu habere se dicebant in ipsa vicaria et fructibus ac proventibus eiusdem nostro penitus arbitrio supponentibus – se et totum ius suum predictum in premissis voluntati et ordinationi nostre sponte simpliciter et pure submittentes, prout in litteris ipsorum super hoc confectis continetur, iuramento nichilominus hinc inde corporaliter prestito, promittentes se super eisdem ordinationem nostram accepturos, et in omnibus ac per omnia fideliter observaturos; nos itaque, communicato virorum prudentium consilio super prefata vicaria et fructibus ac proventibus eiusdem, Deum habentes pre oculis, ordinamus in hunc modum: videlicet quod eadem vicaria et omnes sui fructus ac proventus accrescant parsonatui ecclesie memorate, ipsamque vicariam et fructus ac proventus suos eidem personatui consolidamus imperpetuum; ita sane quod dictus magister Robertus et successores sui qui pro tempore fuerint dicto Ricardo quinque marcas sterlingorum de bonis prefate ecclesie, nomine simplicis beneficii, in maiori ecclesia Exon' per manus subthesaurarii eiusdem ecclesie solvant annuatim ad duos anni terminos, scilicet ad Pascham duas marcas et dimidiam et ad festum S. Michaelis duas marcas et dimidiam, quoad vixerit vel donec eidem in beneficio ecclesiastico fuerit uberiori provisum. Si vero dictus magister Robertus seu successores sui memorato Ricardo dictas quinque marcas annuas, terminis prenotatis, infra octo dies postquam legittime ab eodem Ricardo super hoc fuerint requisiti, plene non solverint, [Fo.12] liceat ipsi Ricardo, non obstantibus submissione seu iuramento supradictis, libere ingredi portiones quas prius habuit in ecclesia antedicta. Datum apud Lodr' viii kalendas Februarii anno Domini mccl nono consecrationis nostre anno ii. In cuius rei testimonium etc.

216 CUSTODY. 6 February 1260, Branscombe. The lord bishop collated Robert de Wisley,[h] priest, to the custody of the vacant church of Lawhitton, at the bishop's pleasure.

217 INSTITUTION. 6 February 1260, Branscombe. At the presentation and full will of the prior and convent of Barlinch, true patrons of Mariansleigh church, the lord bishop admitted Master Robert de Polamford to the said vacant church, and instituted him in the same.

218 PREACHING. 7 February 1260, Loders. The lord bishop admitted brothers and envoys of the hospital of San Jacopo d'Alto Pascio to seek and gather alms from Christ's faithful in the diocese of Exeter, without calling together or preaching by word of mouth; and they had letters.

219 ORDINANCE [OF A VICARAGE] 8 February 1260, Loders. The lord bishop ordained as follows between Master Robert Everard, rector of the church of Uplyme, and Richard de Sherborne, priest, formerly vicar of the said church: To all etc, Walter, bishop of Exeter, etc. Let all know that since a matter of contention had arisen between our beloved sons Master Robert Everard, rector, and Richard de Sherborne, priest, who was acting as vicar for the church of Uplyme in our own diocese, over the vicarage of the same church, at length – when the aforesaid Master Robert and Richard were submitting themselves and the whole claim which they had, or alleged they had, in the said vicarage, and the fruits and proceeds of the same, utterly to our decision – yielding themselves and their whole aforesaid claim in the foregoing voluntarily, completely and unconditionally to our will and ordinance, as is contained in the letters which they drew up on this matter. And moreover, having taken a corporal oath on either side, they promised that they would accept and would faithfully observe in all particulars and in all respects our ordinance on the same matters; we therefore, after taking advice from men of learning concerning the aforementioned vicarage and the fruits and proceeds of the same, and keeping God before our eyes, ordain in this manner: to wit, that the same vicarage, and all its fruits and proceeds, should accrue to the parsonage of the aforementioned church; and we consolidate the said vicarage and its fruits and proceeds with the same parsonage in perpetuity; on such terms indeed that the said Master Robert, and his successors for the time being, should pay annually to the said Richard five marks sterling – in the name of a simple benefice – from the property of the aforementioned church, in Exeter cathedral by the hand of the sub-treasurer of the same cathedral, at two dates in the year, namely two and a half marks at Easter and two and a half marks at Michaelmas, as long as [Richard] shall live or until provision should be made for the same in a more fruitful ecclesiastical benefice. If, indeed, the said Master Robert or his successors should not pay in full to the aforementioned Richard the said five marks a year, at the above-noted points, within eight days after they have been lawfully claimed by the same Richard in this regard, it is allowed to the said Richard, notwithstanding the above submission or oath, freely to enter the portions which he previously held in the aforesaid church. Given etc. In testimony whereof etc.

[h] Or possibly Whistley.

220 INSTITUTIO. Universis etc. Walterus, miseratione etc. Ad universitatis etc. quod nos ad presentationem dilecti filii magistri Ricardi de S. Gorono, rectoris ecclesie de Toriton', ad ipsius ecclesie vicariam Umfredum, presbiterum, divino caritatis intuitu admisimus et ipsum in eadem canonice instituimus vicarium; ordinantes et taxantes quod idem vicarius omnes proventus altalagii, quocumque nomine censeantur, nomine vicarie annuatim percipiat, [et] xii marcas argenti in festo Nativitatis S. Iohannis Baptiste et Natalis Domini vel infra octabis eorundem; reservata nobis nichilominus – cum ad partes illas veniremus – augendi minuendi hanc nostram taxationem seu ceteras portiones eidem vicario, nomine vicarie predicte, de voluntate rectoris eiusdem aut ipsius amicorum consilio, assignandi potestate. In cuius rei testimonium etc. Datum apud Horslegh' in festo Cathedre S. Petri, consecrationis nostre anno ii.

221 COMMENDATIO. Universis etc. Ad universitatis vestre notitiam tenore presentium volumus pervenire quod nos, ad presentationem dilecti filii Rogeri de Sanfford', veri patroni ecclesie de Sokebroc, ecclesiam ipsam vacantem dilecto filio Gregorio de S. Melano, subdiacono, titulo commendationis assignavimus usque ad completum annum integre possidendam. In cuius etc. Datum apud Horslegh' ix kalendas Martii consecrationis anno ii.

222[19] ORDINATIO VICARIE ECCLESIE DE ERMINTON'. Omnibus Christi fidelibus ad quos presens scriptum pervenerit Willelmus miseratione divina Exon' episcopus salutem in Domino. Cupientes quantum cum debito possumus utilitatibus omnium ecclesiarum nostre diocesis salubriter pro-videre, in ecclesia de Erminton' de consensu patronorum, videlicet religiosorum virorum prioris et conventus Montis Acuti, Cluniacens' ordinis, patronorum medietatis, et nobilis viri Hugonis Peverel, patroni, et Ricardi Peverel, persone alius {sic} mediaetatis eiusdem ecclesie, de vicaria perpetua in eadem de proborum consilio taliter duximus ordinandum: scilicet ut quicumque pro tempore fuerit vicarius in eadem canonice institutus percipiat ratione vicarie omnes obventiones altalagii et decimas minutas totius ecclesie parochie, exceptis decimis molendinorum, pomorum et feni; solvendo inde annuatim persone medietatis eiusdem ecclesie, qui ex presentatione dicti nobilis vel heredum suorum in eadem fuerit canonice institutus, unam marcam argenti ad duos anni terminos, scilicet in Pascha et in festo S. Michaelis pro equis portionibus; qui quidem vicarius habebit mesuagium in quo habitare solebat Martinus clericus cum gardino et aliis pertinentiis, et praeterea terram illam de Kyngeston' quam Robertus de Womewell' tenere solebat ad firmam de sanctuario ecclesie memorate. Dictus vero vicarius totius predicte ecclesie onera ordinaria, debita et consueta tantum in se sustinebit. In quorum omnium testimonium nos, una cum sigillis patronorum persone et vicarie {sic}, huic scripto signum nostrum apposuimus.

---

[19] This entry was probably added at some quiet time by Bronescombe's registrar on the blank lower half of the folio; the next folio starts with a new year of the episcopate.

220 INSTITUTION. 22 February 1260, Horsley. To all etc, Walter, by [divine] compassion etc. [We wish it to be known] to all [of you by the tenor of these presents] that at the presentation of our beloved son Master Richard de St Gorran, rector of Torrington church, we have admitted at the prompting of divine charity Humphrey, priest, to the vicarage of the said church, and have canonically instituted him vicar in the same; ordaining and assessing that the said vicar should take annually, on account of the vicarage, all the proceeds of the altarage, under whatever heading they are reckoned, [and] 12 silver marks at the feast of St John the Baptist and Christmas or within the octaves of the same. We reserve to ourselves, nevertheless, when we shall come to those parts, the power to increase or diminish this our assessment, or to assign other portions for the same vicar, on account of the aforesaid vicarage, at the wish of the rector of the same or on the advice of his friends. In testimony whereof etc. Given etc.

221 COMMENDATION. 21 February 1260, Horsley. To all etc. We wish it to be known to all of you by the tenor of these presents that, at the presentation of our beloved son Roger de Sanford, true patron of Shobrooke church, we have assigned the said vacant church to our beloved son Gregory de S Melano [St Mellion or Mullion], subdeacon, by title of commendation, to be possessed in its entirety for a full year. In testimony etc. Given etc.

222 ORDINANCE OF THE VICARAGE OF ERMINGTON CHURCH. No date; 1224–44. To all Christ's faithful to whom the present document shall come, William, by divine compassion bishop of Exeter, greeting in the Lord. Being desirous – so far as we can in accordance with our duty – to make wholesome provision for the needs of all the churches of our diocese, in the church of Ermington, with the consent of its patrons, to wit, the religious men the prior and convent of Montacute, of the Cluniac order, patrons of one mediety, and the noble lord Hugh Peverel, patron, and Richard Peverel, parson, of the other mediety of the same church, we have thought fit, with the advice of reliable persons, to lay down as follows for a perpetual vicarage in the same; namely, that whoever shall for the time being be the canonically instituted vicar in the same church shall, on account of the vicarage, take all the occasional offerings of the altarage and the lesser tithes of the whole parish church, except for the tithes from mills, apples and hay; and from this he shall pay each year to the parson of the mediety of the same church, who shall have been canonically instituted in the same at the presentation of the said noble [lord] or his heirs, one silver mark at two dates in the year, namely at Easter and at Michaelmas, in equal instalments; which same vicar shall have the dwelling-house in which Martin the clerk used formerly to live, with the garden and other appurtenances and, furthermore, that land at Kingston which Robert de Wonwell used to hold at farm from the sanctuary of the aforementioned church. The said vicar, indeed, shall bear on himself only the ordinary, due and customary burdens of the whole aforesaid church. In testimony of all of which we have affixed our seal to this document together with the seals of the patrons, parson and vicar.

[Fo.12v]   **223**   PREDICATIO. Consecrationis domini Walteri Exon' episcopi anno tertio die S. Edwardi regis et martiris apud Horsleg' dominus episcopus admisit fratres hospitalis S. Thome martiris in Acon' ad querendum et colligendum Christi fidelium elemosinas in episcopatu suo infra annum, et habuerunt litteras.

224   OBEDIENTIA. Anno die et loco eisdem abbas de Heyles prestitit manualem obedientiam domino episcopo pro ecclesia S. Keverane in Cornub' quam habet in proprios usus.

225   INSTITUTIO. Anno eodem die S. Cuthberti episcopi ibidem dominus episcopus, ad presentationem Ricardi Peverel, rectoris medietatis ecclesie de Ermington', admisit, de consensu prioris et conventus de Monte Acuto, Gotefridum de Salesbir', presbiterum, ad vicariam predicte ecclesie, et habet litteras institutionis et inductionis.

226   CUSTODIA SEQUESTRI DE ACFORD'. Anno eodem xii kalendas Aprilis ibidem dominus episcopus commisit Manasero filio Mathei custodiam ecclesie et sequestri sui de Acford' usque ad proxime venturum festum S. Michaelis ut exinde respondeat, et super hoc dedit litteras.

227   CUSTODIA SEQUESTRI S. CLEDERI. Anno eodem die Annunciationis Dominice apud Merton' dominus episcopus commisit Reginaldo de Bray custodiam ecclesie S. Clederi et sequestri sui in eadem donec magister W., nuper eiusdem rector, annum probationis compleverit, quod erit vii idus Decembris, vel donec votum professionis emiserit; ita quod de ipso sequestro respondeat; et de hoc dedit litteras. Postea ut infra anno eodem iii nonas Ianuarii.[20]

228   FORMA. Universis etc., W. etc. Ad universitatis vestre notitiam tenore presentium volumus pervenire quod nos, ad presentationem dilecti filii Ricardi Peverel, rectoris medietatis ecclesie de Ermington', veri hac vice patroni ipsius ecclesie vicarie, dilectum filium Gotefridum de Salesbir', presbiterum, ad vicariam ipsam vacantem de consensu prioris et conventus monasterii Montis Acuti, qui aliam ipsius ecclesie medietatem dicuntur obtinere, divine caritatis intuitu admisimus ipsumque G. in eadem canonice vicarium institutimus. In cuius etc. Datum xiii kalendas Aprilis anno tertio.

229   INSTITUTIO PRIORIS. Anno eodem iii kalendas Aprilis apud Horsleg' comparuerunt frater Nicolaus de S. Remigio, presentatus ad prioratum de Tregoni, et frater Galfridus, ordinatus procurator omnium bonorum abbatis et conventus ecclesie S. Marie de Valle in Norm', canonici loci predicti, petentes admitti ad suas administrationes; et quia propter repugnantiam mandatorum non potuerunt admitti de iure, supposuerunt se ordinationi

---

[20] 'Postea' onwards is an addition; it refers to **283**.

223 PREACHING. 18 March 1260, Horsley. In the third year of the consecration of the lord Walter, bishop of Exeter, the lord bishop admitted brothers of the hospital of St Thomas the Martyr at Acre to seek and gather alms from Christ's faithful in his diocese within the year; and they had letters.

224 OBEDIENCE. 18 March 1260, Horsley. The abbot of Hales kissed the bishop's hand in token of obedience to the lord bishop for his appropriated church of St Keverne in Cornwall.

225 INSTITUTION. 20 March 1260, Horsley. The lord bishop, at the presentation of Richard Peverel, rector of a mediety of Ermington church, with the consent of the prior and convent of Montacute, admitted Godfrey de Salisbury, priest, to the vicarage of the aforesaid church; and he has letters of institution and induction.

226 CUSTODY OF THE SEQUESTRATION OF OAKFORD. 21 March 1260, Horsley. The lord bishop committed to Manaserus fitzMatthew the custody of the church at Oakford and its sequestrated property until the next Michaelmas, from which date he is to render his accounts, and he granted letters concerning this matter.

227 CUSTODY OF THE SEQUESTRATION OF ST CLETHER. 25 March 1260, Merton. The lord bishop committed to Reginald de Bray the custody of the church of St Clether, and its sequestrated property there, until Master W. [de Trewinnoc], recently rector of the same, should finish his year of probation [as a monk], which will be on 7 December, or until he is allowed to withdraw from his vow of profession, on terms that [Reginald] shall render his accounts for the said sequestration; and he granted letters on this matter. Later, as below, on 3 January 1261.

228 FORMULA. 20 March 1260. To all etc, Walter, etc. We wish it to be known to all of you by the tenor of these presents that, at the presentation of our beloved son Richard Peverel, rector of a mediety of Ermington church, on this account true patron of the vicarage of the said church, we have admitted, at the prompting of divine charity, our beloved son Godfrey de Salisbury, priest, to that vacant vicarage, with the consent of the prior and convent of the monastery of Montacute, who are alleged to possess the other mediety of the said church, and we have canonically instituted the said Godfrey as vicar in the same. In testimony etc. Given etc.

229 INSTITUTION OF A PRIOR. 30 March 1260, Horsley. There appeared Brother Nicholas de S Remigio, who had been presented to the priory of Tregony, and Brother Geoffrey, appointed proctor for all the property of the abbey and convent of Ste Marie le Val in Normandy, [both] canons of the aforesaid place, seeking to be admitted to their spheres of administration. Because [their] mandates were contradictory, they could not be admitted as of

et gratie domini episcopi, et de hoc confecerunt litteras suas. Unde dominus episcopus de gratia sua fratrem Nicolaum ad regimen dicti prioratus admisit, dummodo inconsulto episcopo non recedat ab eo. Item fratri Galfrido commisit custodiam omnium bonorum dictorum abbatis et conventus in Devon', dummodo bona mobilia et immobilia non alienat vel transferat seu ad ecclesias vacantes presentet inconsulto episcopo donec aliud sufficiens mandatum exhibeat.

230 COMMENDATIO. Anno eodem feria v Pasche, hoc est vi idus Aprilis, ad presentationem prioris et conventus Totton dominus episcopus commendavit magistro Iohanni de Blakedon' ecclesiam de Asprington vacantem titulo commendationis usque ad annum possidendam, et habet litteras.[21]

231 HOMAGIUM. Anno eodem die Mercurii proxima ante festum S. Georgii martiris apud Chedeham' dominus episcopus concessit Willelmo de Pageham, militi, in feudum illam partem wasti sui que inter stratam regiam que ducit de Cycestr' et Portesmue et fossatum magne crofte iuxta mare in parte meridionali ab occidente molendini domini episcopi, tenendam sibi etc., reddendo inde annuatim tres capones albos. Et inde homagium suum recepit; ita tamen quod dictus miles periculum communis pasture in se suscipiat, et totaliter contra omnes homines sustineat suis sumptibus.

232 INSTITUTIO. Anno eodem die S. Georgii London' ad presentationem domini Iohannis de Curtenay, veri patroni, dominus episcopus admisit Iohannem de Broclande, clericum, ad prebendam que fuit Theobaldi, clerici, vacantem pro eo quod idem Theobaldus uxoratus est, sicut constat et declaratur per sententiam officialis Exon'.

[Fo.13] **233** INSTITUTIO. Die et loco eisdem ad presentationem Ricardi de Spekcot et Willelmi de Fuleford', pro rata patronorum ecclesie de Belston', dominus episcopus admisit Willelmum de Speccot, subdiaconum, legitimatum, ad ecclesiam ipsam de Belston' vacantem per sententiam officialis.

234 CUSTODIA. Anno eodem die S. Marci evangeliste ibidem ad presentationem domini Iohannis de Curtenay, veri patroni, dominus episcopus admisit Willelmum de Stanford' ad custodiam prebende que fuit Iohannis de Brocland' in ecclesia de Cheaumeleg', vacantis eo quod aliam recepit in eadem et per resignationem sponte factam, usque ad festum S. Michaelis duraturam. Non habet litteras.[22]

235 PREDICATIO. In vigilia Inventionis Sancte Crucis anno eodem London' exivit littera predicationis pro hospitali S. Ascentii de Anagnia. Ita tamen predicator nullatenus admittatur.

---

[21] 'Non habet litteras' was added in tiny letters just after this entry, presumably as a reminder to himself by the registrar to get it done. This occurs again in **234**.
[22] Cf. **230**.

right. They therefore submitted themselves to the decision and the grace of the lord bishop, and they drew up letters of their own on this matter. Wherefore the lord bishop of his grace admitted Brother Nicholas to the governance of the said priory, provided that he did not withdraw from it without consulting the bishop. Further, he committed to Brother Geoffrey the custody of all the said abbot and convent's property in Devon, provided that he did not alienate or convey the moveable and immoveable property or make presentations to vacant churches, without consulting the bishop, until he should display some other adequate mandate.

230 COMMENDATION. 8 April 1260. At the presentation of the prior and convent of Totnes, the lord bishop commended Master John de Blakedon to the vacant church of Ashprington, to be possessed for a year by right of commendation; and he has letters.

231 HOMAGE. 21 April 1260, Chidham. The lord bishop granted in fee to Sir William de Pagham, knight, that part of his uncultivated land which lies between the highway (which leads from Chichester to Portsmouth) and the ditch of the large croft beside the sea to the south, and the lord bishop's mill to the west, to be held of him etc, for the rent thence each year of three white capons. And he received his homage on that account, on such terms, however, that the said knight takes on himself the risk of [meeting claims to] common pasture, which he is, at his own expense, to maintain entirely against all men.

232 INSTITUTION. 23 April 1260, London. At the presentation of Sir John de Courtenay, the true patron, the lord bishop admitted John de Brocland, clerk, to the prebend [at Chulmleigh] formerly held by Theobald, clerk, vacant because the same Theobald was married, as was established and declared by the judicial sentence of the official of Exeter.[i]

233 INSTITUTION. 23 April 1260, London. At the presentation of Richard de Speccott and of William de Fulford, alternating patrons of Belstone church, the lord bishop admitted William de Speccott, subdeacon, having been legitimized, to the said church of Belstone, vacant by the judicial sentence of the official.

234 CUSTODY. 25 April 1260, London. At the presentation of Sir John de Courtenay, the true patron, the lord bishop admitted William de Stanford to the custody, until Michaelmas, of the prebend in the church of Chulmleigh which had been John de Broclond's, vacant because [the latter] had received another [prebend] in the same [church] and voluntarily resigned [this one]. [William] did not have letters.

235 PREACHING. 2 May 1260, London. A licence to preach was issued on behalf of the hospital of the Ascension at Anagni. On condition, however, that a preacher was in no way to be admitted.

---

[i] What is evidently a later marginal note says that John did not have letters.

236   INSTITUTIO. Anno eodem die Ascensionis Domini apud Horslegh' ad presentationem domini regis Alemannie et Ogeri, rectoris ecclesie de Helleston', dominus episcopus admisit Milonem de Quokham, presbiterum, ad vicariam ipsius ecclesie de Helleston', consistentem in altalagio toto, dummodo idem vicarius solvat rectori vii marcas annuas; et habet litteras super hoc; et debet vicarius omnia onera debita sustinere.

237   CUSTODIA. Anno eodem die Pentecostes apud Horsleg' ad presentationem domini R. de Dodescumb' dominus episcopus commisit custodiam ecclesie de Leg' vacantis Henrico Snellard, clerico, usque ad festum S. Michaelis; ita quod nisi infra idem tempus fuerit in sacris aut gratiam obtinuerit specialem, extunc nichil iuris habeat in ea si canonicum impedimentum eum non excusat.

238[23]   ORDINES. Anno eodem in vigilia Sancte Trinitatis apud Horsleg' dominus episcopus celebravit ordines.

239   INSTITUTIO VICARIE DE THORNCUMB'. Anno eodem in crastino Sancte Trinitatis ibidem ad presentationem abbatis et conventus de Forde dominus episcopus admisit Iohannem de Thorncumb', presbiterum, ad vicariam ecclesie de Thorncumb'; salvo tamen iure ipsius cui per apostolicam sedem de eadem fuerat provisum si voluerit experiri; qui quidem Iohannes bona fide promisit spontaneus se velle cedere et sine difficultate resignare si contingat ipsum cui fuerat provisum iure suo experiri; et habet dictus Iohannes litteras inductionis tantum in forma prescripta. Non recepit curam, nec prestitit obedientiam. Postmodum xvi kalendas Septembris apud Exon recepit curam, prestitit obedientiam et iuravit se facturum residentiam; et habet litteras, salvo iure cuiuslibet.[24]

240[25]   CARTA LIBERTATUM CORNUB'. Reginaldus, Henrici regis filius, comes Cornubie, omnibus hominibus suis, Francis, Anglis et Walensibus, salutem. Sciatis me ecclesiam de Lanst' cum omnibus suis pertinentiis, tam ecclesiasticis quam laicis, et canonicos ibidem in honore Dei et B. prothomartiris Stephani ministrantes, et pro statu tranquillitate et pace H., regis Anglie, similiter et regni et pro salute anime Henrici regis, patris mei, et omnium antecessorum et successorum nostrorum, Deum assidue interpellantes, sub protectione Dei et domini H., regis Anglie, et mea suscepisse. Quare volo et concedo et hac carta mea confirmo quod predicti canonici habeant et teneant memoratam ecclesiam de Lanst' et omnes terras et tenuras suas in Cornub' quas rationabiliter habent vel adquirere poterunt in posterum ita libere et quiete, pacifice et honorifice sicut umquam ipsi vel antecessores sui liberius et melius tenuerunt; scilicet cum soch' et sach', tol et

---

[23] This entry was inserted at the end of the previous one, so was presumably added a little later.

[24] These last two sentences – 'Non recepit' on – seem an addition, as they are somewhat squeezed.

[25] This entry and the next three were obviously just written in by the registrar at this point.

236 INSTITUTION. 13 May 1260, Horsley. At the presentation of the lord king of Germany, and of Oger, rector of Helston church, the lord bishop admitted Miles de Quokham, priest, to the vicarage of the said church of Helston, which consisted of the whole altarage, provided that the vicar paid the rector seven marks a year; and he has letters concerning this; and the vicar must bear all the due burdens.

237 CUSTODY. 23 May 1260, Horsley. At the presentation of Sir R. de Doddiscombe, the lord bishop gave Henry Snellard, clerk, custody of the vacant church of Doddiscombsleigh until Michaelmas; on such terms that, unless within the same time he should have received holy orders or obtained a special remission, he should have no claim thereafter on that [church], if there was no canonical impediment to excuse him.

238 ORDINATION. 29 May 1260, Horsley. The lord bishop held an ordination.

239 INSTITUTION TO THE VICARAGE OF THORVERTON. 31 May 1260, Horsley. At the presentation of the abbot and convent of Forde, the lord bishop admitted John de Thorncombe, priest, to the vicarage of Thorncombe church; saving, however, the claim of anyone who should be provided to the same by the apostolic see, if he wished to exercise it. John indeed promised, in good faith and of his own free will, that he was willing to yield and to resign without objections, if it should happen that the man who was provided exercised his claim. And the said John has letters of induction only, in the prescribed form. He did not receive the cure of souls, nor did he furnish an assurance of obedience. Subsequently, on 17 August at Exeter, he received the cure of souls, promised obedience and swore that he would be resident; and he has letters, saving the claim of anyone else.

240 CHARTER OF PRIVILEGES OF CORNWALL [Between 1154 and 1175]. Reginald, son of King Henry [I], earl of Cornwall,ʲ to all his men, French, English and Welsh, greeting. You should know that I have taken under the protection of God and of the lord Henry [II], king of England, and of myself, the church of Launceston, with all its appurtenances, both ecclesiastical and lay, and the canons who minister in that same place in honour of God and of the blessed proto-martyr Stephen, and are assiduously interceding with God for the safety, calm and peace of H[enry], king of England, and likewise of the kingdom, and for the salvation of the soul of King Henry, my father, and all our ancestors and descendants. Wherefore I desire and grant and by this my charter confirm that the aforesaid canons are to have and to hold the aforementioned church of Launceston and all their lands and tenements in Cornwall, which they have in due form or shall be able to acquire in the future, as freely and with immunity, peacefully and honourably as ever they or their predecessors held them, on the freest or the best terms; namely, with soke and sake, toll and theam, and infangthief, and with all other privileges for themselves and their men concerning suit of court at the pleas and plaints of

ʲ 1141-75.

theam, et infangenthef, et cum omnibus aliis libertatibus sibi et hominibus suis de sectis scyrarum et hundredorum placitis et querelis, clyvewardis et omnibus aliis auxiliis, et omni seculari servicio et exactione et omnibus aliis occasionibus et consuetudinibus secularibus, sicut puram et perpetuam elemosinam. Preterea ad notitiam omnium volo pervenire quod R., prior de Lansc', in pleno comitatu coram me apud castellum de Dunehavede, preposito et burgensibus eiusdem ville presentibus, sufficienter et legitime disrationavit quod, tempore quo comes Moreton' mercatum diei Dominice de villa S. Stephani de Lansc' ad novam villam castelli de Dunhevet transtulit, canonici de Lanst' de assensu et voluntate memorati comitis de Moreton' retinebant sibi et burgo suo de Lanst' et burgensibus in ea manentibus omnes libertates ad liberum burgum spectantes cum eadem integritate quas ab antiquo habuerant preter mercatum diei Dominice tantummodo unum; et ipsi canonici habent de prepositura castelli xx solidos annuatim ad festum S. Martini; et quod easdem libertates integre et quiete et sine contradictione toto tempore H. regis Anglie, patris mei, habuerunt et tenuerunt. Quapropter ego omnes [Fo.13v] libertates ad liberum burgum spectantes memoratis canonicis et ville sue de Lanst' et hominibus in ea focum et locum habentibus cum memoratis xx solidis annui census concessi et hac carta mea confirmavi. Testibus: Roberto Dunstanvill', Ricardo de Raddun', vicecomite Cornub', Roberto filio Anketil, Hugone de Dunstanvill', Jordane de Trekarl, preposito, Mordont Sprakelyn.

241 CARTA LIBERTATUM CORNUB'. Ricardus, comes Pictav' et Cornub', omnibus baronibus suis et militibus et omnibus libere tenentibus in comitatu salutem. Sciatis nos concessisse et hac presenti carta nostra confirmasse Deo et ecclesie S. Stephani de Lanst' et canonicis ibidem Deo servientibus, pro statu et pace domini H., regis Anglie, fratris nostri, simul et regni, et pro salute anime domini Iohannis, regis Anglie, patris nostri, et pro salute anime mee et omnium antecessorum et successorum nostrorum, ut habeant omnes ecclesias suas et omnia ecclesiastica beneficia et possideant cum omnibus pertinentiis suis integre libere et pacifice que habent ex donationibus regum, comitum, baronum et aliorum bonorum virorum; terras etiam suas omnes et tenementa sua omnia que habent in burgo vel extra burgum cum omnibus pertinentiis suis libertatibus et liberis consuetudinibus suis que habent vel habuerunt ab antiquo, sicut carta donatorum testatur, vel in futurum rationabiliter acquirere poterint libere quiete et plenarie; et hec omnia, tam in ecclesiis quam in capellis terris rebus et possessionibus et omnibus pertinentiis suis, memoratis canonicis et successoribus suis concessimus habenda et possidenda in puram et perpetuam elemosinam libere honorifice et quiete ab omni seculari servicio et servili et de omnibus consuetudinibus secularibus et occasionibus omnimodis imperpetuum; et ne quis ponat predictos canonicos in placitum de aliquo tenemento suo nisi coram nobis ipsis vel coram ballivis nostris de Cornub'. Hiis testibus: Andrea de Chanceaus, Ricardo de Turre, Henrico Teutonico, Henrico de Franchenne, Ricardo de Punchardun', Yvone, fratre comitis, Herberto de Novila, Alano Hurri, Henrico de Bodrigan, Radulpho Bloyo, Simon' de Brekelay.

the shire and hundred courts, [also] service of cliff-ward and all other aids, and all secular service and exaction and all other secular occasions and customary services, as in unconditional and perpetual frankalmoign. Furthermore, I wish it to be known to all that R., prior of Launceston, in full shire court before me at Dunheved castle, in the presence of the provost and burgesses of the same town, adequately and lawfully established that, at the time when the count of Mortain[k] transferred' the Sunday market from the township of St Stephen of Launceston to the new township of Dunheved castle,[l] the canons of Launceston, with the assent and agreement of the aforementioned count of Mortain, retained for themselves and their borough of Launceston, and for the burgesses dwelling therein, all the privileges relating to a free borough in the same entirety which they had had from of old, save only for the Sunday market alone; and the said canons have from the reeve's office of the castle twenty shillings yearly at Martinmas; and that they had and held the same privileges entirely and with immunity and without objection throughout the time of Henry, king of England, my father. Wherefore I have granted and by this my charter confirmed to the aforementioned canons and to their township of Launceston, and to the men who have hearth and room in it, all the privileges relating to a free borough together with the aforementioned 20 shillings of annual payment. Witnesses: Robert Dunstanville,[m] Richard de Raddun, sheriff of Cornwall, Robert fitzAnketil, Hugh de Dunstanville, Jordan de Trekarl, reeve, Mordont Sprakelyn.

241   CHARTER OF PRIVILEGES OF CORNWALL [Between 1225 and 1272[n]]. Richard, count of Poitou and earl of Cornwall, to all his barons and knights and all those with free tenure in the county, greeting. You should know that we have granted and by this our present charter confirmed to God, and to the church of St Stephen at Launceston and to the canons serving God in that same place, for the safety and peace of the lord Henry, king of England, our brother, as also of the kingdom, and for the salvation of the soul of the lord John, king of England, our father, and for the salvation of my soul and of all our ancestors and descendants, that they may have all their churches and all the ecclesiastical benefices, which they have as gifts from kings, earls, barons and other good men, and may possess [them] with all their appurtenances entirely, freely and peacefully; as well as all their lands and all their tenements within or outside the borough with all their appurtenances, privileges and their free customs which they have or have had from of old, as the charter[s] of the donors give witness, or which they shall be able to acquire in due form in the future, freely, with immunity and completely; and all these things, both in churches and in chapels, lands, property and possessions, and all their appurtenances, we have granted to the aforementioned canons and their successors, to have and to possess in unconditional and perpetual frankalmoign, freely, honourably and with immunity from all secular and

---

[k] William, son of King Stephen, was count 1154–59; Stephen himself had been count 1115–35.
[l] Both are within the modern town.
[m] Prominent in Dorset, Wilts and Devon, Pipe Roll 2 Henry II– 13 Henry II.
[n] Or more probably before 1257 when Richard became King of the Romans.

242 DE EODEM. Ricardus, comes Cornub' et Pictav', vicecomiti et omnibus ballivis Cornub' salutem. Sciatis quod prioratus de Lanst' et prior et canonici eiusdem prioratus et omnes eorum homines ecclesie tenure et possessiones sunt sub mantenemento et protectione nostra. Quare volumus et firmiter precipimus quod prioratum illum et priorem et canonicos omnes dicti prioratus et omnia sua, tam ecclesiastica beneficia quam laica tenementa, tanquam dominica nostra propria custodiatis et manteneatis et defendatis, nullam eis iniuriam vel molestiam inferentes nec ab aliquo eis inferri permittentes. Et si quis eis in aliquo forisfacere presumpserit plenariam eis inde iustitiam sine dilatione faciatis, in omnibus conservantes libertates omnimodas iuxta formam cartarum suarum quas habent de predecessoribus nostris et de nobis.

243 DE EODEM. Ricardus, comes Pictavie et Cornub', omnibus fidelibus etc. salutem. Sciatis quod nos concessimus dedimus et carta nostra etc. quod burgum nostrum de Dunhevet liberum sit, et burgenses nostri de eodem burgo et omnes homines ad libertates dicti burgi pertinentes ubicumque fuerint, et quod quieti sint per totam terram nostram de puntage astallage guyllage et omnibus aliis consuetudinibus. Concessimus etiam ipsis et heredibus suis pro nobis et heredibus nostris habere electionem de preposito suis, et respondere de firma ipsius burgi ad Pascham et ad festum S. Michaelis annuatim, nobis vel ballivis nostris, scilicet de c solidis, et prioratui de S. Stephani de Lanst' de sexaginta quinque solidis et decem denariis, et leprosis S. Leonardi de Lanst' de c solidis, de elemosina nostra; ita tamen quod si prepositi per eos electi in aliquo evidenter deliquerint vel presumpserint hoc ipsum secundum delictum et presumptionem illam emendabunt. Concessimus etiam ipsis et heredibus suis pro nobis et successoribus nostris quod non placitent nisi infra burgum suum prenominatum de placitis vel rebus quibuscumque pertinentibus ad burgum suum, nisi de placitis ad coronam domini regis pertinentibus. Concessimus etiam ipsis et heredibus suis pro nobis et heredibus nostris habere octo comitatus per annum in burgo nostro prenominato, incipiendo a proximo comitatu post Clausum Pasche usque ad finem octo comitatuum proximorum sequentium. Concessimus etiam ipsis et heredibus suis pro nobis et heredibus nostris ut habeant et teneant unam placeam in eodem [Fo.14] burgo ad quandam aulam gillatoriam erigendam, tenendam de nobis et heredibus nostris, ubi[26] decentius et honorabilius providerint per unam libram piperis annuatim reddendam in festo S. Michaelis pro omni servicio querela et exactione. Concessimus etiam pro heredibus nostris et nobis ipsis et heredibus suis quando aliquis ballivorum

---

[26] MS has 'e.bi'.

servile service and from all secular customs and exactions of any kind for ever; nor is anyone to bring suit against the aforesaid canons for any holding of theirs except before us ourselves or before our bailiffs of Cornwall. Witnessed by: Andrew de Chanceaus, Richard de Turre, Henry the German, Henry de Franchenne, Richard de Punchardun, Ivo, brother of the earl, Herbert de Novila, Alan Hurri, Henry de Bodrigan, Ralph Bloyo, Simon de Brekelay.

242 ON THE SAME [Between 1225 and 1272[o]]. Richard, Earl of Cornwall and Count of Poitou, to the sheriff and all the bailiffs of Cornwall, greeting. You should know that the priory of Launceston, the prior and canons of the same priory, and all their men, churches, tenements and possessions are under our support and protection. Wherefore we desire and firmly order that you should guard, support and defend that priory, the prior and all the canons of the said priory and all their property, both ecclesiastical benefices and secular holdings, as though they were our own demesne, doing no injury or wrong to them, and not allowing it to be done to them by anyone [else]. And if anyone should presume to wrong them in any matter, you shall on that account forthwith do them full justice without delay, preserving in all matters their privileges of every kind, in accordance with the terms of their charters which they hold from our predecessors and from us.

243 ON THE SAME [Between 1225 and 1257/72]. Richard, Count of Poitou and Earl of Cornwall, to all his faithful etc, greeting. You should know that we have granted, given and by this our charter etc, that our borough of Dunheved should be free, and that our burgesses of the same borough, and all men – wherever they may be – to whom the privileges of the said borough are applicable, may have immunity throughout all our land of pontage, stallage, gillage and all other customary dues. We have also granted to them and their heirs on behalf of us and our heirs that they may elect their own reeves and answer annually for the farm of the said borough at Easter and at Michaelmas, namely to us or our bailiffs for 100 shillings, and to the priory of St Stephen's, Launceston, for 65 shillings and 10 pence, and to the lepers of St Leonard's, Launceston, for 100 shillings, of our charity; on condition, however, that if the reeves elected by them should evidently default in or usurp any matter, they shall make this same thing good in proportion to the default or that usurpation. We have also granted to them and their heirs on behalf of us and our successors that they shall not plead except within their own aforenamed borough on pleas or any other sort of thing pertaining to their borough, except for pleas pertaining to the crown of the lord king. We have also granted to them and their heirs on behalf of us and our heirs that they may hold eight shire courts a year within our aforenamed borough, beginning from the next shire court after Low Sunday up to the end of the next eight courts following. We have also granted to them and their heirs on behalf of us and our heirs that they should have and hold an open space in the same borough for the erection of a guild-hall, to be held from us and our heirs, for which they may provide fittingly and properly for all service, suit and civil due through the payment annually of a pound of pepper at Michaelmas. We have granted also to them

[o] Again, presumably before 1257.

nostrorum prisam fecerit in castello de cervisia quod non tenetur habere nisi primam bikam de uno ubolo minus quam alibi vendita fuerit secundum quod assisa facta fuerit per burgenses; si autem plus quam unam bikam habere vel capere voluerint mercabuntur singulas et quantum ceperint sicut alibi poterunt venundari. Concessimus etiam ipsis et heredibus suis pro nobis vel heredibus nostris quod nullus vicecomes vel alius ballivus noster trahet eos in placitum nisi iuste et rationabiliter et sine incausatione. Concessimus etiam ipsis et heredibus suis pro nobis et heredibus nostris quod nullus vicecomes vel alius ballivus noster emat vel capiat pro voluntate sua aliquod in prenominato burgo nisi de bona voluntate et spontaneo consensu venditoris ipsius mercature. Concessimus etiam ipsis et heredibus suis pro nobis et heredibus nostris quod non gildent cum comitatu de aliquo servicio vel tallagio et labore, et quod non tallantur per nos vel heredes nostros nisi ad tempus quando dominus rex omnes burgos suos per Angliam talliaverit. Et ut concessio hec etc.

244 DEPOSITUM APUD NOVUM LOCUM. Anno eodem iii nonas Iulii dominus episcopus deposuit apud novum locum duo instrumenta de firma ecclesie S. Uvelis, obligationem comitis Glouc' et archidiaconi Surr', cirographum abbatis de Kirkestede super ecclesia de Cuningesby, et obligationem domini H., primogeniti regis Aleman', de xl marcis.

245 PREDICATIO. Anno et die eisdem exivit littera predicationis scilicet pro ecclesia S. Marie de Bethleem' usque ad annum duratura, apud Horsleg'.

246 CARTA DOMINI REGIS DE HOMAGIO CUSTODIA ET RELEVIO COMITIS GLOUC'. Henricus, Dei gratia rex Anglie, dominus Hybern', dux Norm', Aquit', comes Andeg', archiepiscopis, episcopis, abbatibus, prioribus, comitibus, baronibus, iusticiariis, vicecomitibus, prepositis, ministris, et omnibus ballivis et fidelibus suis salutem. Sciatis quod cum Nicholaus de Wancy tenuerit de episcopo Exon' in capite feodo duorum militum cum pertinentiis in Wolaumpton', que idem Nicholaus postmodum dedit Iohanni de Gatesden', tenenda de se et heredibus suis per servicium feodi duorum militum et unius denarii vel unius paris albarum cyrotecarum per annum; quod servicium etiam idem Nicholaus postea dedit dilecto et fideli nostro Ricardo de Clare, comiti Glouc' et Herteford', habendum et tenendum de prefato episcopo et ecclesia sua Exon'; ita quod idem comes et heredes sui medii sint inter prefatum Iohannem et heredes suos et predictum episcopum et successores suos; nos, pro salute anime nostre antecessorum et heredum nostrorum, concedimus Deo et ecclesie B. Petri Exon' et venerabili patri Waltero, Exon' episcopo, et successoribus suis pro nobis et heredibus nostris quod, licet dictus comes de nobis tenet in baroniam, quotienscumque tamen heredes eiusdem comitis infra etatem et in custodia nostra extiterint, idem episcopus et successores sui et ecclesia sua supradicta habeant quicquid ad capitale dominium nomine custodie pertinere poterit de feodis predictis, sive dictus comes et eius heredes ea tenuerint in serviciis sive eis aliquomodo tempore in dominico acciderint; ita quod nos vel heredes nostri nichil nobis

and their heirs, on behalf of our heirs and ourselves, that, whenever one of our bailiffs makes a prise of beer in the castle, he is entitled to have no more than the first measure at a halfpenny less than what it shall be sold for elsewhere, in accordance with the assize held by the burgesses; but if [the bailiffs] wish to have or to take more than one measure, they shall pay for each of them, and for what they take – just as they would buy it elsewhere. We have also granted to them and their heirs, on behalf of us or our heirs, that no sheriff or other bailiff of ours is to exercise jurisdiction over them, except according to law and in due form and not without cause. We have also granted to them and their heirs, on behalf of us and our heirs, that no sheriff or other bailiff of ours shall buy or take at his will anything in the aforenamed borough, except with the good will and free consent of the seller of that merchandise. We have also granted to them and their heirs, on behalf of us and our heirs, that they shall not pay geld along with the shire in lieu of any service, tallage or [forced] labour, and they shall not be tallaged by us or our heirs except at a time when the lord king tallages all his boroughs throughout England. And that this grant etc.

244 DEPOSIT IN A NEW PLACE. 5 July 1260. The lord bishop deposited in a new place two instruments concerning the farm of St Eval church, a bond of the Earl of Gloucester and the archdeacon of Surrey, an indenture of the abbot of Kirkstead relating to the church of Coningsby, and a bond for 40 marks of the lord Henry, eldest son of the King of the Germans.

245 PREACHING. 5 July 1260, Horsley. A licence to preach was issued, namely on behalf of the church of St Mary, Bethlehem, valid for a year.

246 CHARTER OF THE LORD KING CONCERNING THE HOMAGE, WARDSHIP AND RELIEF OF THE EARL OF GLOUCESTER. 18 July 1259, Westminster. Henry, by the grace of God king of England, lord of Ireland, duke of Normandy and Aquitaine, count of Anjou, to his archbishops, bishops, abbots, priors, earls, barons, justices, sheriffs, reeves, officials, and all bailiffs and his faithful people, greeting. You should know that since Nicholas de Wancy held [land] at Woolavington in chief from the bishop of Exeter by the fee of two knights with appurtenances, which the same Nicholas later gave to John de Gatesden to be held from him and his heirs for the service of the fee of two knights and of one penny, or one pair of white gloves, a year; and also the same Nicholas afterwards gave this service to our beloved and faithful Richard de Clare, earl of Gloucester and Hertford, to be had and held from the aforementioned bishop and his church of Exeter, on terms that the same earl and his heirs should be mesne lords between the aforementioned John and his heirs and the aforesaid bishop and his successors; we, for the salvation of our soul and [of the souls] of our ancestors and heirs, have granted to God and to the church of the Blessed Peter at Exeter and to the venerable father Walter, bishop of Exeter, and his successors, on behalf of us and our heirs that, although the said earl holds from us in barony, yet whenever the heirs of the same earl are in their nonage and under our wardship, the same bishop and his successors and his previously mentioned church are to have whatever on account of the wardship can pertain from the aforesaid fees to the chief

ratione custodie predicte vendicabimus in feodis predictis. Hiis testibus: venerabilibus patribus R. Lincoln' et W. Wygorn' episcopis, Rogero le Bygod, comite Nortfolch' et marescallo Angl', Humfrido de Boun, comite Hereford' et Essex', Hugone le Bygod, iusticiario Angl', Iohanne Maunsel, thesaurario Ebor', Henrico de Tracy, Egidio de Argentem', Alano la Zuche, et aliis. Datum per manum nostram apud Westm' decimo octavo die Iulii anno regni nostri quadragesimo tertio.

[Fo.14v] **247** INSTITUTIO VICARIE DE PEYNCTON'. Anno eodem idus Iulii ad presentationem M., rectoris ecclesie de Peynton, et ad plenam voluntatem domini episcopi, idem dominus admisit Stephanum de London', presbiterum, ad ipsius ecclesie taxandam vicariam, et habet litteras inductionis, et iuravit obedientiam et residentiam se facturum in forma canonica postea.

248 CONFIRMATIO. Anno eodem xi kalendas Augusti London' exivit littera confirmationis in hec verba: W. miseratione divina etc. dilecto filio Roberto de Handlo, clerico, rectori ecclesie de Edwisleg', salutem in Auctore salutis. Presentationem canonicam ad ecclesiam de Edwisleg' dudum vacantem de te factam ab ipsius ecclesie tunc vero patrono et institutionem tuam in eadem subsecutam ratam et gratam habentes, eam quantum in nobis est pontificali auctoritate confirmamus et presentis scripti patrocinio communimus. In cuius rei etc. Datum anno die et loco supradictis.

249 OBLIGATIO XV LIBRARUM. Anno eodem in vigilia S. Iacobi apostoli London' exivit littera obligatoria xv librarum sterling' solvendarum Lugdun' nepoti domini Tarentasien' archiepiscopi per manus mercatorum Florent'; alioquin reddatur cautio mercatoribus Londonien' facta; et debent solvi mercatoribus Lond' in festo Omnium Sanctorum dicte xv libre.

250 INSTITUTIO. Anno eodem vii idus Augusti ad presentationem Mathei de Baunton', veri patroni ecclesie de Cumb' S. Nicholai, admisit dominus episcopus Willelmum de Allenestun', presbiterum, ad dictam ecclesiam vacantem, et habet litteras actas apud Ford Abbatis [sic].

251 INSTITUTIO. Anno eodem in vigilia S. Laurentii apud Hambiri ad presentationem Willelmi de Tregrille, veri patroni ecclesie de Mahiniet, dominus episcopus admisit Stephanum Heym, clericum, ad ecclesiam ipsam vacantem, et habet litteras in forma communi.

252 INSTITUTIO. Anno eodem in crastino Assumptionis S. Marie apud Exon' dominus episcopus, ad presentationem abbatis et conventus de Buffestr', verorum patronorum ecclesie de Trisme, admisit Willelmum dictum de Brideford', presbiterum, ad ecclesiam ipsam vacantem, et habet litteras in forma communi.

lordship, whether the said earl and his heirs hold them for services or whether at some time they should accrue to their demesne; on such terms that we or our heirs will claim nothing in the aforesaid fees for ourselves on account of the aforesaid wardship. Witnessed by: the venerable fathers Richard, bishop of Lincoln, and Walter, bishop of Worcester, Roger le Bigod, earl of Norfolk and marshal of England, Humphrey de Bohun, earl of Hereford and Essex, Hugh le Bigod, justiciar of England, John Mansel, treasurer of York, Henry de Tracy, Giles de Argentin, Alan la Zuche, and others. Given etc. in the forty-third year of our reign.

247 INSTITUTION TO THE VICARAGE OF PAIGNTON. 15 July 1260. At the presentation of M.,[P] rector of Paignton church, and with the complete agreement of the lord bishop, the same bishop admitted Stephen de London, priest, to the vicarage – to be assessed – of the said church; and he has letters of induction, and he swore obedience and that he would be resident afterwards in canonical form.

248 CONFIRMATION. 22 July 1260, London. A confirmatory letter was issued in these words: W[alter], by divine compassion etc, to our beloved son Robert de Handlo, clerk, rector of Iddesleigh church, greeting in the Author of salvation. We hold that the presentation made of you to the recently vacant church of Iddesleigh, by him who was at that time true patron of the said church, was canonical, and that your subsequent institution in the same was right and approved and, as far as in us lies, we confirm them by pontifical authority and we reinforce them by the protective power of the present document. In testimony whereof etc. Given etc.

249 BOND FOR £15. 24 July 1260, London. There was issued a letter obligatory for fifteen pounds sterling to be paid at Lyons to the nephew[q] of the lord archbishop of Tarentaise by the hands of the Florentine merchants; otherwise the security given to the London merchants[r] is to be surrendered, and the said fifteen pounds must be paid to the merchants at London on 1 November.

250 INSTITUTION. 7 August 1260. At the presentation of Matthew de Baunton, true patron of the church of Combe Raleigh, the lord bishop admitted William de Allenestun, priest, to the said vacant church; and he has letters enacted at Forde Abbey.

251 INSTITUTION. 9 August 1260, Broadhembury. At the presentation of William de Tregrille, true patron of Menheniot church, the lord bishop admitted Stephen Haym, clerk, to the said vacant church; and he has letters in common form.

252 INSTITUTION. 16 August 1260, Exeter. At the presentation of the abbot and convent of Buckfast, true patrons of Trusham church, the lord bishop admitted William, called of Bridford, priest, to the said vacant church; and he has letters in common form.

P Michael de Fiennes? See 6 December 1265.
q Peter de Vienne; see 3 July 1259.
r Presumably the London branch of the Florentine bank.

253 INSTITUTIO. Anno eodem xvi kalendas Septembris apud Exon' dominus episcopus, ad presentationem prioris de Monte Acuto et conventus eiusdem loci, verorum patronorum ecclesie de Holecumb', admisit Adam de Kentelesber', presbiterum, ad vacantem vicariam ecclesie predicte, et habet litteras in forma communi et iuravit se facturum residentiam.

254 INSTITUTIO. Anno eodem xvii[27] kalendas Septembris dominus episcopus admisit Iohannem filium Roberti, canonicum Exon', ad ecclesiam S. Felicitatis vacantem ad presentationem Margerie de Connerton, ipsius ecclesie vere patrone, et habet litteras in forma communi.

255 INSTITUTIO. Anno eodem v kalendas Septembris apud Cumb' Martini ad presentationem Ricardi de Trendelesho, veri patroni eiusdem loci, admisit dominus episcopus Henricum, presbiterum, dudum ipsius ecclesie vicarium, ad vacantem pensionem duarum marcarum et dimidie in eadem ecclesia; et, pensatis ipsius ecclesie facultatibus, cum non sufficiat duobus, in eadem ecclesia tota instituit, et habet litteras inductionis et institutionis.

256 INSTITUTIO. Anno die et loco eisdem ad presentationem Willelmi de Raleg', veri patroni ecclesie de Lokeshor', consolidavit dominus episcopus vacantem vicariam ecclesie de Lockeshor' cum personatu, et Rogerum, presbiterum, ipsius ecclesie rectorem, in ipsa ecclesia tota instituit, et habet litteras in forma communi.

257 ADMISSIO AD TYDECUMB'. Anno eodem viii idus Septembris apud Lawitton Alanus de Sancta Cruce obtinuit litteras institutionis in hec verba: Universis etc. Walterus Dei etc. Ad universitatis vestre notitiam tenore presentium volumus pervenire quod cum dilecta filia, nobilis mulier Amicia, comitissa Devon', Alanum de Sancta Cruce, domini pape subdiaconum, ad prebendam de Tydecumb' in ecclesia de Tiverton' vacantem nobis presentaverit, et ius patronatus eiusdem prebende per breve ultime presentationis in curia domini regis evicerit, nos eundem Alanum ad prebendam ipsam, ad ipsius comitisse presentationem, salvo iure Iohannis Blundell', clerici, per priorem monasterii S. Iacobi iuxta Exon' ad eandem presentati, si quod [Fo.15] habet, intuitu caritatis admisimus. In cuius rei etc. Datum apud Lawitton etc. ut supra.

258 LITTERA REGI DIRECTA. Anno eodem in vigilia Nativitatis S. Marie apud Lawitteton' frater Aluredus, electus Tavistoch', obtinuit litteras in hac forma: Serenissimo et reverendo domino H., Dei gratia illustri regi Angl', domino Hybern', et duci Aquit', Walterus, Eiusdem miseratione Exon' episcopus, salutem in Eo Qui dat salutem regibus et post trihumphum {sic}coronam. Excellentie vestre tenore presentium notum facimus quod, vacante abbatia Tavistoch' nostre diocesis, et potestate providendi monasterio loci predicti de ydoneo pastore propter vitium in forma electionis inventum ad nos secundum statuta canonum devoluta, nos, ipsius monasterii statum

---

[27] These entries are in this order.

253 INSTITUTION. 17 August 1260, Exeter. At the presentation of the prior of Montacute and the convent of the same place, true patrons of Holcombe Rogus church, the lord bishop admitted Adam de Kentelesbere, priest, to the vacant vicarage of the aforesaid church; and he has letters in common form, and he swore that he would be resident.

254 INSTITUTION. 16 August 1260. The lord bishop admitted John fitzRobert, canon of Exeter, to the vacant church of Phillack at the presentation of Margery de Connerton, true patron of the said church; and he has letters in common form.

255 INSTITUTION. 28 August 1260, Combe Martin. At the presentation of Richard de Trentishoe, true patron of the same place, the lord bishop admitted Henry, priest, formerly vicar of the said church, to a vacant pension of two and a half marks in the same church and, having assessed the means of the said church, since they are insufficient for two persons, [the bishop] instituted [him] to the whole of the same church; and he has letters of induction and institution.

256 INSTITUTION. 28 August 1260, Combe Martin. At the presentation of William de Raleigh, true patron of the church of Loxhore, the lord bishop consolidated the vacant vicarage of Loxhore church with the parsonage, and he instituted Roger, priest, rector of the said church, to the whole of the said church; and he has letters in common form.

257 ADMISSION TO TIDCOMBE. 6 September 1260, Lawhitton. Alan de Sancta Cruce obtained letters of institution in these words: To all etc, Walter, by God's etc. We wish it to be known to all of you by the tenor of these presents that, since our beloved daughter, the noble dame Amice, countess of Devon, has presented to us Alan de Sancta Cruce, papal subdeacon, to the vacant prebend of Tidcombe in the church of Tiverton and, by a writ of darrein presentment in the king's court, demonstrated her right of patronage over the same prebend, we, at the prompting of charity, have admitted the same Alan to the said prebend at the presentation of the said countess, saving the right – should he have any – of John Blundell, clerk, presented to the same by the prior of the monastery of St James by Exeter. In testimony whereof etc. Given etc. as above.

258 LETTER ADDRESSED TO THE KING. 7 September 1260, Lawhitton. Brother Alured, [abbot-]elect of Tavistock, obtained letters in these terms: To the most serene and reverend lord H[enry], by God's grace the illustrious king of England, lord of Ireland and duke of Aquitaine, Walter, by the compassion of the Same bishop of Exeter, greeting in Him Who gives salvation to kings and after [their] triumph a crown. We make it known to your excellency by the tenor of these presents that, since the abbey of Tavistock in our diocese is vacant and since, in accordance with what is laid down in the canons, the power of providing a suitable shepherd to the monastery of the aforesaid place

attendentes, de dilecto filio Aluredo, eiusdem monasterii priore, licet minus sollempniter electo viro utique, sicut pro certo didiscimus, provido et discreto ac in temporalibus et spiritualibus circumspecto, auctoritate pontificali eidem monasterio de gratia speciali duximus providendum; serenitati vestre sup[p]licantes, quatinus quod vestrum est in hac parte quoad administrationem temporalium, vestra circa eam exequi dignetur celsitudo. Datum apud Lawitteton' in vigilia festi Nativitatis B. Virginis, consecrationis nostre anno tertio.

259   INSTITUTIO. Anno eodem apud Lawitteton' in crastino Nativitatis S. Marie dominus episcopus admisit Rogerum de Telmer, presbiterum, ad taxatam et vacantem vicariam ecclesie S. Wenne ad presentationem abbatis et conventus Theokebir', verorum patronorum ipsius ecclesie, et iuravit se facturum residentiam et habet litteras in forma communi tam institutionis quam inductionis, et cavetur in eis quod agnoscet onera consueta.

260   IN FORMA PAUPERUM. Anno eodem die S. Lamberti apud Polton' Ricardus dictus Longus de Churchton' exhibuit litteras apostolicas preceptorias in forma pauperum impetratas Anagn' viii kalendas Aprilis pontificatus Alexandri pape anno sexto: Mendaces etc.

261   TAXATIO VICARIE DE STRATTON'. Anno eodem in crastino Nativitatis S. Marie exivit littera sub hac forma: Universis presentes litteras inspecturis Walterus, miseratione divina Exon' episcopus, salutem in Domino sempiternam. Officii nostri debitum exequentes, ut tenemur, ecclesiam de Stratton' quam prior et conventus de Lanceveton' in usus proprios dicuntur obtinere plene iure collatam vicaria canonice taxata carentem invenimus. Cum igitur nostrum sit ex officio subditorum nostrorum scissuras resarcire, ad instantiam et de expresso consensu eorundem .. prioris et conventus et Iohannis de Lisnewith, presbiteri, qui se dicit eiusdem ecclesie vicarium, ordinationi nostre se pure supponentium et eam servare bona fide promittentium, ad ipsius ecclesie ordinationem et dicte vicarie taxationem, competenti estimatione proventuum ipsius ecclesie premissa, duximus procedendum; taliter ordinantes quod, eodem Iohanne ipsius ecclesie perpetuo vicario remanente, idem vicarius et successores sui post ipsum omnes obventiones redditus et proventus maiores et minores ipsius ecclesie et totam terram sanctuarii, annuo censu libere tenentium dumtaxat excepto, integre percipiant et de eis disponant pro sue libito voluntatis, et omnia ipsius ecclesie onera debita et consueta taliter agnoscant, ac predictis priori et conventui viginti quinque marcas argenti in conventuali ecclesie S. Stephani de Lanceveton' in festo Omnium Sanctorum vel infra quindenam et in festo Resurrectionis Dominice vel infra quindenam, equis portionibus, annuatim persolvant; necnon et quicquid de ipsius ecclesie proventibus preter dictas viginti quinque marcas superfuerit nomine vicarie habeant tanquam suum; ita tamen quod si idem vicarius vel successores sui post ipsum in dicte pecunie solutione cessaverint, si infra triduum postquam cessaverint moniti non

---

[28] Superscribed here is 'Churiton', i.e. Cheriton.

has devolved on us (on account of a defect found in the form of election), we, looking to the state of the said monastery, have, with pontifical authority, thought fit to provide to the same monastery of our special grace our beloved son Alured, prior of the same monastery; even though [he was] elected with insufficient regard to the solemnities, yet [he is], as we are reliably informed, a provident and discreet person and circumspect in both temporal and spiritual matters. We beseech your serenity, that , because your interest in this affair extends to the administration of the temporalities, your highness should deign to give effect to this. Given etc in the third year of our consecration.

259 INSTITUTION. 9 September 1260, Lawhitton. The lord bishop admitted Roger de Telmer, priest, to the assessed and vacant vicarage of the church of St Wenn at the presentation of the abbot and convent of Tewkesbury, true patrons of the said church; he swore that he would be resident, and he has letters in common form, both of institution and induction, and he gives security in them that he will undertake the customary burdens.

260 IN FORMA PAUPERUM. 17 September 1260, Pawton. Richard called Long of Churchton showed papal letters of instruction *in forma pauperum* which had been obtained at Anagni on 25 March 1260: *Mendaces* etc.

261 ASSESSMENT OF STRATTON VICARAGE. 9 September 1260. A letter was issued in these terms: To all who inspect the present letters Walter, by divine compassion bishop of Exeter, eternal greeting in the Lord. In executing the duty of our office, as we are bound to do, we have found the church of Stratton, which the prior and convent of Launceston are alleged to hold – after its collation with full right – as impropriators, to be lacking a canonically assessed vicarage. Since therefore it is our duty to mend the breaches between our subjects, at the instance and with the express consent of the same prior and convent and of John de Lisnewith, priest, who alleges that he is vicar of the same church, (who submit themselves unconditionally to our ordinance and promise to observe it in good faith) we have thought fit, after first making an adequate assessment of the income of the said church, to proceed to the ordinance of the said church and the assessment of the said vicarage, laying down as follows: While the same John remains perpetual vicar of the said church, the same vicar and his successors after him should take in their entirety all the occasional offerings, revenues and proceeds, greater and lesser, of the said church and all the sanctuary land, excepting only the annual payment of the free tenants, and they are to dispose of them at their own free will; they are likewise to undertake all the due and customary burdens of the said church, and they shall pay each year to the aforesaid prior and convent in the conventual church of St Stephen at Launceston 25 silver marks, in equal instalments on the feast of All Saints (or within the fortnight) and at Easter (or within the fortnight). They shall also have whatever remains over from the proceeds of the said church, beyond the said 25 marks, as their own on account of the vicarage; on condition, however, that if the same vicar, or his

satisfecerint, extunc liceat priori et canonicis predictis ad vicariam ipsam tanquam de iure vacantem ydoneam parsonam canonice presentare. In cuius rei testimonium presentes litteras eisdem canonicis et vicario duximus concedendas. Actum publice in conventuali capitulo de Lanceveton' in crastino festi Nativitatis S. Marie, ab Incarnatione Domini mcc sexaginta et consecrationis nostre anno tertio.

[Fo.15v] **262** Anno eodem in crastino Nativitatis S. Marie dominus episcopus visitavit prioratum Lanceveton'.

263 Anno eodem die Dominica proxima ante festum Exaltationis Sancte Crucis dominus episcopus visitavit monasterium de Tywardrait.

264 Anno eodem die Exaltationis Sancte Crucis dominus episcopus consecravit altare capelle de Tregaer in honore Sancte Crucis.

265 Anno eodem xiv kalendas Octobris, hoc est die Sabbati post Exaltationem Sancte Crucis, dominus episcopus celebravit ordines apud Bodmin'.

266 NOTA EXCOMMUNICATIO PRO DUELLO CLERICI.[29] Anno die et loco eisdem dominus episcopus solempniter excommunicavit omnes illos qui Willelmum dictum Blundum, clericum, decreverunt duellum suscipere et inire susceptum contra canonicas sanctiones, et omnes illos qui ad hoc consilium, auxilium, favorem seu consensum prebuerunt; item omnes illos qui eidem decreto et duello interfuerunt, in vituperium et scandalum ecclesiastice libertatis; quo facto, magna multitudo militum liberorum villanorum reatum suum agnoscens, prestito iuramento de parendo mandatis ecclesie, absolutionis beneficium obtinuit; propter quod reservata maiori deliberationi penitentia eorum qui decretum ipsum forciaverunt dictaverunt et tuebantur et ei ex affectu consenserunt, ceteros qui gratia spectabuli advenerunt pro penitentia iniunxit ut, discincti et discalciati ac capitibus discoopertis, a conventuali ecclesia S. Petroci Bodminie usque ad ecclesiam Fratrum Minorum in humilitate spiritus reverenter et processionaliter incederent, disciplinam penitentialem et solempnem ibidem recipientes. Et ita factum est.

267 Anno eodem die Dominica proxima post festum Exaltationis Sancte Crucis dominus episcopus visitavit priorem et conventum Bodmin', et fecit ibi correctiones quas eis in scriptis dedit.

268 Anno eodem die S. Mathei apostoli dominus episcopus visitavit priorem et conventum de S. Germano.

---

[29] Heading was added later, but not much, I think.

successors after him, should fail in the payment of the said money, [and] if within three days of this failure, having been warned, they do not make satisfaction, it is to be lawful thereafter for the aforesaid prior and canons to present a suitable parson, in accordance with the canons, to the said vicarage just as if it were vacant *de iure*. In testimony whereof we have thought fit to grant the present letters to the same canons and to the vicar. Enacted publicly in the conventual chapter-house at Launceston on 9 September 1260 and in the third year of our consecration.

262 [VISITATION]. 9 September 1260. The lord bishop visited Launceston Priory.

263 [VISITATION]. 12 September 1260. The lord bishop visited the monastery of Tywardreath.

264 [CONSECRATION]. 14 September 1260. The lord bishop consecrated an altar in honour of the Holy Cross in the chapel of 'Tregaer'.

265 [ORDINATION]. 18 September 1260. The lord bishop held an ordination at Bodmin.

266 [EXCOMMUNICATION RECORDED BECAUSE OF A CLERK'S TRIAL BY BATTLE]. 8 September 1260, Bodmin. The lord bishop solemnly excommunicated all those persons who gave judgment that William called Blund, clerk, should undertake trial by battle and go through with the undertaking contrary to canonical prohibitions, and all those who lent their advice, help, favour or agreement to this; also all those who were present at the same judgment and trial to the disparagement and scandal of the Church's privilege. After this was done, a great multitude of knights, free men and villeins acknowledged their guilt and, after taking an oath to obey the commands of the Church, obtained the benefit of absolution. Wherefore, reserving for fuller deliberation the penance for those who enforced, formulated and observed the said judgment and who acquiesced to it, he enjoined as penance on the others, who were present for the sake of the spectacle, that they should reverently walk in procession in humility of spirit, ungirdled, without shoes and with their heads uncovered, from the conventual church of St Petrock, Bodmin, as far as the church of the Franciscans, there to receive solemn and penitential discipline. And it was so done.

267 [VISITATION]. 19 September 1260. The lord bishop visited the prior and convent of Bodmin, and he made corrections there, which he gave them in writing.

268 [VISITATION]. 21 September 1260. The lord bishop visited the prior and convent of St Germans.

269   Anno eodem die Iovis proxima post festum S. Mathei apostoli dominus episcopus visitavit priorem et conventum Plimton', et fecit ibi statuta et correctiones quas eis in scriptis tradidit sigillatas.

270   Anno eodem die Iovis in crastino S. Michaelis apud Exon' dominus episcopus admisit Clementem, vicarium Exonien', ad ecclesiam de Ionestow' vacantem ad presentationem magistri Iohannis Wiger, veri patroni, et habet litteras inductionis tantum.

271   Anno eodem v nonas Octobris apud Cokespitt' dominus episcopus instituit magistrum Bartholomeum de Lardar' in ecclesia S. Gerendi, et habet litteras institutionis.

272   TAUTON'. Anno eodem die Lune ante festum S. Michaelis[30] Henricus de Trascy arrainavit assisam nove disseisine super Walterum, Exon' episcopum, apud Toriton' coram domino Henrico de Bracton apud Toriton'[31] de libero tenemento suo in Tauton', ut dicit. Et est amicabiliter compositum inter eos: ita scilicet quod dictus Henricus possit firmare bedum molendini sui in terra episcopi ubi incepit vel alibi ad commodum suum; et pro hoc dedit domino episcopo et ecclesie sue Exon' terram que dicitur Itinges cum pertinentiis, et medietatem piscarie debite concessit. Et est facta scriptura concessionis et feofactionis hinc inde que residet penes decanum et capitulum Exon'.

273   Anno eodem die S. Michaelis apud Exon' in maiori ecclesia Exon' dominus episcopus benedixit Aluredum, priorem Tavistok', electum abbatem eiusdem loci; et fecit professionem, quam obtulit super principale altare.

274   PREDICATIO. Anno eodem die Dominica ante festum apostolorum Simonis et Iude London' exivit littera predicationis cum indulgentia xx dierum[32] pro fabrica Wygorn' ecclesie duratura usque ad triennium.

275   Anno eodem in crastino S. Martini apud Horsleg' dominus episcopus commisit custodiam sequestri sui in portione ecclesie S. Endelient' Iohanni Blohiou, clerico, ad eandem presentato, usque ad Pasche.

[Fo.16]   **276**   ORDINATIO DE LEGH CANONICORUM.[33] Hec est amicabilis compositio facta inter priorem et canonicos de Plympton' ex parte una et priorem et canonicos de Leg' ex altera parte super controversiis inter ipsos motis coram venerabili patre S[imone], Dei gratia Exon' episcopo, scilicet cum prior in ecclesia de Legh' fuerit eligendus hoc episcopo Exon' debet pronuntiari ut in propria persona per se vel per aliquem alium quem voluerit

[30] This and the two preceding entries have marginal notes – letters – showing the correct order in time.
[31] Is the repetition a sign of indignation? Or just an error?
[32] The period was added at the end of the line.
[33] 'Aliter nunc' is here written, possibly in Grandisson's hand.

269 [VISITATION]. 23 September 1260. The lord bishop visited the prior and convent of Plympton, and he made decrees and corrections there, which he delivered to them in writing under seal.

270 [ADMISSION]. 30 September 1260, Exeter. The lord bishop admitted Clement, vicar[s] of Exeter, to the vacant church of Instow at the presentation of Master John Wiger, the true patron; and he has letters of induction only.

271 [INSTITUTION]. 3 October 1260, Cokesputt. The lord bishop instituted Master Bartholomew de Lardario to the church of Gerrans; and he has letters of institution.

272 [BISHOP'S] TAWTON. 27 September 1260, Great? Torrington. Henry de Tracy brought an assize of novel disseisin against Walter, bishop of Exeter, before Sir Henry de Bracton concerning his free holding – as he alleges – in Bishop's Tawton. And an amicable composition was made between them, namely on terms that the said Henry can construct a race for his mill on the bishop's land, either where he began [it] or elsewhere, as is convenient for him; and in return for this he gave to the lord bishop and his church of Exeter the land which is called 'Itinges' with its appurtenances, and he duly granted half the fishing rights. And a charter of the grant and the infeoffment herein was drawn up and is deposited with the dean and chapter of Exeter.

273 [BLESSING]. 29 September 1260, Exeter. The lord bishop blessed Alured, prior of Tavistock and abbot-elect of the same place, in the cathedral; and he made his profession [of obedience], which he offered at the high altar.

274 LICENCE TO PREACH. 24 October 1260, London. A letter of preaching was issued, together with twenty days' indulgence, on behalf of the building works at Worcester cathedral, to be valid for three years.

275 [CUSTODY]. 12 November 1260, Horsley. The lord bishop committed the custody, until Easter, of his sequestration in the portion of the church of St Endellion to John Bloyo, clerk, after he was presented to the same.

276 ORDINANCE CONCERNING CANONSLEIGH. 6 June 1219. This is the amicable composition made between the prior and canons of Plympton, on the one part, and the prior and canons of Canonsleigh, on the other part, concerning the disputes arisen between them, before the venerable father S[imon],[t] by God's grace bishop of Exeter, namely that when a prior is to be chosen for the church of Canonsleigh this must be notified to the bishop of

---

[s] Vicar choral of the cathedral?
[t] Simon de Apulia, 1214–23.

loco sui destinare intersit electioni. Similiter priori de Plimpton' debet nuntiari ut ipse intersit electioni si voluerit, ita tamen quod non habebit vocem in electione, nec per episcopum nec per priorem impediatur quominus ille prior constituatur quem eligerint canonici de Legh' de corpore ecclesie sue de Leg'. Si autem non consenserint in aliquem de gremio ecclesie sue de Legh' tunc priusquam ad aliquam aliam decurratur ecclesiam de ecclesia de Plimpton' aliquem sibi eligent in priorem. Si autem non consenserint – quod absit – in aliquam personam predictarum ecclesiarum, de aliqua conventuali ecclesia eiusdem ordinis et regulari aliquam idoneam personam in priorem sibi assument. Ex quo autem fuerit ibi prior secundum supradictum modum electus et per Exoniensem episcopum confirmatus, habeat plenam potestatem canonicorum recipiendorum et regendorum et plenam administrationem omnium ad ecclesiam de Legh' pertinentium. Preterea prior de Legh' corriget excessus canonicorum de Legh' et alia emendabit que fuerint ibidem emendanda cum consensu canonicorum suorum. Si autem tantus et talis fuerit excessus – quod absit – ut per priorem et canonicos de Legh' sine scandalo non valeat emendari, tunc prior et canonici de Leg' significabunt priori de Plimpton' ut caritative ad domum eorum veniat, consilium eis in corrigendis excessibus impensurus. Et per hanc compositionem sopita sunt omnia litigia inter eos prius exorta, et omnes exactiones et contentiones huiusmodi sunt remisse. Si non per consilium predictorum excessus in dicta domo non poterint emendari, Exon' episcopus qui pro tempore fuerit eos secundum Deum emendabit. Acta sunt hec Exon' mcc nonodecimo, presente domino Exon' episcopo, Henrico, archidiacono Exon', S., archidiacono Totton', Radulpho, archidiacono Barnastap', magistris Ysaac et I., canonicis Exon', et multis aliis.

277 EXITUS ET REVERSIO. Anno eodem die S. Martini exivit W. de Capella apud Horsleg' et rediit ibidem in vigilia S. Katerine. Et iterum exivit apud Ferndon' die Conceptionis S. Marie et rediit apud Horsleg' in crastino S. Thome apostoli.

278 INSTITUTIO. Anno eodem die Sabbati proxima post festum S. Lucie apud Chedeham' dominus episcopus admisit Iohannem Blohyou, quem eadem die ordinavit subdiaconum, ad portionem ecclesie S. Endeliente vacantem ad presentationem Roberti Modred, et habuit litteras inductionis.

279 INSTITUTIO. Anno eodem in vigilia S. Thome apostoli apud Tyting' ad presentationem domini I. de Curtenay, veri patroni, dominus episcopus admisit Iohannem Pinell', subdiaconum, ad ecclesiam de Musbir' vacantem, et habet litteras institutionis et inductionis.

Exeter so that he may be present at the election, either himself in person or through some other whom he shall wish to designate in his place. Similarly the prior of Plympton must be notified so that he may be present if he wishes at the election, on condition that he shall have no vote in the election, nor may there be any hindrance, whether by the bishop or by the prior, to the appointment as prior of that man whom the canons of Canonsleigh shall choose from the body of their church of Canonsleigh. But if they shall not agree on someone from their own number at Canonsleigh then, before recourse is had to any other church, let them choose someone from the church of Plympton to be their prior. But if they shall not agree – which God forbid – on anyone from the aforesaid churches, they shall take to themselves as prior some suitable person from any conventual church of the same Order and Rule.ᵘ Moreover, from the time when a prior has been elected there according to the aforesaid method, and confirmed by the bishop of Exeter, he shall have full power to receive and rule over the canons, and complete administration of all matters pertaining to the church of Canonsleigh. Furthermore, the prior of Canonsleigh shall check the excesses of the canons of Canonsleigh, and he shall, with the agreement of his canons, correct other matters which need correction there. But if the excess should be on such a scale and of such a kind – which God forbid – that it cannot properly be corrected by the prior and canons without scandal, then the prior and canons of Canonsleigh shall make this known to the prior of Plympton, so that of his charity he may come to their house to give them the benefit of his advice in putting right the excesses. And by this composition all the lawsuits which earlier sprang up between them have been laid to rest, and all charges and discords of this kind set aside. If the excesses in the said house are not capable of being corrected by the advice of the aforesaid persons, the bishop of Exeter in office at the time shall correct them in accordance with the will of God. These things were enacted at Exeter in 1219 in the presence of the lord bishop of Exeter, Henry [de Melville], archdeacon of Exeter, S., archdeacon of Totnes, Ralph, archdeacon of Barnstaple, Masters Isaac and I., canons of Exeter, and many others.

277 DEPARTURE AND RETURN. 11 November 1260, Horsley. Master W[illiam] de Capella left Horsley, and he returned there on 24 November. And on 8 December at Faringdon he again left, and returned to Horsley on 22 December.

278 INSTITUTION. 18 December 1260, Chidham. At the presentation of Robert Modred, the lord bishop admitted John Bloyo, whom on the same day he ordained subdeacon, to the vacant portion of the church of St Endellion; and he had letters of induction.

279 INSTITUTION. 20 December 1260, Tyting. At the presentation of Sir J[ohn] de Courtenay, the true patron, the lord bishop admitted John Pinell, subdeacon, to the vacant church of Musbury; and he has letters of institution and induction.

ᵘ I.e. Augustinian.

280   INSTITUTIO. Anno die et loco predictis ad presentationem eiusdem I. dominus episcopus admisit Henricum de Esse, clericum, ad prebendam capelle castri Exon' de Cuteton' vacantem, et habuit litteras inductionis et institutionis, et fecit litteras suas obligatorias de honestate futura etc.

281   INSTITUTIO. Anno eodem die S. Thome apostoli apud Horsleg' dominus episcopus admisit Thomam de Doune, subdiaconum, ad ecclesiam de Estdoune vacantem ad presentationem Philippi de Doune, veri patroni eiusdem, et habuit litteras inductionis et institutionis in forma communi.

282   PROVISIO PRIORIS DE LEGH'. Anno eodem xvi kalendas Ianuarii apud Leg' Canonicorum magister R. de Tefford, officialis Exon', assidentibus sibi Exon' et Barnest' archidiaconis, per specialem commissionem domini episcopi cassavit electionem de fratre Willelmo de Chaggeford' in priorem electo factam; et per aliam commissionem specialiorem de fratre Henrico [de][34] Trewvinok', canonico Lanst', ipsius ecclesie scilicet providet-de priore incontinenti.

283   INSTITUTIO. Anno eodem London' iii nonas Ianuarii ad presentationem Philippi Basset, veri patroni ecclesie S. Clederi, dominus episcopus admisit Reginaldum de Bray, subdiaconum, ad ipsam ecclesiam vacantem per cessionem magistri W. [Fo.16v] de Trewinnoc qui, elapso anno et amplius, ordinem Cistercien' est ingressus,[35] et habet litteras institutionis et inductionis.

284   CUSTODIA SEQUESTRI PREBENDE. Anno et die eisdem ibidem dominus episcopus commisit custodiam sequestri sui in vacante prebenda capelle castri Exon' ultra Exam Nicholao de Castro, clerico magistri Thome de Wymundeham', usque ad beneplacitum sue voluntatis, et habet litteras inductionis.

285   INSTITUTIO. Anno eodem ii idus Ianuarii apud Horslegh' ad presentationem domine Iohanne de Campo Arnulphi dominus episcopus admisit Robertum filium Roberti, subdiaconum, ad ecclesiam S. Wineri vacantem et ad eius presentationem spectantem, et habet litteras institutionis, alias prius fuit inductus nomine custodie per litteras domini.

286   LITTERA LX MARCARUM. Anno eodem die S. Hilarii apud Horsleg' dominus episcopus recepit litteras domini Henrici, filii regis Aleman', de lx marcis solvendis in quindenam Pasche; W. de Capella liberavit easdem.

287   INSTITUTIO. Anno eodem vii idus Februarii London' ad presentationem domini I. de Curtenay, veri patroni prebende castri Exon' ultra Essam, dominus episcopus admisit magistrum Thomam de Wimundeham ad prebendam ipsam vacantem, et habuit litteras inductionis et institutionis.

[34] There is a hole in the page.
[35] Cf. **227**.

280 INSTITUTION. 20 December 1260, Tyting. At the presentation of the same J[ohn], the lord bishop admitted Henry de Esse, clerk, to the vacant Cutton prebend in the chapel of Exeter Castle; and he had letters of induction and institution, and he gave written security for his future good behaviour, etc.

281 INSTITUTION. 21 December 1260, Horsley. The lord bishop admitted Thomas de Down, subdeacon, to the vacant church of East Down, at the presentation of Philip de Down, true patron of the same; and he had letters of induction and institution in common form.

282 PROVISION OF A PRIOR TO CANONSLEIGH. 17 December 1260, Canonsleigh. Master R[obert] de Tefford, the official of Exeter, with the archdeacons of Exeter and Barnstaple acting as his assessors, by the special commision of the lord bishop quashed the election of Brother William de Chagford, [who had been] elected as prior; and by another very special commission he immediately provided Brother Henry de Trewvinok, canon of Launceston, namely as prior of the said church.

283 INSTITUTION. 3 January 1261, London. At the presentation of Philip Basset, true patron of the church of St Clether, the lord bishop admitted Reginald de Bray, subdeacon, to the said church, vacant by the resignation of Master W. de Trewinnoc who, after the passing of a year or more, has entered the Cistercian Order;[v] and he has letters of institution and induction.

284 CUSTODY OF THE SEQUESTRATION OF A PREBEND. 3 January 1261, London. The lord bishop committed – at his pleasure – the custody of his sequestration in the vacant Beyond the Exe prebend of the chapel of Exeter Castle to Nicholas de Castro, clerk of Master Thomas de Wymondham; and he has letters of induction.

285 INSTITUTION. 12 January 1261, Horsley. At the presentation of the Lady Joan de Champernowne, the lord bishop admitted Robert fitz Robert, subdeacon, to the vacant church of Gwinnear which was in her patronage; and he has letters of institution, having sometime previously been inducted on account of being given custody through letters of the lord [bishop].

286 LETTER CONCERNING 60 MARKS. 13 January 1261, Horsley. The lord bishop received letters from the Lord Henry, son of the King of the Germans, concerning 60 marks to be paid within the period of fifteen days after Easter [before 8 May 1261]; William de Capella paid the same.

287 INSTITUTION. 7 February 1261, London. At the presentation of Sir J[ohn] de Courtenay, true patron of the prebend Beyond the Exe in Exeter Castle, the lord bishop admitted Master Thomas de Wymondham to the said vacant prebend; and he had letters of induction and institution.

v Cf. **227**.

288 INSTITUTIO. Anno die et loco eisdem ad presentationem eiusdem patroni dominus episcopus admisit Willelmum de Stanf', clericum, ad prebendam dicti castri in Aysseclist vacantem per resignationem magistri Thome de Wimundeham, et habuit litteras inductionis et institutionis.

289 INSTITUTIO. Anno eodem in crastino S. Valentini London' dominus episcopus admisit Willelmum de Capella, domini pape subdiaconum, ad totam ecclesiam de Lanant' vacantem per obitum Andrei de Montibus, secundum tenorem ordinationis domini I., titulo S. Laurentii in Lucin' presbiteri cardinalis, et confirmationis domini pape ad dudum factam presentationem prioris et conventus de Tywardrait, verorum patronorum ipsius ecclesie. Presentibus magistris I. Nobili et I. Wygg' in camera sua ante caminum hora fere prima.

290 INFEODATIO LONDON'. Anno eodem London' in octabis S. Hillarii facte sunt cirographate littere ad cautelam duplicate inter dominum episcopum, decanum et capitulum Exon' ex parte una et priorem et conventum Sancti Sepulchri de Warwik' ex altera de conventione divisaria terre inter eos, et de quieta clamantia gabuli aule domini episcopi, et de feofamento cuiusdam portionis terre continentis in longitudine xvii ulnas et dimidiam inter corneram aule et postem wa[r]derobe episcopi.

291 INSTITUTIO VICARIE DE HERTILOND'.[36] Anno eodem ii kalendas Martii London', cum post trinam monitionem taxanda vicaria parrochialis ecclesie de Hertilond' tanto tempore vacaverit quod ipsius ordinatio ad dominum episcopum extitit devoluta pro {sic} statuta Lateran' concilii, idem dominus eam contulit Henrico de Hertilond', presbitero, reservata sibi taxatione, et habet litteras institutionis et inductionis ad instar de Axeminstr' in forma communi.

292 ORDINATIO DE LIDEFORD. Anno eodem apud Credeton' xiii kalendas Septembris exivit littera: Universis etc., episcopus etc. Fidedignorum assertione intelligentes quod quidam parochiani ecclesie de Lideford', villulag' que dicuntur Babbeneye et Pushyll' inhabitantes, adeo distant ab eorum ecclesia matrice predicta quod eam pro nimia distantia nullo modo visitare possunt quotiens eis fuerit oportunum, dilecto filio officiali archidiaconi Totton' nostris litteris dedimus in mandatis ut, facta inquisitione sollempni in pleno capitulo eiusdem loci, nos litteratorie reddet certiores an homines predicti ad erectionem sufficerent oratorii; item que parochialis ecclesia villulis ipsis vicinior existat in qua iidem homines sine preiudicio iuris alieni audire divina et ecclesiastica percipere valeant sacramenta, et quanto eedem {sic} villule distant a matrice ecclesia predicta, et si, tempestatibus et inundationibus aquarum exortis, parochianis ipsis matricem ecclesiam predictam visitare volentibus via longior debeatur. Cumque per certificationem officialis memorati invenerimus quod, incolis ipsis ad constructionem oratorii minime sufficientibus, parochialis ecclesia de Wydecumba locis

---

[36] Marginal sign here, referring on to third next folio, i.e. **335**.

288 INSTITUTION. 7 February 1261, London. At the presentation of the same patron the lord bishop admitted William de Stanford, clerk, to the prebend of Ashclyst in the said castle, vacant by the resignation of Master Thomas de Wymondham; and he had letters of induction and institution.

289 INSTITUTION. 15 February 1261, London. In the presence of Master J[ohn] Noble and Master J[ohn] Wyger, before the hearth in his chamber, about the first hour, the lord bishop admitted William de Capella, papal subdeacon, to the whole church of Lelant, vacant through the death of Andrew de Montibus, in accordance with the tenor of the ordinance of the Lord John,[w] cardinal priest with the title of St Laurence in Lucin', and of the confirmation by the lord Pope of the presentation formerly made by the prior and convent of Tywardreath, the true patrons of the said church.

290 INFEOFFMENT AT LONDON. 20 January 1261, London. Chirograph letters – duplicate for security – were drawn up between the lord bishop and the dean and chapter of Exeter, on the one part, and the prior and convent of the Holy Sepulchre at Warwick, on the other, concerning an agreement about the division of land between them, the quitclaim concerning the gable of the lord bishop's hall, and the infeoffment of a certain portion of land, some seventeen and a half ells in length, between the corner of the hall and the doorpost of the bishop's wardrobe.

291 INSTITUTION TO HARTLAND VICARAGE. 28 February 1261, London. Since, after three warnings, the vicarage – to be assessed – of Hartland parish church has been vacant for so long that its ordinance has devolved upon the bishop by the statutes of the Lateran Council, the same bishop collated to it Henry de Hartland, priest, reserving its assessment to himself; and [Henry] has letters of institution and induction in common form, on the model of Axminster.

292 ORDINANCE CONCERNING LYDFORD. 20 August ?1260, Crediton. A letter was issued: To all etc, the bishop etc. Understanding from the declaration of trustworthy persons that certain parishioners of Lydford church, living in the hamlets called Babeny and Pizwell, are so far distant from their aforesaid mother church that, because of the excessive distance, they can in no wise visit it as often as would be beneficial for them, we have given our written instructions to our beloved son, the official of the archdeacon of Totnes. He is to conduct a solemn inquiry in full chapter of the said place, and he is to inform us in writing whether the aforesaid persons are of sufficient number for the building of an oratory; as also what parish church might be closer to the said hamlets, in which those same persons could hear divine worship and receive the sacraments of the Church, without prejudice to anyone else's rights; and how far distant are the same hamlets from the aforesaid mother church; as also whether, in times of storms and floods, a longer journey is necessary for the said parishioners who wish to visit the aforesaid mother church. And since we have found, by the attestation of the

w John de Toledo, an English Cistercian, held this title 1244–62 while bishop of Porto.

ipsis plus aliis omnibus est vicina, et quod loca predicta a matrice ecclesia de
Lideford' sereno tempore per octo et tempestatibus exortis in circuitu per
quindecim distant miliaria, salutem animarum sicut nec debemus negligere
nulla ratione volentes, ecclesiarum ipsarum rectores ad nostram fecimus
presentiam evocari. Rectoribus igitur predictis coram nobis constitutis, et
exposito eisdem huiuscemodi periculo, ac depresso {sic} consensu utriusque
ecclesie patronorum, ordinationi nostre se supponentibus promittentibusque
bona fide voluntati nostre parere in hac parte ac nostram ordinationem
predictam [Fo.17] observare inperpetuum, de consilio prudentium virorum
nobis assistentium taliter ordinavimus: videlicet quod predictorum et
adiacentium locorum incolis, sicut in veritate sunt, parochianis ecclesie de
Lideford' perpetuo remanentibus, in ecclesia de Wydecumb' inposterum
divina audiant, et omnia in vita et morte ecclesiastica percipiant sacramenta.
In coopertura et fabrica ecclesie de Wydecumb', clausura cimiterii, subsidio
luminarium, et deferendo pane benedicto, cum ipsius ecclesie parochianis
contribuant; consuetudines ipsius ecclesie in visitationibus infirmorum,
benedictionibus nubentium, in purgationibus post partum, in baptismatibus
parvulorum, in mortuariis et sepulturiis morientium observent; offerant
quoque ibidem sollempniter ter in anno et decimam nichilominus agnorum
eidem ecclesie cum integritate persolvant. In signum vero subiectionis et
agnitionem iuris parochialis quilibet incola dictorum locorum terram tenens
semel in anno, videlicet die S. Petroci, in ecclesia de Lideford' sollempniter
offerat, et omnes decimas et obventiones maiores et minores, hiis dumtaxat
exceptis que superius enumerantur, matrici ecclesie sue de Lideford' sine
qualibet diminutione et contradictione persolvant. In cuius etc.

293 CARTA CANCELLARIO EBOR' FACTA. Anno eodem London' v idus Iulii
exivit littera: W. miseratione divina etc. magistro I., Ebor' cancellario, etc.
Cum ex officii nostri debito nostram visitantes parochiam vicariam ecclesie de
Axminist' tanto tempore vacavisse inveniremus quod ipsius collatio ad nos
esset devoluta, nosque, sollempni premissa monitione quod decanus et
capitulum Ebor' seu hii quorum tunc intererat personam ydoneam infra
certum tempus ad eam presentarent, vicariam ipsam dilecto filio Waltero de
Aulescumb', presbitero, mense Novembris caritatis intuitu contulerimus,
salva canonicis Ebor' ecclesie antiqua et debita portione de eadem ecclesia in
pecunia numerata per vicarium ipsum annuatim solvenda; nolentes tamen
bona vestra ibidem vel alibi sub districtu nostro existentia inutiliter distrahi
aut consumi, omnes fructus et proventus portionis vestre quam in dicta
ecclesia de Axminist' optinetis ratione prebende vestre Ebor' vos contingentes, salva ministrorum dicte ecclesie congrua sustentatione, dilecto filio
.. archidiacono Exon' sub nostrorum testimonio commisimus quousque,
auctore Domino, in Angliam redieritis bona fide conservandos. In cuius etc.

aforementioned official, that the said inhabitants are in no way sufficient to justify the building of an oratory, that the parish church of Widdecombe is nearer than any other to the said places, and that the aforesaid places are distant from the mother church of Lydford eight miles in fine weather and fifteen by a roundabout journey in times of storms, and since we have no wish – and ought not – to neglect the salvation of souls for any reason, we have had the rectors of the said churches summoned to our presence. The aforesaid rectors therefore have appeared before us, and have had explained to them the danger of this nature and, with the express consent of the patrons of each church, submit themselves to our ordinance, promising in good faith to obey our wishes in this matter and to observe in perpetuity our aforesaid ordinance, and we, with the advice of the learned men who assist us, have laid down as follows: To wit, that while the inhabitants of the aforesaid and neighbouring places are for ever to remain – as in truth they are – parishioners of the church of Lydford, they may hereafter hear divine worship, and receive all the Church's sacraments, in life and at death, in Widdecombe church. In the roofing and repair of the church of Widdecombe, the fencing of the graveyard, the provision of money for candles and the offering of blessed bread, they are to contribute along with the parishioners of the said church; they are to observe the customs of the said church as regards visiting the sick, the blessing of those marrying, the churching of women after child-birth, the baptism of infants, services for the dead and funerals. They are also to make a solemn offering in that same place three times a year, and, moreover, to pay in its entirety the tithe of lambs to the same church. In token, however, of their subjection and in recognition of the rights of the parish, each single inhabitant of the said places who holds land is to make a solemn offering in the church of Lydford once in the year, to wit, on the feast of St Petrock, and they are to pay all tithes and occasional offerings, greater and lesser, excepting only those set out above, to their mother church of Lydford, without any sort of reduction or objection. In testimony whereof etc.

293 CHARTER DRAWN UP FOR THE CHANCELLOR OF YORK. 11 July 1260, London. A letter was issued: W[alter], by divine compassion etc, to Master J[ohn de Exeter], chancellor of York, etc. When, in accordance with the duty of our office, we made a visitation of our parochial vicarage of Axminster church, we found that it had been so long vacant that the collation of the same had devolved on us. Having first issued a solemn warning that the dean and chapter of York, or those who had an interest at the time, should within a set period present a suitable parson to it, in the month of November we collated to the said vicarage, at the prompting of charity, our beloved son Walter de Awliscombe, priest, reserving for the canons of York cathedral the ancient and due portion of the same church to be paid annually in coin by the said vicar. Not wishing, however, that your property, whether in that place or elsewhere within our jurisdiction, should be fruitlessly squandered or wasted, we have entrusted to our beloved son the archdeacon of Exeter, as witnessed by our household, all the fruits and incomes of that portion of yours which you hold in the said church of Axminster, and which belong to you by reason of your prebend at York (save for what is appropriate for the maintenance of the ministers of the said church) which are to be preserved by him in good faith until, God willing, you return to England. In testimony whereof etc.

294   OBLIGATIO MAGISTRI W. DE WALEBY. Anno eodem London iv idus Iulii exivit littera: Universis presentes litteras inspecturis magister Willelmus de Waleby, canonicus Ebor' etc. Cum venerabilis pater dominus W. Exon' episcopus ad instantiam meam michi concesserit quod fructus portionis mee in ecclesia de Axminist' ad prebendam meam Ebor' spectantes, associato michi uno de suis, colligere possim et conservare dummodo de fructibus ipsis, deductis expensis necessariis laborantium, citra proximo venturum festum Nativitatis Dominice nichil penitus destruatur; ego eidem domino episcopo tenore presentium in verbo veritatis et bona fide promitto quod fructus ipsos et proventus, per ministeriales meos et certum custodem a dicto domino episcopo ad hoc deputandum, fideliter colligi et conservari salvoque reponi faciam, et quod de fructibus ipsis nichil penitus distraham aut distrahi permittam usque procurator, plenam habens potestatem ordinationi seu taxationi vicarie ipsius ecclesie consentiendi in Angliam prius venerit, et hoc de eiusdem domini episcopi procedat volunte. Volo etiam et concedo quod de bonis portionis mee in ipsa ecclesia congrua sustentatio ministris ipsius interim ministretur. Pro hac quoque concessione et gratia omnibus impetratis et impetrandis in hoc facto absolute renuntio. In cuius etc.

295   PREDICATIO S. ANTONII. Memorandum quod anno eodem tertia die post festum S. Michaelis venit apud Cockyspitte quidam frater questiarius de S. Antonio cum litteris precatoriis archidiaconi Cantuar' quem dominus precepit admitti per litteras officialis sui quia cancellarius non fuit tunc presens, et idem sic admissus in Quadragesima fecit collectam.

[Fo. 17v]³⁷   **296**   PROCURATIO CONFERENDI BENEFICIA IN CURIA. Consecrationis domini Walteri Exon' episcopi anno quarto xvii Kalendas Aprilis apud Horsleg' exivit patens littera domini episcopi continens quod Ricardus de Honeton', clericus, habet potestatem conferendi beneficia omnia spectantia ad collationem domini episcopi que tenent persone tunc existentes in Curia vel illi quos ad eam venire contigerit dum ibidem moram fecerit R. de Honetone.

297   EXITUS W. Anno eodem apud Horsleg' die S. Gregorii exivit W. de Capella, et rediit in vigilia Annuntiationis Dominice apud Forde, et interim habuit R. de Honyton' procurationem et potestatem conferendi beneficia vacantia in Curia.³⁸

298   INSTITUTIO. Anno eodem Exon' iii nonas Aprilis ad presentationem abbatis et conventus de Hertilond' dominus episcopus admisit Hugonem de Molton', presbiterum, ad vacantem vicariam ecclesie de Lanceles quam iidem canonici habent appropriatam, et habet litteras institutionis et inductionis.

---

³⁷ Written in a later hand (Grandisson's?) at the head of the page are the words: Hoc anno ivit episcopus ad concilium Lugdunense.
³⁸ 'Et interim . . .' was added later.

294 BOND OF MASTER W. DE WALESBY. 12 July ?1260, London. A letter was issued: To all who inspect the present letters, Master William de Walesby, canon of York, etc. Since the venerable father, lord W[alter], bishop of Exeter, has at my instance granted me, in association with one of his own clergy, the power to collect and keep the fruits of my portion in the church of Axminster which relate to my prebend at York, provided that none of the said fruits – after deducting the necessary expenses of the labourers – is to be consumed at all until the Christmas next following, I promise to the same lord bishop, by the tenor of these presents in the words of truth and in good faith, that I will have the same fruits and proceeds faithfully collected, kept and safely set aside by means of my agents and of a certain custodian, to be deputed for the purpose by the said lord bishop; and that, of the said fruits, I will spend, or allow to be spent, nothing whatsoever until such time as my proctor, having full power to agree to the ordinance or assessing of the vicarage of the said church, arrives in England; and this is to proceed with the agreement of the same lord bishop. I also desire and grant that in the meantime an appropriate subsistence is to be provided for the ministers of the same church from the property of my portion in it. Also, in return for this concession and favour, I renounce absolutely all suits and applications for suits in this matter. In testimony whereof etc.

295 PREACHING OF ST ANTONY'S. 2 October ?1260, Cokesputt. It is recorded that in the same year, on the third day after the feast of St Michael, there came to Cokesputt a certain friar of the convent of St Antony seeking alms, with supplicatory letters from the archdeacon of Canterbury, whom the lord bishop ordered to be admitted by means of letters from his official, since the chancellor was not present at the time; and having been thus admitted, he took a collection on the first Sunday in Lent.

296 PROXY FOR CONFERRING BENEFICES AT THE CURIA. 16 March 1261, Horsley. The lord bishop issued letters patent giving Richard de Honiton, clerk, the authority to confer all benefices within the collation of the lord bishop which are held by persons then at the Curia or those who should happen to come to it while R. de Honiton continues to stay there.[x]

297 W.'S DEPARTURES. 12 March 1261, Horsley. W. de Capella departed and returned on 24 March at Forde, and meanwhile R. de Honiton had the proxy and power to confer benefices vacant at the Curia.

298 INSTITUTION. 3 April 1261, Exeter. At the presentation of the abbot and convent of Hartland the lord bishop admitted Hugh de Molton, priest, to the vacant vicarage of Launcells church, appropriated to the same canons; and he has letters of institution and induction.

[x] Cf. **323**.

299 CONFIRMATIO ELECTI HERTILOND'. Anno eodem et loco electionem de fratre Ogero de Kernic celebratam dominus episcopus confirmavit, salvo iure domini Oliveri de Dineham', si quid habet, infra mensem postquam venerit in Angliam coram domino episcopo declarando.

300 ORDINES. Anno eodem die Sabbati qua cantatur Sitientes, hoc est v idus Aprilis, dominus episcopus celebravit ordines apud Plymton' de beneficiatis et religiosis tantum.

301 INSTITUTIO. Anno die et loco eisdem ad presentationem domine Albrede de Botrell' dominus episcopus admisit Iohelem Walerand', subdiaconum, ad vacantem ecclesiam de Plymtr' cum honere {sic} residendi, et habet litteras inductionis tantum.

302 INSTITUTIO. Anno die et loco eisdem ad presentationem Philippi de Columbar' dominus episcopus admisit Rogerum de Ridon', subdiaconum, ad vacantem ecclesiam de Boflumiet cum honere {sic} residendi, et habet litteras inductionis tantum.

303 INSTITUTIO. Anno die et loco eisdem ad presentationem Willelmi de Punchardon' dominus [episcopus] admisit Galfridum de Santon', subdiaconum, ad vacantem ecclesiam de Westboklond' cum onere residendi, et habet consimiles litteras.

304 INSTITUTIO. Anno die et loco eisdem ad presentationem trium patronorum scilicet [. . .][39] dominus episcopus admisit Rogerum de Memmyslond', subdiaconum, ad vacantem ecclesiam de Honycherche cum onere residendi, et habet consimiles litteras.

305 INSTITUTIO DE CASTELLO EXON'. Anno die et loco eisdem ad presentationem domini Iohannis de Cortenay dominus episcopus admisit Henricum de Esse, subdiaconum, ad vacantem prebendam castri Exon' de Coteton', et habet litteras.

306 BENEDICTIO ABBATIS HERTILOND'. Anno et loco eisdem Dominica in Passione, hoc est iv idus Iunii [sic], dominus benedixit solempniter fratrem Ogerum abbatem de Hertilond', et habuit litteras administrationis in forma consueta.

307 COMMENDATIO. Anno eodem xii kalendas Maii, hoc est die Mercurii ante Pascha, apud Chydelegh' ad presentationem prioris et conventus Totton' dominus episcopus simpliciter commendavit vacantem ecclesiam de Asprington' magistro Iohanni de Blakedon' et, salvis prioribus litteris inductionis, habet litteras huiusmodi commendationis.

---

[39] This gap left in the MS for the missing names takes almost a whole line.

299 CONFIRMATION OF THE PERSON ELECTED AT HARTLAND. 3 April 1261, Exeter. The lord bishop confirmed the solemn election of Brother Oger de Kernic [as abbot of Hartland], saving the right of Sir Oliver de Dineham, if he has any, which must be declared before the lord bishop within a month of his coming to England.

300 ORDINATION. 9 April 1261, Plympton. The lord bishop held an ordination for beneficed clergy and religious only.

301 INSTITUTION. 9 April 1261, Plympton. At the presentation of the Lady Albreda de Botrell the lord bishop admitted Joel Walerand, subdeacon, to the vacant church of Plymtree with the duty of residence; and he has letters of induction only.

302 INSTITUTION. 9 April 1261, Plympton. At the presentation of Philip de Columbar' the lord bishop admitted Roger de Ridon', subdeacon, to the vacant church of Botus Fleming with the duty of residence; and he has letters of induction only.

303 INSTITUTION. 9 April 1261, Plympton. At the presentation of William de Ponchardon the bishop admitted Geoffrey de Santon', subdeacon, to the vacant church of West Buckland with the duty of residence; and he has identical letters.

304 INSTITUTION. 9 April 1261, Plympton. At the presentation of the three patrons, namely . . ., the lord bishop admitted Roger de Memmyslond', subdeacon, to the vacant church of Honeychurch with the duty of residence; and he has identical letters.

305 INSTITUTION CONCERNING EXETER CASTLE. 9 April 1261, Plympton. At the presentation of Sir John de Courtenay the lord bishop admitted Henry de Esse, subdeacon, to the vacant prebend of Cutton in Exeter Castle;[y] and he has letters.

306 BLESSING OF THE ABBOT OF HARTLAND. 10 April 1261, Plympton. The bishop gave a solemn blessing to Brother Oger, abbot of Hartland; and he had letters of administration in customary form.

307 COMMENDATION. 20 April 1261, Chudleigh. At the presentation of the prior and convent of Totnes, the lord bishop commended completely Master John de Blakedon' to the vacant church of Ashprington; and, saving his earlier letters of induction, he has such letters of commendation.

y Cf. **280**.

308 SOLUTIO RELEVII: PEYNTON'. Anno die et loco eisdem magister Iohannes de Blakedon' solvit domino episcopo c solidos pro relevio terre de Coleton' in manerio de Peynton' quod accidit per mortem Alani de Formans, ita quod de voluntate domini episcopi dicta terra pro relevio nec pro homagio heredis dicti Alani sine speciali mandato domini episcopi [oneretur].

309 ORDINES. Anno eodem ix kalendas Maii dominus episcopus celebravit ordines privatos in ecclesia S. Petri Exon'.

310 INSTITUTIO. Anno die et loco eisdem ad presentationem domini Radulphi de Dodescumb' dominus episcopus admisit Henricum Snellard', subdiaconum, ad vacantem ecclesiam de Legh' Gobold', et habet litteras institutionis et inductionis.

311 INSTITUTIO. Anno die et loco eisdem ad presentationem Walteri de Merton' dominus episcopus admisit Iohannem de [Fo.18] Merton' subdiaconum ad vacantem ecclesiam de Merton', salva taxata ipsius ecclesie vicaria, et habet litteras institutionis et inductionis in forma prescripta.

312 INSTITUTIO. Anno die et loco eisdem ad presentationem Radulphi de Esse dominus episcopus admisit Ricardum de Esse, subdiaconum, ad vacantem ecclesiam de Esse, et habet litteras institutionis et inductionis.

313 INSTITUTIO. Anno die et loco eisdem ad presentationem Manasseri, rectoris ecclesie de Acford', dominus episcopus admisit Robertum de Plymton', presbiterum, ad vicariam ecclesie de Acford' tunc taxandam que constitit in [. . .]⁴⁰ etc.

314 INSTITUTIO. Anno et loco eisdem die Pasche cum dominus Philippus Basset hac vice contulit potestatem per litteras suas patentes domino episcopo providendi ecclesie Sancte Crucis de Rosewyck' de rectore ydoneo, idem dominus episcopus contulit eandem ecclesiam vacantem magistro Henrico de Bollegh', et habet litteras institutionis et inductionis.

315⁴¹ ORDINES. Eodem die dominus [episcopus] ordines [sic] octo accolitos de choro Exon'.

316 CONSOLIDATIO. Anno et loco eisdem in crastino Pasche dominus episcopus consolidavit vacantem vicariam ecclesie de Hamm' cum personatu eiusdem salva decano Exon' et eius successoribus annua pensione xx solidorum debita ratione ecclesie de Braunton' decanatui Exon' annexe solvenda annuatim in festo Nativitatis S. Iohannis et Omnium SS.; et assignavit eandem magistro Olivero de Tracy eiusdem ecclesie rectori.

⁴⁰ Two lines were left blank.
⁴¹ This entry was squeezed in beween its neighbours.

308 PAYMENT OF RELIEF FOR PAIGNTON. 20 April 1261, Chudleigh. Master John de Blakedon' paid to the lord bishop one hundred shillings as relief for the land at Collaton St Mary in the manor of Paignton which had come to him on the death of Alan de Formans, on terms that, by the wish of the lord bishop, the said land [was liable neither] for relief nor homage from the heir of the said Alan without special command of the lord bishop.

309 ORDINATION. 23 April 1261, Exeter. The lord bishop celebrated private orders in St Peter's cathedral.

310 INSTITUTION. 23 April 1261, Exeter. At the presentation of Sir Ralph de Doddiscombe the lord bishop admitted Henry Snellard, subdeacon, to the vacant church of Doddiscombsleigh; and he has letters of institution and induction.

311 INSTITUTION. 23 April 1261, Exeter. At the presentation of Walter de Merton the lord bishop admitted John de Merton, subdeacon, to the vacant church of Merton, reserving a assessed vicarage for the said church; and he has letters of institution and induction in prescribed form.

312 INSTITUTION. 23 April 1261, Exeter. At the presentation of Ralph de Esse the lord bishop admitted Richard de Esse, subdeacon, to the vacant church of Roseash; and he has letters of institution and induction.

313 INSTITUTION. 23 April 1261, Exeter. At the presentation of Manasser, rector of the church of Oakford, the lord bishop admitted Robert de Plympton, priest, to the vicarage of Oakford church, then to be assessed, which consists of . . .

314 INSTITUTION. 24 April 1261, Exeter. When Sir Philip Basset on this occasion gave power by his letters patent to the lord bishop to provide a suitable rector to the church of Holy Cross, Grade,[z] the same lord bishop collated to the same vacant church Master Henry de Bollegh; and he has letters of institution and induction.

315 ORDINATION. 24 April 1261. The lord bishop ordained eight acolytes from the choir of Exeter.

316 CONSOLIDATION. 25 April 1261, Exeter. The lord bishop consolidated the vacant vicarage of Georgeham church together with the parsonage of the same, saving to the dean of Exeter and his successors an annual pension of twenty shillings, due by reason of the annexation of Braunton church to the deanery of Exeter, to be paid each year on the Nativity of St John [24 June] and All Saints' Day [1 November]; and he assigned the same to Master Oliver de Tracy, rector of the same church.

---

[z] Identified as Grade by Hingeston-Randolph, p.143, citing Bishop Stafford's Register.

317 INSTITUTIO. Anno eodem in crastino S. Marci evangeliste apud Crydeton' ad presentationem Ricardi de Greinville dominus episcopus admisit Henricum de Bratton ad vacantem ecclesiam de Bedeford', et habuit litteras inductionis.

318 INSTITUTIO. Anno et die eisdem apud Exoniam ad presentationem prioris et conventus Lanceveton' dominus episcopus admisit Thomam de S. Columba, presbiterum, ad vacantem vicariam de Lanweneck', et habet litteras institutionis et inductionis.

319 CONSOLIDATIO. Eodem die ibidem dominus episcopus consolidavit vicariam ecclesie de Lawhyton' et assignavit eam rectori eiusdem titulo commendationis perpetuo possidendam. Actum est hoc Exon' v kalendas Maii.

320 INSTITUTIO. Anno die et loco eisdem ad presentationem domini Iohannis Cortenai dominus episcopus admisit Iohannem le Pruz, clericum, ad vacantem prebendam sine onere et cura que fuit Luce Kent in ecclesia de Chaumelegh', et habet litteras institutionis et inductionis.

321 INSTITUTIO. Anno eodem die S. Dunstani Londonie dominus episcopus contulit prebendam de Apeldoreham in ecclesia de Boseham vacantem Thome de Herteford', canonico Exon', et habet litteras inductionis.

322 INSTITUTIO. Anno die et loco predictis dominus episcopus contulit vacantem thesaurariam Crydeton' ecclesie magistro Iohanni Nobili, et habet litteras inductionis.

323 PROCURATIO CONFERENDI BENEFICIA IN CURIA. Anno et loco predictis xii kalendas Iunii dominus episcopus concessit magistro B. de Lardar' procurationem et potestatem conferendi, per se vel per alium, vacantia beneficia ad collationem domini spectantia in Curia Romana dum ibi fuerit, non obstante priore commissione facta post eius recessum nichilominus valitura.

324 SERVICIUM CURIE: MUTUUM. Anno die et loco predictis idem magister B. recepit litteras ad recipiendum in Curia Romana centum marcas solutas London', item alias c marcas ibidem nomine mutui London' facti.

325 MUTUUM: PROCURATIO CURIE. Anno die et loco predictis idem magister B. recepit potestatem per patentes litteras domini contrahendi mutuum quinquaginta marcarum in Curia, et procurationem ad impetrandum et contradicendum; [item ad componendum nomine domini episcopi in causis Iohannis de Camerario et .., cancellarii Eboracen'].[42]

---

[42] This clause was cancelled by a 'va . . . cat'.

317 INSTITUTION. 26 April 1261, Crediton. At the presentation of Richard de Grenville the lord bishop admitted Henry de Bracton to the vacant church of Bideford; and he had letters of induction.

318 INSTITUTION. 26 April 1261, Exeter. At the presentation of the prior and convent of Launceston the lord bishop admitted Thomas de S. Columb, priest, to the vacant vicarage of Lewannick; and he has letters of institution and induction.

319 CONSOLIDATION. 26 April 1261, Exeter. The lord bishop consolidated the vicarage of the church of Lawhitton and he assigned it to the rector of the same[a] to be held in perpetuity by a title of commendation. This was enacted at Exeter on 27 April.

320 INSTITUTION. 26 April 1261, Exeter. At the presentation of Sir John Courtenay the lord bishop admitted John le Pruz, clerk, to the vacant prebend, without duty or cure of souls, which Luke Kent had held in the church of Chulmleigh; and he has letters of institution and induction.

321 INSTITUTION. 19 May 1261, London. The lord bishop collated Thomas de Hertford, canon of Exeter, to the vacant prebend of Appledram in the church of Bosham; and he has letters of induction.

322 INSTITUTION. 19 May 1261, London. The lord bishop collated Master John Noble to the vacant treasurership of the church of Crediton; and he has letters of induction.

323 PROXY FOR CONFERRING BENEFICES AT THE CURIA.[b] 21 May 1261, London. The lord bishop granted Master B. de Lardario a proxy and authority to confer, by himself or through another, vacant benefices within the collation of the bishop at the Roman Curia, while he should be there, notwithstanding the previous commission made after his departure still remaining valid.

324 EMPLOYMENT AT THE CURIA – A LOAN. 21 May 1261, London. The same Master B. received letters for the receipt at the Roman Curia of a hundred marks paid in London, and further for another hundred marks in that same place on account of a loan made in London.

325 LOAN: PROXY AT THE CURIA. 21 May 1261, London. By the bishop's letters patent the same Master B. received authority to contract a loan of fifty marks at the Curia, and a proxy for raising and defending actions; {also for reaching a ordinance in the name of the lord bishop in the causes of John de Camerario and the chancellor of York.}

[a] R. de Wisley?
[b] Cf. **296**.

326 PREDICATIO. Anno eodem x kalendas Iunii London' exivit littera predicationis pro hospital' S. Iacobi de Alto Passu in forma communi.

[Fo.18v] **327** CONFIRMATIO DOMINI EPISCOPI DE ECCLESIA S. GERENDI. Anno eodem quarto decimo kalendas Iunii London' exivit talis littera London': Universis presentes litteras inspecturis Walterus miseratione divina Exon' episcopus salutem in Domino sempiternam. Litteras bone memorie quondam Henrici Exon' episcopi, predecessoris nostri, non cancellatas non abolitas in nulla sui parte vitiatas, inspeximus in hec verba: Sciant omnes ad quos presens scriptum pervenerit quod hec est compositio facta inter dominum H. Exon' episcopum et I. priorem et conventum de Plympton' super ecclesia S. Gerendi; videlicet quod idem episcopus et successores eius Exon' episcopi post eum plenum ius habebunt imperpetuum conferendi cuicumque voluerint totam decimam dominii sui tam de frugibus quam de rebus aliis ad predictam ecclesiam spectantibus, et preterea medietatem decimarum omnium et obventionum omnium altaris ex parochia provenientium; predicti vero I. prior et conventus de Plimpton' cum omni integritate percipiant alteram medietatem decimarum parochie tam in decimis frugum quam rerum aliarum, cum medietate omnium obventionum altaris in usus suos imperpetuum convertendam. Dominus vero episcopus et successores eius capellanum invenient qui ecclesie deserviat et episcopis de honere {sic} ecclesie respondeat. Et idem capellanus iuratoriam prestabit cautionem dictis priori et conventui quod prenominatam portionem illorum quantum in eo est ad usus eorum fideliter custodiet, et cum omni integritate eis persolvat. Et ut hec compositio rata permaneat imperpetuum tam sigillis eiusdem H. episcopi et capituli Exon' quam prioris et conventus Plympton' utrobique est roborata. Facta autem est hec compositio apud S. Germanum viii idus Iulii pontificatus H. Exon' episcopi anno ix. His testibus: Augero priore S. Germani, magistro .. de Warwyk', magistro H. de Wylton', canonicis Exoniens', Roberto de Ilstinton, canonico Plymton', magistro W. Pate, Serlone capellano, magistro Thoma de Socton', Iohanne de Gloucestr', Gilberto clerico. Nos igitur dictam compositionem quantum in nobis est ratam et gratam habentes pontificali auctoritate confirmamus et presentis scripti patrocinio communimus. In cuius rei testimonium presentibus litteris sigillum nostrum apponi fecimus. Datum London' xiv kalendas Iunii anno gratie mcc sexagesimo primo et consecrationis eiusdem W. quarto.

328 TRADITIO LITTERARUM. Anno eodem kalendis Maii, hoc est Clausi Pasche, apud Cockespyt W. de Capella liberavit magistro de Tyfford' quatuor litteras patentes ecclesiam de Lanceveton' contingentes sigillatas per quoddam filum iterate sibi reddendas. Redierunt postea et ideo [. . .]43

---

43 This entry is cancelled with a 'vacat'.

326 PREACHING. 23 May 1261, London. A licence to preach, in common form, was issued on behalf of the hospital of S. Iacopo d'Altopascio.

327 CONFIRMATION BY THE LORD BISHOP CONCERNING THE CHURCH OF GERRANS. 19 May 1261, London. A letter as follows was issued in London: To all who inspect the present letters Walter, by divine compassion bishop of Exeter, eternal greeting in the Lord. We have inspected letters of Henry of blessed memory, former bishop of Exeter,[c] our predecessor; they are not cancelled, not annulled, nor in any part defective, and run in these words: Let all persons to whom this present document should come know that this is the settlement made between the lord H[enry], bishop of Exeter, and prior J[ohal][d] and the convent of Plympton concerning the church of Gerrans. To wit, that the same bishop and his successors as bishops of Exeter after him shall have full right in perpetuity to confer on whomsoever they will the whole tithe of their demesne, both in fruits and in other things belonging to the aforesaid church, and furthermore a half of all the tithes and of all the occasional offerings of the altar yielded from the parish. But the aforesaid prior J[ohal] and the convent of Plympton may take in their full totality the other half of the tithes of the parish, tithes both of fruits and of other things, together with a half of all the occasional offerings of the altar, to be turned to their own use in perpetuity. But the lord bishop and his successors shall find a chaplain who shall officiate in the church and be responsible to the bishops for the charges of the church. And the same chaplain shall under oath give security to the said prior and convent that he will, as far as in him lies, preserve faithfully their aforementioned portion for their use, and pay it over to them in full totality. And so that this settlement may be ratified in perpetuity, it has been strengthened on both sides with the seals of the same bishop H[enry] and the chapter of Exeter[e] and of the prior and convent of Plympton. And this settlement has been made at St German's on 8 July 1203. Witnessed by: Auger, prior of St German's, Master de Warwick, Master H. de Wilton, canons of Exeter, Robert de Ilstinton', canon of Plympton, Master W. Pate, Serlo, chaplain, Master Thomas de Socton', John de Gloucester, Gilbert, clerk. We therefore, as far as in us lies, confirm the said settlement holding it right and approved by our pontifical sanction and we reinforce it with the protective power of the present document. In testimony whereof we have had our seal affixed to the present letters. Given etc.

328[f] DELIVERY OF LETTERS. 1 May 1261, Cokesputt. W. de Capella handed over to Master de Tyfford'[g] four letters patent, sealed by a certain thread, touching the church of Launceston, to be returned to him again. They were afterwards returned and therefore . . .

---

[c] Henry Marshal, 1194–1206.
[d] Johal was prior 1188–?1202.
[e] The deanery was not established until Bishop Brewer's time.
[f] This entry was cancelled.
[g] The bishop's official? or possibly the chancellor of the cathedral.

329 PREDICATIO. Anno eodem viii kalendas Iunii apud Horslegh' exivit littera predicationis pro hospitali Sancti Spiritus de Roma ad annum in forma communi.

330 INSTITUTIO PILTON'. Anno eodem iv nonas Maii apud Hurseleg' iuxta Winton' ad presentationem abbatis et conventus Malmesbir' dominus episcopus admisit fratrem Adam de Betesleg', monachum, ad regimen prioratus de Pilton, et habet litteras inductionis.

331 COMPOSITIO REALIS DE PILTON'. Anno eodem xi kalendas Maii inter episcopum decanum et capitulum Exon' ex parte una et abbatem et conventum Malmesbir' ex altera facta est realis compositio in hec verba: Hec compositio realis et perpetua anno gratie mcc sexagesimo primo facta inter Walterum, episcopum, decanum et capitulum ac ecclesiam Exon' ex parte una et Willelmum, abbatem, conventum ac monasterium Malmesbir', Salesbir' diocesis, ex altera: videlicet cum inter episcopum decanum capitulum Exon'[44] abbatem conventum et monasterium predicta super iure et possessione officii visitationis iure ordinario exercendi in cella B. Marie de Pilton', Exon' diocesis, ad predictum monasterium Malmesbir' pertinente, necnon et modo instituendi et destituendi priores seu administratores in cella memorata, suborta esset materia questionis, tandem inter partes ipsas de litium fluctibus ad pacis quietam transire volentes, questio predicta in hunc modum realiter conquievit: videlicet quod predictus episcopus et successores sui post ipsum nomine suo et ecclesie Exon' cellam predictam Pilton' iure ordinario sine reclamatione decetero visitabunt, et quo correctione indigebunt, in rebus et personis canonice visitabunt;[45] hoc adhibito moderamine ad gravamen sumptuum monasterii et celle predicte visitandum in hac parte, quod eiusdem loci priores [Fo.19] dicto episcopo et eius successoribus nomine cuiuslibet procurationis ratione visitationis debite seu debende viginti solidos sterlingorum dumtaxat impendant. Prefati itaque abbas et conventus Malmesbir' et eorum successores dicta cella Pilton' per mortem cessionem resignationem seu alio modo legittime vacante idoneas successive personas priores seu administratores instituendos ibidem dicto domino episcopo et eius successoribus decetero presentabunt, qui curam administrationem seu regimen ab eodem episcopo et eius successoribus recipient et, nisi eis aliquid canonicum obsistat, sine difficultate admittentur. Et ut hoc perpetuo inviolabiliter observetur inter partes episcopus decanus capitulum abbas et conventus predicti tenore presentium hinc inde se obligant in perpetuum et presenti scripto sigilla sua ad perpetuam rei memoriam alternatim apposuerunt. Actum et datum anno gratie mcc sexagesimo primo.[46]

---

[44] MS has *ecclesiam* instead of *Exon'*.
[45] I have translated this as *corrigent*.
[46] A gap was left here, perhaps in case the note of the settlement had been longer.

329 PREACHING. 25 May 1261, Horsley. A licence to preach, in common form, was issued for a year on behalf of the hospital of the Holy Spirit at Rome.

330 INSTITUTION TO PILTON. 4 May 1261, Hursley. At the presentation of the abbot and convent of Malmesbury the lord bishop admitted Brother Adam de Beteslegh, monk, to the government of Pilton Priory; and he has letters of induction.

331 BINDING ORDINANCE CONCERNING PILTON. 21 April 1261. A binding ordinance was made between the bishop, dean and chapter of Exeter on the one part and the abbot and convent of Malmesbury on the other in these words: This is a binding and perpetual ordinance made in the year of grace 1261 between Bishop Walter, the dean and chapter and church of Exeter on the one part and abbot William and the convent and monastery of Malmesbury, in the diocese of Salisbury, on the other. To wit, since a matter of dispute had arisen between the bishop, dean, chapter and church [of Exeter] and the aforesaid abbot, convent and monastery concerning the title and possession of the office of visitation – to be exercised under the ordinary's right – of the daughter-house of the Blessed Mary, Pilton, in the diocese of Exeter, which belongs to the aforesaid monastery of Malmesbury, and concerning also the method of instituting and depriving priors or administrators in the aforementioned daughter-house, at length the aforesaid issue was brought in this way to a binding agreement between the parties, who themselves wished to pass from the stormy seas of litigation to the haven of peace. To wit, that the aforesaid bishop and his successors after him, in their own name and that of the church of Exeter, shall henceforth, by right of being the ordinary, visit the aforesaid daughter-house at Pilton without challenge, and they shall canonically reform what needs correction in things and persons, subject to this limit on the costs of visitation of the monastery and the aforesaid daughter-house, in this respect, that the priors of the same place are to pay to the said bishop and his successors on account of any kind of procuration, due or falling due by reason of the visitation, no more than 20 shillings sterling. And so the aforementioned abbot and convent of Malmesbury and their successors, when the said daughter-house of Pilton is lawfully vacant through death, retirement, resignation or in any other way, shall henceforth present to the said lord bishop and his successors suitable persons successively to be instituted as priors or administrators in that same place, who shall receive the cure, administration or rule from the same bishop and his successors and, unless there is some canonical objection to them, shall be admitted without hindrance. And so that this may be inviolably observed for ever between the parties, the aforesaid bishop, dean and chapter, and abbot and convent by the tenor of these presents henceforth bind themselves in perpetuity, and have mutually had their seals affixed to the present document for a permanent record of the event. Enacted and given in the year of grace 1261.

332 APPROPRIATIO ECCLESIE DE DONEKEWELL. Omnibus sancte matris ecclesie filiis ad quos presentes littere pervenerint Willelmus miseratione divina Exon' episcopus salutem in Domino eternam. Noverit universitas vestra quod, considerata cotidiana hospitalitate que in domo B. Marie de Donckewell' ultra quam facultates ipsius domus subpetere videantur devote excercetur, de consensu et voluntate dilectorum filiorum .. decani et capituli Exon', ecclesiam de Donekewell' parochialem cum omnibus pertinentiis suis que ad patronatum .. abbatis et conventus dicte domus pertinere dinoscitur, divine caritatis intuitu in augmentum hospitalitatis eiusdem misericorditer duximus concedendam et in proprios usus imperpetuum confirmandam. Et quia abbatia de Donekewell' infra limites parochie dicte ecclesie sita est, volumus ut eandem per honestum capellanum imperpetuum faciat deservire. Volumus etiam ut dictis .. abbati et conventui occasione dicte ecclesie contra tenorem privilegiorum suorum nichil servitutis accrescat. In huius rei testimonium presenti scripto sigillum nostrum apponi fecimus. Datum apud Cerde ii kalendas Octobris anno gratie mccxlii.

333 CONFIRMATIO .. DECANI ET CAPITULI EXON' SUPER DICTA ECCLESIA DE DONEKEWELLE ET ETIAM ECCLESIA DE SILDEN'. Omnibus Christi fidelibus ad quos littere presentes pervenerint Rogerus decanus et .. capitulum B. Petri Exon' salutem. Noveritis nos de communi assensu et voluntate ratam et gratam habere confirmationem quam fecit venerabilis dominus et pater Willelmus Exon' episcopus .. abbati conventui et abbatie de Donekewell' de ecclesiis de Donekewell' et Schilden' cum pertinentiis in proprios usus inperpetuum libere possidendis secundum tenorem cartarum eiusdem domini Exon' super hoc eisdem confectarum; dictamque concessionem presentium tenore et sigilli nostri appositione, quantum ad nos pertinet, confirmamus. Datum apud Exon' die Epiphanie anno gratie mccxl tertio.[47]

334 EXITUS. Die Veneris ante Pentecosten, hoc est iv idus Iunii, apud Ferndon' exivit W. de Capella et rediit v nonas Iulii apud Cumton'.

335 TAXATIO ET COLLATIO VICARIE DE HERTILOND'.[48] Universis presentes litteras inspecturis W. miseratione divina Exon' episcopus salutem in Domino sempiternam. Ad universitatis vestre notitiam tenore presentium volumus pervenire quod cum taxanda vicaria ecclesie parochialis S. Nectani de Hertilond' tanto tempore vacavit quod ipsius collatio per negligentiam abbatis et conventus Hertilond', qui ecclesiam ipsam in proprios usus obtinent, pleno iure concessam secundum statuta Lateranen' concilii ad nos extitit devoluta, nos periculum animarum precavere et earum saluti prospicere cupientes vicariam ipsam dilecto filio Henrico de Hertilond' presbitero, divine caritatis intuitu contulimus et ipsum in eadem canonice vicarium instituimus.

[47] Again, space for two more lines left free, as with the next entry.
[48] Sign in the margin refers to **291**.

332   APPROPRIATION OF THE CHURCH OF DUNKESWELL. To all the sons of
Holy Mother Church to whom the present letters shall come, William,[h] by
divine compassion bishop of Exeter, eternal greeting in the Lord. Let all know
that, in consideration of the daily hospitality which is zealously exercised in
the house of the Blessed Mary of Dunkeswell, beyond what the resources of
the said house seem to be equal to, with the consent and agreement of our
beloved sons the dean and chapter of Exeter, at the prompting of divine
charity, we have mercifully thought fit to grant the parish church of
Dunkeswell, with all its appurtenances, which is recognized as belonging to
the patronage of the abbot and convent of the said house, for the increase of
the same hospitality, and to confirm it as appropriated [to the abbot and
convent] in perpetuity. And because the abbey of Dunkeswell is situated
within the boundaries of the parish of the said church, we wish [the abbey] to
see to it that the same [church] is served in perpetuity by a respectable
chaplain. We wish also that no burden of service should be added to the said
abbot and convent by reason of the said church, contrary to the wording of
their privileges. In testimony hereof we have had our seal affixed to this
present document. Given at Chard, 30 September 1242.

333   CONFIRMATION BY THE DEAN AND CHAPTER OF EXETER CONCERNING
THE SAID CHURCH OF DUNKESWELL AND ALSO THE CHURCH OF SHELDON.
To all Christ's faithful to whom the present letters shall come, Roger, dean,
and the chapter of [the cathedral church] of the Blessed Peter at Exeter,
greeting. You are to know that we, by our common assent and agreement,
hold as right and approved the confirmation made by the venerable lord and
father William, bishop of Exeter, to the abbot, convent and abbey of
Dunkeswell concerning the churches of Dunkeswell and Sheldon, with their
appurtenances, for them to possess as appropriated, in perpetuity [and] freely,
in accordance with the wording of the charters of the same bishop of Exeter,
drawn up for the same [persons] on this matter; and as far as it concerns us,
we confirm the said grant by the tenor of these presents and by the affixing of
our seal. Given at Exeter, 6 January 1243.

334   DEPARTURE. 10 June 1261. W[illiam] de Capella left from Farringdon
and returned at *Cumton*[i] on 3 July.

335   ASSESSMENT OF AND COLLATION TO THE VICARAGE OF HARTLAND.
29 May 1261, London. To all who shall inspect the present letters, Walter, by
divine compassion bishop of Exeter, eternal greeting in the Lord. We wish it
to be known to all of you by the tenor of these presents that, since the vicarage
– to be assessed – of the parish church of St Nectan of Hartland has been
vacant for so long through the negligence of the abbot and convent of
Hartland, who have the said church, granted with full right, appropriated to
themselves, that its collation has devolved upon us in accordance with the
canons of the Lateran Council, we, desiring to avoid the risk of danger to

h William Brewer, bishop 1224–44.
i Perhaps one of the two Comptons in Hampshire, or one of the Comptons (Abbas or
Valence) in Dorset, west of Dorchester.

Ordinantes de expresso consensu partium, ordinationi nostre in verbo
veritatis et sacerdotii in scriptis sacrosanctis per omnia stare promittentium,
quod idem vicarius per manus et liberationem abbatis predicti, vel eius
procuratoris, centum solidos sterlingorum ad quatuor anni terminos principales equis portionibus annuatim, esculenta quoque et pocu[Fo.19v]lenta
cotidiana sicut unus de canonicis loci predicti pro se et uno servitore sibi
ministrante ac pabulum pro uno equo nomine vicarie tantummodo percipiat;
reservata nobis cum expedire viderimus ad utriusque partis utilitatem
huiusmodi assignationem mutandi potestate. Volumus etiam quod abbas et
conventus predicti omnia onera ipsius ecclesie et capellarum ex ea
dependentium debita et consueta totaliter agnoscant, et per unum de eorum
canonicis, quem ad hoc eligerint, de ipsarum fructibus ac proventibus
universis disponant pro sue libito voluntatis. Idem vero vicarius per se et
unum clericum dumtaxat in matrice ecclesie predicta personaliter continue
ministrabit. Abbas vero et conventus predicti presbiteros idoneos, quos ad hoc
elegerint in capellis ex dicta ecclesia dependentibus suis sumptibus minis-
traturos, per eorum procuratorem et vicarium predictum archidiacono loci,
cum opus fuerit, presentabunt. In cuius rei testimonium presentes litteras
eidem vicario concessimus patentes. Datum Lond' iv kalendas Iunii
consecrationis nostre anno quarto.

336 COMPOSITIO REALIS DE BOSEHAM. Cum controversia verteretur inter
dominum Exon' et capitulum suum ex una parte et dominum Cicestr' et
capitulum suum ex altera super subiectione ecclesie seu capellarie de Boseham
quam ecclesia Cicestr' sibi lege diocesana subiectam sicut et alias ecclesias
diocesis sue asserebat, tandem mediante E., Elyen' episcopo, eadem
controversia in hunc modum amicabiliter est sopita: Ecclesia sive capellaria de
Bosham cum omni populo suo et ministris suis et possessionibus et pertinentiis
suis in Cicestr' diocesi constitutis plene subiecta erit ecclesie Cistrens' lege
diocesana, exceptis solis canonicis eiusdem ecclesie de quibus ita provisum est
et ordinatum: dominus Exon' libere prebendas conferet et canonicos
installabit non requisito consensu vel auctoritate ecclesie vel episcopi Cicestr'.
Item canonici ex eo quod canonici cautionem obedientie non exponent
ecclesie aut episcopo Cicestr' venient tamen ad sinodum episcopi Cicestr'; si
quid corrigendum fuerit circa personam alicuius canonicorum ad admonitio-
nem Cicestr' ecclesie dominus Exon' faciet illud corrigi et emendari. Si vero
actio civilis et mere personalis inter eosdem canonicos invicem mota fuerit,
iurisdictio erit domini Exon' ita ut si causam illam infra competentem
terminum iudicialiter sive amicabiliter terminare pretermiserit, Exon'
iurisdictio ad Cicestr' pertinebit. Si vero canonicus agat criminaliter adversus
canonicum, sive actionem in rem aut quacumque [sic] alia persona sive
civiliter sive criminaliter agat adversus canonicum, iurisdictio ad Cicestr'
spectabit. Si vero aliquis canonicorum ministraverit i[n] populo curam habens
animarum quam diu sic ministraverit erit obediens ecclesie Cicestr' sicut et

souls and to have an eye to their salvation, at the prompting of divine charity, have collated to the said vicarage our beloved son, Henry de Hartland, priest, and have instituted him as vicar in the same in accordance with the canons. Ordaining with the express consent of the parties, who promise upon the holy scriptures, on their word of truth and as priests, to observe our ordinance in all things, that the same vicar shall receive annually, in the name of the vicarage, by the hands and payment of the aforesaid abbot or his proctor 100 shillings sterling at the principal quarter days, in equal instalments, also daily food and drink, just like one of the canons of the aforesaid place, for himself and for one servant looking after him, and fodder for one horse. We reserve to ourselves the power of altering this particular disposition when we shall see this as furthering the interest of either party. We wish also the aforesaid abbot and convent to bear all the due and customary burdens of the said church and its dependent chapels in their entirety and, through one of their canons whom they shall choose for this purpose, they shall dispose at will of all the fruits and proceeds of the same. The same vicar, on the one part, shall officiate, through himself and no more than one clerk, in person and continuously in the aforesaid mother church; the aforesaid abbot and convent, on the other part, shall when necessary present to the archdeacon of the place through their proctor and the aforesaid vicar suitable priests, whom they shall choose for this purpose, to officiate at their own expense in the chapels dependent from the said church. In testimony whereof we have granted the present letters patent to the same vicar.

336 BINDING AGREEMENT CONCERNING BOSHAM. 1198/1215. Since a dispute was going on between the bishop of Exeter and his chapter on the one part and the bishop of Chichester and his chapter on the other concerning the rule over the church or chaplaincy of Bosham, which the church of Chichester was alleging to be subject to itself by diocesan right, just like other churches in its diocese, at length through the mediation of E[ustace],j bishop of Ely, the same dispute was amicably settled in this way: The church or chaplaincy of Bosham, with all its people and ministers and possessions and appurtenances situated in the diocese of Chichester, shall be fully subject to the church of Chichester by diocesan right, except only the canons of the same church, for whom it has been appointed and laid down in these terms: the bishop of Exeter shall freely confer the prebends and shall instal the canons, without the consent or sanction of the church or bishop of Chichester being required. Further, the canons, although as canons they shall not provide security for obedience to the church or bishop of Chichester, shall nevertheless come to the synod of the bishop of Chichester. If anything should need to be corrected in regard to the person of any of the canons, the bishop of Exeter, on the warning of the church of Chichester, shall see to its being corrected and put right. If, however, a civil action, a purely personal claim, should be raised mutually between these same canons, the bishop of Exeter will have jurisdiction, provided that if he shall neglect to settle that suit by judicial decision or amicable agreement within the due term, Exeter's jurisdiction shall belong to Chichester. But if a canon raises a criminal action against a[nother] canon or a

j Bishop of Ely 1198-1215.

alii ministrantes et curam animarum habentes. Pro delicto tertio canonici suspendi poterit ecclesia de Boseham' auctoritate episcopi Cicestr' ecclesie set non pro delicto canonici numerus canonicorum in senario stabit. Canonicus habens prebendam suam ex o[b]ventionibus parochie de Boseham semel in anno archidiaconum Cicestr', si eidem archidiacono placuerit, procurabit. Ad maiorem huiusmodi compositionis firmitatem episcopus Cicestr' et capitulum suum sigilla sua apposuerunt una cum sigillo E., Elyen' episcopi, quo mediante pax formata est.

337 INSTITUTIO. Anno eodem vi idus Iulii apud Braneys dominus episcopus admisit magistrum Arnoldum, Ricardi Romanorum regis illustris prothonotarium, ad ecclesiam de Braneys, et habet litteras institutionis ad presentationem regis predicti.

338 INSTITUTIO. Anno eodem idus Iulii dominus episcopus admisit Walterum David, clericum et subdiaconum, ad personatum viginti denariorum vacantem in ecclesia de Brawode Kelly per resignationem Petri de Fishacre et habet litteras institutionis.

339 INSTITUTIO. Anno eodem v idus Iulii apud Polslo dominus episcopus ad presentationem priorisse de Polslo admisit Stephanum, capellanum, ad vicariam de Buddeleg' et habet litteras.

340 INSTITUTIO. Anno eodem iv idus Iulii apud Exoniam dominus episcopus admisit Willelmum, presbiterum, ad vicariam ecclesie de Oteryton' ad presentationem prioris loci ipsius et habet litteras.

341 INSTITUTIO. Anno loco et die eisdem ad presentationem prioris de Cowik dominus episcopus admisit Henricum, presbiterum, ad vicariam ecclesie S. Andree de Cowik' et habet litteras.

342 INSTITUTIO. Anno die et loco eisdem ad presentationem priorisse de Polslo dominus episcopus admisit Gregorium, presbiterum, ad vicariam ecclesie de Aylesber', et habet litteras.

343 VISITATIO. Anno eodem xv kalendas Augusti Bonifacius, Cantuar' archiepiscopus, visitavit Walterum, Exon' episcopum.

344 VISITATIO. Anno eodem xiv kalendas Augusti idem archiepiscopus visitavit .. decanum et capitulum Exon'.

real action, or [if] any other person at all raises either a civil or a criminal action against a canon, jurisdiction will pertain to Chichester. If, however, any one of the canons shall officiate among the people with the cure of souls, as long as he shall thus officiate, he shall be obedient to the church of Chichester, just like any others officiating with the cure of souls. For a canon's third offence, he can be suspended from the [collegiate] church of Bosham by the authority of the bishop of the church of Chichester but, despite any offence by a canon, the number of canons shall remain at six. A canon holding his prebend on the occasional offerings of Bosham parish shall, once in the year, entertain the archdeacon of Chichester, if this is agreeable to the same archdeacon. For the greater confirmation of this particular ordinance, the bishop of Chichester and his chapter have affixed their seals, together with the seal of E[ustace], bishop of Ely, through whose mediation this concord was made.

337 INSTITUTION. 10 July 1261, Bradninch. The lord bishop admitted Master Arnold, protonotary to the illustrious Richard, King of the Romans, to the church of Bradninch; and he has letters of institution at the presentation of the aforesaid king.

338 INSTITUTION. 15 July 1261. The lord bishop admitted Walter David, clerk and subdeacon, to the parson's benefice of 20 pence in the church of Broadwood Kelly vacant through the resignation of Peter de Fishacre; and he has letters of institution.

339 INSTITUTION. 11 July 1261, Polsloe. At the presentation of the prioress of Polsloe the lord bishop admitted Stephen, chaplain, to the vicarage of Budleigh;[k] and he has letters.

340 INSTITUTION. 12 July 1261, Exeter. At the presentation of the prior of Otterton the lord bishop admitted William, priest, to the vicarage of Otterton church; and he has letters.

341 INSTITUTION. 12 July 1261, Exeter. At the presentation of the prior of Cowick the lord bishop admitted Henry, priest, to the vicarage of St Andrew's church, Cowick; and he has letters.

342 INSTITUTION. 12 July 1261, Exeter. At the presentation of the prioress of Polsloe the lord bishop admitted Gregory, priest, to the vicarage of Aylesbeare church; and he has letters.

343 VISITATION. 18 July 1261. Boniface, archbishop of Canterbury, visited Walter, bishop of Exeter.

344 VISITATION. 19 July 1261. The same archbishop visited the dean and chapter of Exeter.

---

k The modern parish of East Budleigh.

[Fo.20] **345** VISITATIO. Anno eodem xii kalendas Augusti idem archiepiscopus per clericos suos visitavit priorem et conventum Totton'.

346 VISITATIO. Anno eodem xi kalendas Augusti idem archiepiscopus per clericos suos visitavit priorem et conventum Plimpton'.

347 Anno eodem apud Crideton' et die comparuerunt coram domino episcopo magister O. de Trascy, rector ecclesie de Hamme, et prior S. Marie Magdalen' Barn', quorum communi consensu et voluntate hinc inde consensum est et provisum quod omnes decime de Crideho, quas dictus prior ibidem consuevit percipere, remaneant in sequestro dicti episcopi ita quod partes per communes amicos tractent de pace, et eam reformatam coram domino episcopo recitabunt confirmandam. Alioquin in crastino celebrationis ordinum comparebunt coram domino episcopo ubicumque fuerit in episcopatu ut, eo mediante, pax si fieri possit plene reformetur.

348 Anno die et loco eisdem procurator decani et capituli Rothomagen' comparens exhibuit transcripta duorum privilegiorum sedis apostolice sub signo domini Cant' et procurationem suam, quorum copia residet penes dominum episcopum. et habet eundem diem . . .[49]

349 OBEDIENTIA. Anno die loco eisdem .. prior B. Marie Magdalen' iuravit domino episcopo canonicam obedientiam et reverentiam; presentibus tunc magistris Olivero de Trascy, archidiacono Surr', Roberto de Tefford', officiali domini episcopi, Iohanne le Noble, Luca Payn, Gervasio de Crideton', et Roberto de Polamford', et aliis.

350 VISITATIO. Anno eodem x kalendas Augusti dominus archiepiscopus per clericos suos visitavit abbatem et conventum Tavistok'.

351 DEDICATIO. Anno et die eisdem dominus episcopus dedicavit ecclesiam de Stokeleg' Pomeray.

352 CONFIRMATIO. Anno eodem die S. Marg' virginis ad instantiam domini episcopi decanus et capitulum Exon' confirmarunt augmentum sex prebendarum in ecclesia Criditon'.

353 APPROPRIATIO. Anno die et loco eisdem dominus episcopus decanus et capitulum Exon' concesserunt ecclesiam de Marineleg', cum eam vacare contigerit, priori et conventui de Berliz in proprios usus perpetuo possidendam pleno iure.

---

[49] The sentence just begun is cancelled with 'vacat quod alibi'.

345 VISITATION. 21 July 1261. The same archbishop through his clerks visited the prior and convent of Totnes.

346 VISITATION. 22 July 1261. The same archbishop through his clerks visited the prior and convent of Plympton.

347 [ORDINANCE CONCERNING GEORGEHAM]. 22 July 1261, Crediton. There appeared before the lord bishop Master O[liver] de Tracy, rector of Georgeham church, and the prior of St Mary Magdalen, Barnstaple, by whose common consent and accord it was henceforth agreed and appointed that all the tithes of Croyde, which the said prior was accustomed to take there, should remain under the sequestration of the said bishop on terms that the parties should negotiate peace through their common friends and, once it was re-established, they should read it out before the lord bishop for his confirmation. Otherwise they shall appear before the lord bishop, wherever he may be in his diocese, on the morrow of the celebration of orders[l] so that by his mediation peace may if possible be fully re-established.

348[m] [PAPAL PRIVILEGES]. 22 July 1261, Crediton. The proctor of the dean and chapter of Rouen appeared and showed the transcripts of two papal privileges under the seal of the archbishop of Canterbury and also his power of attorney; a copy of them remains in the possession of the lord bishop; and he has the same day . . .

349 OBEDIENCE. 22 July 1261, Crediton. The prior of St Mary Magdalen [Barnstaple] swore canonical obedience and respect to the lord bishop; there were present then Masters Oliver de Tracy, archdeacon of Surrey, Robert de Tefford, official of the lord bishop, John le Noble, Luke Payn, Gervase de Crediton and Robert de Polamford, and others.

350 VISITATION. 23 July 1261. The lord archbishop through his clerks visited the abbot and convent of Tavistock.

351 DEDICATION. 23 July 1261. The lord bishop dedicated the church of Stockleigh Pomeroy.

352 CONFIRMATION.[n] 20 July 1261, [Exeter]. At the request of the lord bishop the dean and chapter of Exeter confirmed an increase of six prebends in the [collegiate] church of Crediton.

353 APPROPRIATION. 20 July 1261, Exeter. The lord bishop and the dean and chapter of Exeter granted the church of Mariansleigh, when it should fall vacant, to the prior and convent of Barlinch to be possessed completely as appropriated to them in perpetuity.

[l] Presumably the Sunday after the next Ember Day, i.e. 25 September 1261.
[m] This entry was afterwards cancelled with the note that it was recorded elsewhere, presumably in some other episcopal archive.
[n] Cf. **744** and **926**.

354 EXITUS. Anno die et loco predictis apud Exon' exivit W. de Capella cum clericis domini archiepiscopi visitantibus et rediit die Sabbati ante Ad Vincula apud Sudtauton', et in crastino exivit et postea rediit apud S. Germanum die Lune post Ad Vincula in octabis dicti festi prope Braneis.

355 VISITATIO. Anno eodem ix kalendas Augusti archiepiscopus Cant' per clericos suos visitavit priorem et conventum Lanst'.

356 VISITATIO. Anno eodem die S. Iacobi idem archiepiscopus visitavit priorem et conventum Bodm' per eosdem.

357 VISITATIO. Anno [eodem] vii kalendas Augusti idem archiepiscopus visitavit priorem et conventum de Tywerdrait per eosdem.

358 DEDICATIO. Anno et die eisdem dominus episcopus dedicavit ecclesiam de Berliz.

359 DEDICATIO. Anno [eodem] vi kalendas Augusti dominus episcopus dedicavit capellam B. Katerine ibidem.

360 VISITATIO. Anno eodem v kalendas Augusti dominus archiepiscopus visitavit abbatem et conventum Hertilond' per eosdem.

361 DEDICATIO. Anno et die eisdem dominus episcopus dedicavit ecclesiam de Wlfereswrth'.

362 INSTITUTIO. Anno eodem iv kalendas Augusti apud Cridton' ad presentationem domini Manasseri, rectoris ecclesie de Acford', dominus episcopus admisit Robertum de la Sturte, presbiterum, ad vicariam ipsius ecclesie, ordinans quod omnes obventiones altaris, totam terram sanctuarii, assisum redditum, domum quandam cum orto, unam acram terre, unam acram prati, et xl solidos per manum rectoris ad quatuor anni terminos equis portionibus per manum rectoris[50] percipiat, et debita onera et consueta ipsius ecclesie agnoscat; decima [sic] garbarum et feni et domibus persone rectoris usibus reservatis.

363 DEDICATIO. Anno et die eisdem dominus episcopus dedicavit ecclesiam de Donesford'.

364 DEDICATIO. Anno eodem iii kalendas Augusti dominus episcopus dedicavit ecclesiam de Chaggeford'.

[Fo.20v]　**365** DEDICATIO. Die Dominica ii kalendas Augusti anno eodem dominus episcopus dedicavit ecclesiam de Okempton'.

366 DEDICATIO. Anno eodem in crastino festi S. Petri Ad Vincula dominus episcopus dedicavit ecclesiam de Lyu Trenchard'.

---

[50] *Per manum rectoris* is repeated.

354 DEPARTURE. 20 July 1261, Exeter. W[illiam] de Capella departed with the lord archbishop's clerks who were making visitations and he returned on 30 July at South Tawton; he departed the next day and thereafter returned on 8 August to St Germans near Bradninch.

355 VISITATION. 24 July 1261. The archbishop of Canterbury through his clerks visited the prior and convent of Launceston.

356 VISITATION. 25 July 1261. The same archbishop through the same [clerks] visited the prior and convent of Bodmin.

357 VISITATION. 26 July 1261. The same archbishop through the same [clerks] visited the prior and convent of Tywardreath.

358 DEDICATION. 26 July 1261. The lord bishop dedicated the church of Barlinch.

359 DEDICATION. 27 July 1261, [Barlinch]. The lord bishop dedicated the chapel of St Katherine in that same place.

360 VISITATION. 28 July 1261. The lord archbishop through the same [clerks] visited the abbot and convent of Hartland.

361 DEDICATION. 28 July 1261. The lord bishop dedicated the church of Woolfardisworthy.°

362 INSTITUTION. 29 July 1261, Crediton. At the presentation of Sir Manasser, rector of Oakford church, the lord bishop admitted Robert de la Sturte, priest, to the vicarage of the said church, laying down that he is to receive all the occasional offerings of the altar, all the sanctuary land, the fixed rent, a certain house with garden, one acre of land, one acre of meadow, and 40 shillings at the hands of the rector, in equal instalments on the quarter days, and he is to bear the due and customary charges of the said church, but the garb and hay tithes and the buildings of the parsonage were reserved for the rector's use.

363 DEDICATION. 29 July 1261. The lord bishop dedicated the church of Dunsford.

364 DEDICATION. 30 July 1261. The lord bishop dedicated the church of Chagford.

365 DEDICATION. 31 July 1261. The lord bishop dedicated the church of Okehampton.

366 DEDICATION. 2 August 1261. The lord bishop dedicated the church of Lewtrenchard.

° The Woolfardisworthy north of Crediton, in Witheridge Hundred.

367 DEDICATIO. Anno eodem iii nonas Augusti dominus episcopus dedicavit ecclesiam de Lideford'.

368 DEDICATIO. Anno eodem ii idus Augusti dominus episcopus dedicavit ecclesiam de Lanmoren.

369 DEDICATIO. Anno eodem idibus Augusti dominus episcopus dedicavit ecclesiam S. Michaelis de Penkevel.

370 DEDICATIO. Anno eodem xix kalendas Septembris dominus episcopus dedicavit ecclesiam S. Iusti in Ros.

371 COLLATIO. Anno eodem in crastino Assumptionis apud Penrin dominus episcopus contulit vicariam ecclesie de Moresc taxandam magistro Ricardo de Lanquek', presbitero, que consistit in omnibus obventionibus altaris, excepta decima feni, et in manso et sanctuario; vicarius quoque sustinebit consueta in toto, extraordinaria pro rata.

372 COLLATIO. Anno et die et loco eisdem dominus episcopus contulit vicariam ecclesie S. Hillarii iuxta Montem Iohanni de Penrin, presbitero, que consistit[51] in omnibus obventionibus altaris, excepta decima piscium totius parrochie et exceptis mortuariis de Markasiou de parvo mercato Brevannek Penmened Trewarven provenientibus; item exceptis decimis de nutrimentis animalium prioris; item excepta tota decima Insule Montis. Item vicarius sustinebit omnia onera ordinaria, extraordinaria pro rata.

373 INSTITUTIO. Anno die et loco eisdem ad presentationem prioris et conventus de S. Germano dominus episcopus admisit magistrum Rogerum de S. Iusto, presbiterum, ad vicariam ecclesie de Lanestli que consistit in hiis portionibus quas magister Henricus de Bolleg' habuit, nomine vicarie, salvo iure plus petendi auctoritate Concilii.

374 DEDICATIO. Anno eodem xiii kalendas Septembris dominus episcopus dedicavit ecclesiam S. Stephani iuxta Hyndemor'.

375 INSTITUTIO. Anno eodem v kalendas Septembris apud S. Germanum ad presentationem prioris et conventus de Tywardraith' dominus episcopus admisit Thomam de Hendr', presbiterum, ad vicariam ecclesie de Treneglos, et habet litteras.

376 INSTITUTIO. Anno die et loco eisdem ad presentationem prioris et conventus predictorum dominus episcopus admisit Radulphum, presbiterum, ad taxandam vicariam ecclesie parochialis de Tywardrait que consistit in liberatione unius monachi et iv marcis, [una camera[52]] et pabulo unius equi cum annona, et habet litteras in forma communi.

---

[51] The details, rather squeezed, were clearly added from here on.
[52] Crossed out.

367   DEDICATION. 3 August 1261. The lord bishop dedicated the church of Lydford.

368   DEDICATION. 12 August 1261. The lord bishop dedicated the church of Lamorran.

369   DEDICATION. 13 August 1261. The lord bishop dedicated the church of St Michael Penkevil.

370   DEDICATION. 14 August 1261. The lord bishop dedicated the church of St Just in Roseland.

371   COLLATION. 16 August 1261, Penryn. The lord bishop collated Master Richard de Lanquek', priest, to the vicarage, to be assessed, of St Clement's church, which consists of all the occasional offerings of the altar, except the tithes of hay, and of a house and the sanctuary; the vicar is to bear the whole of the customary [burdens], and the extraordinary ones proportionately.

372   COLLATION. 16 August 1261, Penryn. The lord bishop collated John de Penryn, priest, to the vicarage of St Hilary's church, which consists of all the occasional offerings of the altar, except for the tithes of fish from the whole parish and except for the mortuary dues yielded from Market Jew,P Brevannek', Penmened [and] Trewarvene, and also except for the tithes of the feedstuffs of the prior'sq cattle; also except the whole tithe of St Michael's Mount. Further, the vicar is to bear all the ordinary burdens, and the extraordinary ones proportionately.

373   INSTITUTION. 16 August 1261, Penryn. At the presentation of the prior and convent of St Germans, the lord bishop admitted Master Roger de St Just, priest, to the vicarage of Gulval church, which consists of those portions which Master Henry de Bollegh held on account of the vicarage, saving the right of seeking more in accordance with the authority of the Council.

374   DEDICATION. 20 August 1261. The lord bishop dedicated the church of St Stephen-in-Brannel.

375   INSTITUTION. 28 August 1261, St Germans. At the presentation of the prior and convent of Tywardreath, the lord bishop admitted Thomas de Hendre, priest, to the vicarage of Treneglos church; and he has letters.

376   INSTITUTION. 28 August 1261, St Germans. At the presentation of the aforesaid prior and convent, the lord bishop admitted Ralph, priest, to the vicarage, to be assessed, of the parish church of Tywardreath, which consists of the allowance for one monk, and four marks, (one room) and forage including corn for one horse; and he has letters in common form.

P Better known as Marazion, which Market Jew or the small market – *Parvo Foro*, *Parvo Mercato* – adjoined.
q The prior of St Michael's Mount.

377 INSTITUTIO. Anno die et loco eisdem ad presentationem prioris et conventus Bodmin' dominus episcopus admisit Iohannem dictum Chepman, presbiterum, ad taxandam vicariam parochialis ecclesie S. Petroci Bodmin', ordinans quod consistit in liberatione unius canonici, iv marcis annuis, [una camera competenti⁵³] pabulo unius equi cum annona, et habet litteras in forma communi.

378 RESIGNATIO PRIORATUS LANST'. Anno eodem ii nonas⁵⁴ Septembris apud Lanceveton' prior Robertus eiusdem loci cessit regimini prioratus et dominus concessit conventui licentiam eligendi, et providit priori in hac forma: W. Dei gratia etc. fratri R. de Fissacr' dudum priori etc. salutem etc. Cum etatis vestre auroram et meridiem citra estis et onera ecclesie Lanceveton' predicte supportanda cuius regimini sponte cessistis expenderitis, non indignum iudicamus ut, vobis iuxta cursum nature ad vesperam declinantibus, precipuum honorem pro meritis impendamus; de communi consensu et assensu unanimi totius conventus loci predicti deliberatione provida ordinantes ut infra septa ecclesie predicte camera illa, quam precipuam consuevistis habere, vobis et uni concanonico vestro de anno in annum mutando ad vitam assignetur una cum viridario ad cameram ipsam pertinente; obventiones quoque altalagii ecclesie S. Stephani Superioris Lanstaveton' una cum terra de parco infra muros cum omnibus pertinentiis, et esculenta ac poculenta quantum tribus canonicis domus vestre assignari consuevit per diem, ac uni servitori vobis ministranti pro vestra, concanoni vestri vobis in solatium deputati, et sacerdotis in dicta ecclesia ministrantis persona qui vobis respondeat in temporalibus assignamus; hoc adhibito moderamine quod si altalagii predicti obventiones, processu temporis auctoritate superioris per ordinationem canonicam diminui vel forsan depauperari contingat, in recompen[Fo.21]sationem diminutionis seu depauperationis huiusmodi decem marcas annuas per manum futuri prioris et eius successorum iuxta nostre voluntatis arbitrium ad iv anni terminos principales sine diminutione et difficultate qualibet percipiatis; residuis ipsius altalagii obventionibus et parco predicto in usus prioris et conventus predictorum extunc reversuris. Interpretandi quoque corrigendi mutandi mitigandi ordinationem presentem et dispensandi supra eam, si opus fuerit, et cohercendi rebelles nobis reservamus. In cuius rei testimonium presentibus litteris nos et dictus conventus sigilla nostra apposuimus, quod prior futurus cum creatus fuerit sigillum suum eisdem in signum approbationis et consensus apponat decernentes. Actum in capitulo de Lanstaveton' ii idus Septembris consecrationis nostre anno iv et gratie mcc sexagesimo primo.

379 DEDICATIO. Anno eodem v kalendas Septembris dominus episcopus dedicavit conventualem ecclesiam S. Germani.

⁵³ This phrase has been crossed out.
⁵⁴ A mistake for *idus*?

377 INSTITUTION. 28 August 1261, St Germans. At the presentation of the prior and convent of Bodmin, the lord bishop admitted John called Chepman, priest, to the vicarage, to be assessed, of the parish church of St Petrock, Bodmin, laying down that it should consist of the allowance for one canon, four marks annually, (one appropriate room) forage including corn for one horse; and he has letters in common form.

378 RESIGNATION OF THE PRIOR OF LAUNCESTON. 12 September 1261, Launceston. Robert, prior of the same place, retired from the rule of the priory, and the bishop granted to the convent licence to elect, and he provided for the prior on these terms: Walter, by God's grace etc, to brother Robert de Fishacre, formerly prior etc, greeting, etc. Since you have now passed the dawn and noon of your life, and have spent [yourself in] bearing the burdens of the aforesaid church of Launceston, from the rule of which you have voluntarily retired, we judge it not unworthy, now that you are declining in the course of nature towards your evening, that we should award you special honour in accordance with your merits. We ordain, with careful deliberation, and with the common consent and unanimous accord of the entire convent of the aforesaid place, that, within the precincts of the aforesaid church, that particular room which you were accustomed to occupy should be assigned for life to you and to one of your fellow canons, who is to change each year, together with the pleasure garden pertaining to the said room. We assign [to you] also the occasional offerings of the altarage of the church of St Stephen's, Launceston, together with the parkland within the walls with all its appurtenances, as much food and drink as has customarily been assigned daily for three canons of your house – and for one servant ministering to you – for your own person, for the person of the one of your fellow canons allotted to your service, and for the person of the priest ministering in the said church, who is to answer to you for the temporalities. This is subject to the qualification that if the offerings of the aforesaid altarage, by the passage of time, by the command of a superior, [or] through a canonical ordinance, should chance to be reduced or perhaps impoverished, in recompense for such reduction or impoverishment you should take, as is agreeable to our judgment, ten marks yearly at the hand of the future prior and of his successors, at the main quarter days, without reduction or any sort of difficulty; the residue of the offerings of the said altarage and the aforesaid park shall thereupon revert to the use of the aforesaid prior and convent. We reserve to ourselves also [the power] of interpreting, correcting, altering, or modifying the present ordinance, and dispensing from it if that should be necessary, and of coercing the disobedient. In testimony whereof we and the said convent have affixed our seals to the present letters, decreeing that the future prior, when he shall have been chosen, shall affix his seal to the same as a sign of approval and consent. Enacted in the chapter of Launceston, 4 September 1261.

379 DEDICATION. 28 August 1261. The lord bishop dedicated the conventual church of St Germans.

380 DEDICATIO. Anno eodem die S. Egidii dominus episcopus dedicavit ecclesiam de Curiton'.

381 DEDICATIO. Anno eodem iv nonas Septembris dominus episcopus dedicavit ecclesiam de Bradeston'.

382 INSTITUTIO. Anno eodem die Nativitatis S. Marie apud Tauton' ad presentationem magistri Ricardi de Bolevile, rectoris ecclesie de Liu Toriton', de consensu Nicolai de Bolevile, veri patroni ecclesie predicte, dominus episcopus admisit Ricardus de Aufridecumb', presbiterum, ad ipsius ecclesie vicariam taxandam, ordinans quod in omnibus obventionibus altaris exceptis mortuariis domo et terra ad inhabitandum consistat, et habet litteras in forma communi.

383 STUDIUM. Anno eodem iii idus Septembris apud Crideton' dominus episcopus concessit Willelmo de Haccumb', rectori ecclesie de Stok' Flandr', licentiam Parisi' in iure canonico usque ad triennium, et habet litteras.

384 INSTITUTIO. Anno eodem viii kalendas Octobris apud Totton' ad presentationem domini Nicolai filius Martini, veri patroni ecclesie de Dertington', dominus episcopus admisit Henricum de Sicca Villa, subdiaconum, ad eandem ecclesiam vacantem, et habet litteras institutionis et inductionis in forma communi.

385 CELEBRATIO ORDINUM. Anno eodem viii kalendas Octobris dominus episcopus celebravit ordines ad Totton'.

386 INSTITUTIO. Anno eodem vii kalendas Octobris apud Peyncton' ad presentationem domine Agnetis Bauceyn, vere patrone ecclesie de Clist S. Laurentii hac vice, dominus episcopus admisit Robertum de Hill', subdiaconum, ad predictam ecclesiam vacantem cum onere residendi, et habet litteras institutionis et inductionis in forma communi.

387 PROVISIO ECCLESIE DE BIR'. Anno eodem v nonas Octobris apud Teynton magister N. de Plimpton', archidiaconus de Nortfolch', gerens vices Hugonis de la Penn' auctoritate apostolica providit magistro G. Wale domini pape notario de ecclesia de Biri, et super hoc direxit litteras patentes domino episcopo, quarum auctoritate dominus episcopus ipsius notarii procuratorem in predicte ecclesie possessionem mandavit induci.

388 SENTENTIA PLIMPT'. Anno eodem iii nonas Octobris apud Exon' dominus episcopus diffiniter pronuntiando sequestravit ecclesiam de Eckeboclond' cum fructibus et salvo custodiri precepit quousque de predicta ecclesia, vel saltim vicaria, aliter duxerit ordinandum.

389 DE EODEM. Anno die et loco eisdem dominus episcopus diffinitive pronuntiavit collationem Willelmi quondam Exon' episcopi factam de ecclesia

380 DEDICATION. 1 September 1261. The lord bishop dedicated the church of Coryton.

381 DEDICATION. 2 September 1261. The lord bishop dedicated the church of Bradstone.

382 INSTITUTION. 8 September 1261, Bishop's Tawton. At the presentation of Master Richard de Bolevile, rector of North Lew church, with the consent of Nicholas de Bolevile, true patron of the aforesaid church, the lord bishop admitted Richard de Ilfracombe, priest, to the vicarage, to be assessed, of the said church, laying down that it should consist of all the occasional offerings of the altar, except for the mortuary dues, with a house and land in which to dwell; and he has letters in common form.

383 STUDY. 11 September 1261, Crediton. The lord bishop granted to William de Haccombe, rector of Stoke Fleming, licence [to study] canon law in Paris for up to three years; and he has letters.

384 INSTITUTION. 24 September 1261, Totnes. At the presentation of Sir Nicholas fizMartin, true patron of Dartington church, the lord bishop admitted Henry de Sackville, subdeacon, to the same vacant church; and he has letters of institution and induction in common form.

385 CELEBRATION OF AN ORDINATION. 24 September 1261, Totnes. The lord bishop held an ordination.

386 INSTITUTION. 25 September 1261, Paignton. At the presentation of Lady Agnes Bauceyn, true patron for this turn of Clyst St Lawrence church, the lord bishop admitted Robert de Hill, subdeacon, to the aforesaid vacant church, with the duty of residing; and he has letters of institution and induction in common form.

387 PROVISION TO THE CHURCH OF BERRYNARBOR. 3 October 1261, Bishopsteignton. Master Nicholas de Plympton, archdeacon of Norfolk, acting on behalf of Hugh de la Penn, by papal authority provided Master G. Wale, papal notary, to the church of Berrynarbor, and he addressed letters patent on this matter to the lord bishop, by the authority of which the lord bishop ordered the proctor of the said notary to be inducted into possession of the aforesaid church.

388 JUDICIAL SENTENCE CONCERNING PLYMPTON [PRIORY]. 5 October 1261, Exeter. The lord bishop by a definitive judgment sequestrated the church of Egg Buckland with its fruits, and ordered that it should be kept safely until he should think fit to ordain otherwise concerning the aforesaid church, or at least its vicarage.

389 CONCERNING THE SAME. 5 October 1261, Exeter. The lord bishop gave definitive judgment that the collation made by William [Brewer], former

de Landeho non valere, et per consequens dudum postea subsequtam [sic] confirmationem capituli Exon' tanquam minus legitimam non tenere. Item alia ratione cum conditio et status rei penitus esset immutatus, idem episcopus pronuntiavit dictam ecclesiam legitimo gubernatore destitutam et ad ordinationem suam [Fo.21v] seu collationem devolutam ac eam sue ordinationi seu collationi reservavit. Item anno die et loco eisdem dictos priorem et conventum ecclesiam de Dene vitiose et contra iustitiam ingressos esse pronuntiavit et eos ecclesia ipsa per diffinitivam privavit, magistro Gervasio de Crideton' eam conferendo, in hec verba:[55]

(1) Cum religiosi viri prior et conventus Plimpton' vocati fuissent ut comparerent coram nobis ex officii debito procedentibus ius suum si quod habent in ecclesiis de Ekebokelond', de Landeho, et de Dene quas detinere dinoscuntur ostensuri; dictis religiosis coram commissariis nostris certis die et loco comparentibus, ex parte eorum exhibitum fuit quoddam privilegium bone memorie Alexandri pape IV super ecclesia de Ekeboklond' per quod eis licere dicebant ipsius ecclesie possessionem ingredi cum eam vacare contingeret per cessionem aut decessum rectoris eiusdem, consensu dyocesani minime requisito; hocque pretextu se dictam ecclesiam possidere et licite retinere posse dicebant. Set quia de cessione vel obitu dicti rectoris non constat, nec predecessori nostro constitit, nec dicti privilegii forma si eis prodesse debeat est servata, cum ius dyocesani salvum non fuerit in hac parte maxima cum ad vicariam ipsius ecclesie nobis aut predecessori nostro nullus adhuc canonice fuerit presentatus vicarius instituendus in ea seu admissus, nos, Walterus Exon' episcopus in nomine Patris etc., ecclesiam ipsam cum fructibus sequestrari et salvo custodiri precipimus quousque de ea vel saltim eius vicaria aliter duxerimus ordinandum.

(2) Item super ecclesia de Landeho exhibita fuit littera bone memorie Willelmi Exon' episcopi que videtur innuere quod dicta ecclesia de Landeho, amotis seu decedentibus clericis seu canonicis secularibus ibidem constitutis, canonicis de Plympton' ab eodem episcopo de consensu capituli sui canonice ut dicebant collata fuit; introducentes insuper quoad hoc instrumenta plurium episcoporum que videntur factum ipsius confirmare. Quia vero prefatus W(illelmus) episcopus, qui rerum ecclesie sue procurator erat non dominus, sine legitimo consensu capituli res sue ecclesie alienare non potuit, ad huiusmodi donationem processit. Preterea cum appareat cartam donationis predicti W(illelmi) episcopi quoad predictam ecclesiam de Landeho evacuatam esse, pro eo quod ipso innuente non vacabat ipsa ecclesia set erant ibi canonici seculares toto tempore vite ipsius, prout testantur instrumenta plurium episcoporum subsequentium. In nomine Patris etc., collationem dicti

---

[55] Figures are given in the margin, as indicated, for the following four paragraphs, but there are no paragraph marks, unlike **395** and its series of letters.

bishop of Exeter, of the church of St Kew was invalid, and in consequence the subsequent confirmation, long afterwards, of the chapter of Exeter did not hold good as lacking what is prescribed by law. Further, and for another reason, in particular since the condition and status of the matter had been fundamentally changed, the same bishop gave judgment that the said church lacked a lawful governor and had devolved to his own ordinance or collation, and he reserved it for his own ordinance or collation. Further, in the same year, day, and place, he gave judgment that the said prior and convent [of Plympton] had intromitted defectively and contrary to justice with the church of Dean Prior, and by definitive [sentence] he deprived them of the said church, conferring it on Master Gervase de Crediton in these words:

Since the religious persons, the prior and convent of Plympton, have been summoned to appear before us – who are proceeding in accordance with the duties of our office – to show their right, if they have any, to the churches of Egg Buckland, St Kew and Dean Prior, which they are known to be occupying; when the said religious appeared before our commissaries at the fixed day and place, there was exhibited on their behalf a certain privilege of Pope Alexander IV of blessed memory concerning the church of Egg Buckland, whereby they said it was lawful for them to enter into possession of the said church when it should happen to fall vacant by the resignation or decease of the rector of the same, without any requirement for the diocesan's consent; and on this pretext they said they possessed and could lawfully retain the said church. But because the position as regards the resignation or death of the said rector is not established, and it was not established to our predecessor, nor are the terms of the said privilege – if it is intended to be of use to them – preserved, [then] since the right of the diocesan has not been safeguarded in this most important respect, since hitherto nobody has been canonically presented to the vicarage of that church to us or our predecessor to be instituted vicar in the same, nor been admitted, we, Walter, bishop of Exeter, in the Name of the Father, etc. we order the said church and its fruits to be sequestrated and to be kept safely until we see fit to ordain otherwise concerning it, or at least concerning its vicarage.

Further, there was exhibited a letter of William, bishop of Exeter, of blessed memory, concerning the church of St Kew, which seems to imply that the said church of St Kew, on the removal or decease of the clerks or secular canons established there, was canonically collated by the same bishop, with the consent of his chapter, to the canons of Plympton, as they allege – introducing furthermore, as to this, records of many bishops which seem to confirm the doing of the same. Because, however, the aforementioned Bishop William, who was proctor for, not owner of, the properties of his church, was not able to alienate the property of his church without the legitimate consent of his chapter, he had recourse to a donation of this kind. Furthermore, it appears that the aforesaid William's charter of donation has been made void as regards the aforesaid church of St Kew in that, despite what he implied, the said church was not vacant, but there were secular canons there for the whole period of his life, as is witnessed by the records of many later bishops. In the Name of the Father, etc, we give judgment that the collation of the said Bishop William concerning the said church of St Kew is invalid and thus in

W(illelmi) episcopi de dicta ecclesia de Landeho non valere et sic per
consequens subsecutam dudum postea capituli Exon' confirmationem minus
legitimam non tenere pronuntiamus.
(3) Item cum status rei etsi tenuisset donatio in Omnipotentis Dei iniuriam sit
immutatus penitus per priorem et conventum de Plympton' absque consensu
et auctoritate dyocesani, eo quod in ecclesia de Landeho ab initio fuerint
canonici seculares quibus postea successerunt regulares, nec modo sit ibi
aliquis secularis aut regularis canonicus qui iuxta loci conditionem et
consuetudinem ad iuris exigentiam Deo valeat deservire et cultus divini augeri
debeat non diminui, pronuntiamus dictam ecclesiam legitimo gubernatore
destitutam et ad ordinationem seu collationem nostram esse devolutam ac eam
ordinationi seu collationi nostre reservamus.

(4) Quantum ad ecclesiam de Dene: licet prior et conventus Plympton' nuper
requisitus {sic} super toto iure et possessione quod dicunt se habere in dicta
ecclesia respondissent se possidere a quodam Italico nomine firme pro
quodam censu annuo qui ad eorum presentationem a predecessore nostro
rector fuerat institutus in eadem; modo tamen asserunt dictam ecclesiam in
proprios usus suos esse conversam, exhibentes quoad hoc privilegium felicis
recordationis domini Alexandri pape quarti de quodam alio privilegio
Celestini faciens mentionem, quorum pretextu in predicta ecclesia quoad
proprietatem et possessionem se dicunt satis esse munitos; verum cum constet
dictos religiosos eo tempore quo ingressi sunt dicte ecclesie possessionem
nullam ab alio quam a seipsis auctoritatem habuisse, quia per privilegium
Celestini se defendere non possunt eo quod per contrarium actum ab eo
recessum fuit omnino, sicque ipsum privilegium mortificatum fuerit et viribus
penitus evacuatum, nec per privilegium Alexandri, quia ut apparet ex littera
ante datam ipsius privilegii fuerant possessionem dicte ecclesie nulla tamen
superveniente superioris auctoritate ingressi, relinquitur eos dictam ecclesiam
vitiose assecutos vel ingressos. Item cum constet dicti Alexandri privilegium in
se continere conditionem, videlicet ut veris existentibus premissis – et falsa
sunt pro maiore parte – sicque ipsum privilegium per falsi suggestionem et
fallendo principis conscientiam et quasi per obreptionem obtentum, et
mendax precator carere debeat commodo impetratarum nec etiam ipsi
formam dicti privilegii observarunt, eosdem priorem et conventum dictam
ecclesiam de Dene vitiose et contra iustitiam esse ingressos pronuntiamus, et
eos dicta ecclesia scriptis presentibus in nomine Patris etc. [Fo.22] per
diffinitivam sententiam privamus, magistro Gervasio de Criditon' eam
conferentes intuitu caritatis.

390 RESIGNATIO. Anno die et loco Exonie eisdem magister Robertus de
Polamford' resignavit ecclesiam de Marinelegh' in manus episcopi.

consequence the subsequent confirmation – long afterwards – of the Exeter chapter does not hold good, as lacking what is prescribed by law.

Further, since (even if the donation had held good) the status of the matter has been utterly changed to the injury of Almighty God by the prior and convent of Plympton, without the consent and sanction of the diocesan, insofar as there were from the beginning secular canons in the church of St Kew who were later replaced by regular canons, and since now in that place there is nobody, whether secular or regular canon, available to serve God in accordance with the foundation and custom of the place and the requirement of law, and since divine worship should be increased not diminished, we give judgment that the said church lacks a legitimate ruler and has devolved to our establishment or collation, and we reserve it for our establishment and collation.

As for the church of Dean Prior, although the prior and convent of Plympton, when they were recently challenged over all the right and possession which they allege they have in the said church, replied that they possessed from a certain Italian, who had been instituted rector in the same by our predecessor at their presentation, by title of a farm for a fixed annual payment; now, however, they assert that the said church was appropriated to them, exhibiting as to this a privilege of the lord Pope Alexander IV of happy memory, which makes mention of a certain other privilege of Celestine,[r] by reason of which they allege that they are sufficiently corroborated as to [their] ownership and possession in the aforesaid church. But since it is established that the said religious, at the time at which they entered into possession of the said church, had no sanction from anyone other than themselves, because they are not able to defend themselves by the privilege of Celestine – because it was totally withdrawn by a contrary act on his part, and so the said privilege is deprived of life and completely emptied of its force – nor by the privilege of Alexander because, as appears from the letter, they had entered in possession of the said church before the date of the same privilege – with, however, no supervening sanction from a superior – it remains [the fact] that they gained or entered into the said church defectively. Further, since it is established that the privilege of the said Alexander included a condition, to wit, 'provided that the existing facts given are true' – and they are for the most part false – thus the said privilege [was] obtained by *suggestio falsi* and by deceiving the pope's understanding as through an ambush, and since a lying petitioner ought to be deprived of the benefit of what is claimed – and these men did not even observe the terms of the said privilege – we give judgment that the same prior and convent entered on the said church of Dean Prior defectively and contrary to justice, and in these present documents, in the name of the Father, etc, we deprive them of the said church by definitive sentence, conferring it, at the prompting of charity, on Master Gervase de Crediton.

390   RESIGNATION. 5 October 1261, Exeter. Master Robert de Polamford resigned the church of Mariansleigh into the bishop's hands.

---

[r] Celestine III, 1191–98, or Celestine IV, 1241.

391   RESIGNATIO. Anno eodem die S. Fidis virginis apud Teynton' Robertus de Whysseleye, presbiter, r[esi]gnavit[56] ecclesiam de Lawiteton' in manus episcopi.

392   COLLATIO: INSTITUTIO. Anno die et loco eisdem dominus episcopus contulit ecclesiam de Lawitton' magistro R[oberto d]e Polamford', et habet litteras institutionis et inductionis in forma communi.

393   APPROPRIATIO. Anno die et loco predictis dominus episcopus concessit litteram inductionis priori et conventui de Berliz' in ecclesiam de Marinelegh' quam eis prius, de consensu capituli Exon', appropriaverat.

394   RESIGNATIO. Anno eodem die Veneris in crastino S. Fidis virginis apud Cheddelegh' Baldewynus, prior Plympt', et Walterus, hostiller, et Robertus Blundus, canonici Plympton', habentes ad hoc speciale mandatum, resignaverunt in manus episcopi ecclesiam de Dene et ius quod in ea se habere dicebant auctoritate apostolica. Et ad eam tanquam ad vacantem per eorum resignationem presentaverunt magistrum N. de Plymton', archidiaconum Northfolch', set quia dominus episcopus magistro Gervasio de Criditon' eam prius contulerat auctoritate concilii, ipsum distulit admittere ad eandem. Unde idem magister Gervasius, hoc perpendens et quieti religiosorum prospicere volens quantum in eo fuit, ecclesiam ipsam in manus domini episcopi resignavit. Quo facto idem dominus episcopus dictum archidiaconum admisit ad eandem titulo commendationis, eam sibi assignando usque ad sue beneplacitum voluntatis.

395   HERTILOND'. Has quatuor litteras sequentes inspexit dominus episcopus et eas approbavit in crastino S. Francisci apud Exon' anno predicto.[56] Universis sancte matris ecclesie filiis ad quod presens scriptum pervenerit Willelmus miseratione divina Exon' ecclesie minister humilis salutem in Domino. Noverit universitas vestra quod cum nobis dilucide constaret religiosos viros, abbatem et conventum monasterii B. Nectani de Hertilond', annuam pensionem quinque marcarum ab antiquo de ecclesia de Cnudston' continue percepisse, nos, predicti monasterii paupertati paterna affectione levamen adhibere volentes et religionis ipsorum meritum attendentes, predictam pensionem predictis viris religiosis sicut hactenus percipere consueverunt in perpetuum percipiendam quantum in nobis est concedimus et auctoritate episcopali confirmamus. In cuius rei testimonium presenti scripto sigillum nostrum apponi fecimus. Datum apud Hertilond' ix Kalendas Septembris anno Domini mccxliii et consecrationis nostre xx.

396   HERTILOND'. Universis sancte matris ecclesie filiis ad quos presens scriptum pervenerit Rogerus, Exon' ecclesie decanus, et eiusdem loci capitulum salutem in Domino. Noverit universitas vestra nos, de consensu

---

[56] There is a hole in the parchment.
[57] This sentence is actually written before the paragraph mark.

391 RESIGNATION. 6 October 1261, Bishopsteignton. Robert de Wisley, priest, resigned the church of Lawhitton into the bishop's hands.

392 COLLATION; INSTITUTION. 6 October 1261, Bishopsteignton. The lord bishop collated Master Robert de Polamford to the church of Lawhitton; and he has letters of institution and induction in common form.

393 APPROPRIATION. 6 October 1261, Bishopsteignton. The lord bishop granted a letter of induction to the prior and convent of Barlinch to the church of Mariansleigh which earlier he had appropriated to them, with the consent of the chapter of Exeter.

394 RESIGNATION. 7 October 1261, Chudleigh. Baldwin, prior of Plympton, and Walter Hostiller[s] and Robert Blund, canons of Plympton, holding a special mandate for this, resigned into the bishop's hands the church of Dean Prior and the title to it which they were alleging they had by papal sanction. And they presented to it, as being vacant by their resignation, Master Nicholas de Plympton, archdeacon of Norfolk, but because the lord bishop had earlier collated to it Master Gervase de Crediton by the authority of the Council, he deferred admitting him to the same. Wherefore the same Master Gervase, considering the matter and wishing to have an eye to the peace of the religious to the best of his ability, resigned the said church into the lord bishop's hands. After this was done, the same lord bishop admitted the said archdeacon to the same by right of commendation, assigning it to him at his [the bishop's] pleasure.

395 HARTLAND. 5 October 1261, Exeter. The lord bishop gave his inspeximus to these four letters following, and affirmed them.
24 August 1243, Hartland. To all the sons of Holy Mother Church to whom the present document shall come, William, by divine compassion humble minister of the church of Exeter, greeting in the Lord. Let all know that, since it was clearly established to us that the religious men, the abbot and convent of St Nectan's monastery at Hartland, have from of old been in constant receipt of an annual pension of five marks from the church of Knowstone, we, wishing with a fatherly disposition to alleviate the poverty of the aforesaid monastery and noticing the merit of their religious life, as far as in us lies grant to the aforesaid religious men the aforesaid pension just as they have been accustomed to receive it, to be received in perpetuity, and we confirm this by [our] episcopal authority. In testimony whereof we have had our seal affixed to the present document.

396 HARTLAND. 1 August 1247, Exeter. To all the sons of Holy Mother Church to whom the present document shall come, Roger, dean of the church of Exeter, and the chapter of the same place, greeting in the Lord. Let all

---

[s] It is uncertain whether this is his name or, more likely, his occupation as guest-master.

Iohannis, tunc rectoris ecclesie de Cnudston', unanimi consensu confirmasse viris religiosis, abbati et conventui monasterii B. Nectani de Hertilond', annuam pensionem quinque marcarum a predicto I. eiusque successoribus de dicta ecclesia de Cnudston' imperpetuum percipiendam, quam felicis memorie Willelmus miseratione divina Exon' episcopus quondam eisdem concessit et instrumento suo eisdem super hoc confecto confirmavit, prout in eodem plenius continetur. In cuius rei testimonium presenti scripto sigillum nostrum apponi fecimus. Datum Exon' die B. Petri ad Vincula anno gratie mccxl septimo.

397 HERTILOND'. Omnibus sancte matris ecclesie filiis ad quos presens littera pervenerit Willelmus miseratione divina Exon' episcopus salutem in Domino. Noveritis nos debitam et antiquam pensionem quam viri religiosi, abbas et conventus Hertilond', percipere consueverunt de ecclesie Mollond' dictis abbati et conventui quantum in nobis est confirmasse. In cuius rei testimonium huic scripto sigillum nostrum apponi fecimus. Datum apud Teynton' consecrationis nostre xv mensis Decembris.

398 HERTILOND'. Omnibus Christi fidelibus ad quos presentes littere pervenerint Rogerus, decanus, et capitulum Exon' salutem in Domino. Noveritis nos de communi consensu nostro quinque marcas quas venerabilis pater Willelmus Exon' episcopus concessit et per cartam suam quam inspeximus confirmavit abbati et conventui de Hert' percipiendas annuatim de ecclesia de Mellond' [sic] quantum in nobis est confirmasse secundum tenorem carte memorate. In cuius rei testimonium presenti scripto sigillum nostrum duximus apponendum. Datum Exon' viii Idus Ianuarii anno Domini mccxl secundo.

[Fo.22v] **399** CONFIRMATIO CRIDETONEN'. Universis presentes litteras inspecturis Walterus miseratione divina Exon' episcopus salutem in Domino sempiternam. Litteras bone memorie Ricardi, quondam Exon' episcopi, predecessoris nostri, sigillorum decani et capituli B. Petri Exon' munimine roboratas inspeximus in hec verba: Omnibus sancte matris ecclesie filiis ad quos presens scriptum pervenerit Ricardus Dei gratia Exon' episcopus eternam in Domino salutem. Cum semper pium sit et salubre humane conditionis imperfectioni et impotentie studio pietatis su[bv]enire,[58] tunc maxime precipue devotionis meritum pie completur et laudabiliter cum iuste decedentium voluntati utilita[ti] et necessitati prudenti providetur industria; inde est quod ad universitatis vestre notitiam tenore presentium volumus per[venir]e quod nos de unanimi consensu et assensu dilectorum filiorum decani et capituli Exon' ecclesie, divine pietatis in[tuitu] liberaliter concedimus et tenore presentium confirmamus et deinceps decernimus inviolabiliter observari, s[cilicet] quod quilibet canonicus ecclesie Criditon' in extremis agens ad supplementum testamenti sui et ad relevationem fructuum unius anni qui debentur ex antiqua ordinatione singulis canonicis fabrice predicte ecclesie, sive in vita sive in morte, omnium bonorum prebende sue proximi anni post decessum cuiuslibet canonici liberam in omnibus habeat

[58] There is a hole in the parchment.

know that we, with the consent of John, then rector of Knowstone church, unanimously have confirmed to the religious men, the abbot and convent of St Nectan's monastery of Hartland, the annual pension of five marks to be received in perpetuity from the aforesaid John and his successors from the said church of Knowstone, which William, by divine compassion bishop of Exeter, of happy memory, formerly granted to them and confirmed to them by his instrument drawn up concerning this, just as is more fully included in the same. In testimony whereof we have had our seal affixed to the present document.

397 HARTLAND. December 1239, Bishopsteignton. To all the sons of Holy Mother Church to whom the present letter shall come, William, by divine compassion bishop of Exeter, greeting in the Lord. You are to know that as far as in us lies we have confirmed the due and long-established pension, which the religious men, the abbot and convent of Hartland, were accustomed to receive from the church of Molland, to the said abbot and convent. In testimony whereof we have had our seal affixed to this document.

398 HARTLAND. 6 January 1242, Exeter. To all Christ's faithful to whom the present letters shall come, Roger, dean, and the chapter of Exeter, greeting in the Lord. You are to know that we have, by our common consent, as far as in us lies confirmed the five marks, to be received annually from Molland church, which our venerable father, William, bishop of Exeter, granted and by his charter, which we have inspected, confirmed to the abbey and convent of Hartland according to the tenor of the aforementioned charter. In testimony whereof we have had our seal affixed to the present document.

399 CONFIRMATION [TO THE CANONS] OF CREDITON. 10 October 1261, Chudleigh. To all who shall inspect the present letters, Walter, by divine compassion bishop of Exeter, eternal greeting in the Lord. We have given our inspeximus to the letters of Richard [Blund], formerly bishop of Exeter, of blessed menmory, our predecessor, which have been fortified with the corroboration of the seals of the dean and chapter of St Peter's, Exeter, in these words: To all the sons of Holy Mother Church to whom the present document shall come, Richard, by God's grace bishop of Exeter, lifelong greeting in the Lord. Although it is always pious and wholesome to assist the imperfection and powerlessness of the human condition by the zeal of piety, then most of all are the deserts of special devotion dutifully and laudably fulfilled when, by prudent industry, provision is justly made for the wishes, benefits and needs of the deceased. So it is that we wish it to be known to all of you by the tenor of these presents that we, with the unanimous consent and assent of our beloved sons, the dean and chapter of the church of Exeter, at the prompting of divine compassion, freely grant and by the tenor of these presents confirm, and order to be hereafter inviolably observed, namely, that each canon of the church of Crediton, acting on his deathbed, may have free power of disposal in all ways of all the goods of his prebend for the year following the death of each such canon, in order to supplement his will and for

dispensationem; ita quod illa bona quibus et in quos usus pios voluerit integre poterit assignare. Et ut hec nostra concessio et confirmatio inperpetuum robur firmitatis obtineat presentem paginam sigilli nostri munimine una cum appositione sigillorum decani et capituli predicti facimus roborari. Datum Exon' anno Domini mccl tertio in festo Nativitatis Dominice et consecrationis nostre nono. Nos igitur predictam concessionem et confirmationem ratas habentes eas pontificali auctoritate confirmamus et presentis scripti patrocinio communimus. In cuius rei testimonium presentes litteras sigilli nostri impressione duximus roborandas. Datum apud Cheddel' in crastino S. Dionisii anno gratie mcclx primo et consecrationis nostre quarto.

400 APPROPRIATIO ECCLESIE DE DENE. Walterus Dei gratia Exon' episcopus dilectis filiis priori et conventui de Plimpton' salutem eternam et benedictionem. Pontificalis moderaminis circumspectioni convenit diligenter attendere quod summa est ratio que pro religione facit et viros religiosos pro caritatis affectu confovere. Eapropter, dilecti in Christo filii, humilitatis vestre devotioni paterna affectione subvenire volentes, ad pauperum et peregrinorum ad vos confluentium necessitatem sublevandam ecclesiam de Dene cum fructibus et obventionibus vacantem per resignationem Nicolai de Plimpton', archidiaconi Northfolch', domini pape capellani, cuius ius patronatus ad vos noscitur pertinere, de consensu decani et capituli nostri Exon', vobis et ecclesie vestre in proprios usus concedimus et confirmamus pleno iure perpetuo possidendam, salva congrua portione vicarii nobis et successoribus nostris canonice presentandi. In cuius rei testimonium presentes litteras vobis duximus concedendas. Datum Exon' in crastino S. Kalixte pape et martiris anno gratie mcclx primo et consecrationis nostre anno quarto.

401 Anno eodem apud Exon' in crastino S. Kalixti dominus episcopus decanus et capitulum Exon' appropriaverunt ecclesiam de Dene priori et conventui de Plympton' in forma proxima superius scripta.

402 INSTITUTIO ET TAXATIO VICARIE DE DENE.[59] Anno et die et loco eisdem ad presentationem Baldewini, prioris de Plympton' et conventus, dominus episcopus admisit David de Beare, presbiterum, ad taxandam vicariam de Dene que postmodum taxata consistit in[60] omnibus obventionibus altaris, decima feni, terra assisi redditus, iv solidis et vi denariis, uno ferlingo et dimidio terre sanctuarii immunibus a prestatione decimarum, et xxx solidatis decimarum garbarum, una cum agnitione ordinariorum onerum, extraordinariis pro rata partiendis. Datum xviii Kalendas Maii apud Coccespitt'.

403 INSTITUTIO ET TAXATIO VICARIE DE COWIK'. Anno die et loco eisdem dominus episcopus taxavit vicariam ecclesie de Cowik' in hac forma: Universis etc. Ad universitatis vestre notitiam tenore presentium volumus

---

[59] 'et taxatio ..' was added.
[60] The rest of the paragraph was added later, to judge from its being squeezed in.

a relief of one year's fruits, (which, according to a ordinance of long ago, are due from each of the canons for the fabric fund of the aforesaid church, whether in life or in death); on terms that he is able to assign in their entirety those goods to whom and for what pious uses he wishes. And in order that this our grant and confirmation may have valid strength in perpetuity, we have had the present deed fortified with the corroboration of our seal, together with the affixing of the seals of the dean and chapter aforesaid. Given at Exeter, 25 December 1253. We therefore, ratifying the aforesaid grant and confirmation, confirm them by pontifical authority and reinforce [them] by the protective power of the present document. In testimony whereof we have had the present letters fortified with the impression of our seal.

400 APPROPRIATION OF DEAN PRIOR CHURCH. 15 October 1261, Exeter. Walter, by the grace of God bishop of Exeter, to his beloved sons the prior and convent of Plympton, lifelong greeting and blessing. It is in accordance with the carefulness of our episcopal rule diligently to be mindful of the chief factor which makes for religion, and in a spirit of charity to cherish men of religion. For that reason, beloved sons in Christ, wishing with a fatherly disposition to aid your humble devotion, we grant and confirm to you and your church as appropriated to you, to be possessed for ever with complete title, with the consent of our dean and chapter of Exeter, for the relief of the need of the poor folk and pilgrims who flock to you, the church of Dean Prior, with its fruits and offerings, vacant by the resignation of Nicholas de Plympton, archdeacon of Norfolk and papal chaplain, of which the right of patronage is known to belong to you, save for a suitable portion for the vicar, who is to be canonically presented to us and our successors. In testimony whereof we have had granted to you the present letters.

401 [APPROPRIATION]. 15 October 1261, Exeter. The lord bishop, the dean and the chapter of Exeter appropriated the church of Dean to the prior and convent of Plympton in the form written just above.

402 INSTITUTION AND ASSESSMENT OF THE VICARAGE OF DEAN PRIOR. 15 October 1261, Exeter. At the presentation of prior Baldwin and the convent of Plympton, the lord bishop admitted David de Beare, priest, to the vicarage – to be assessed – of Dean Prior, which, after later being assessed, consists of all the occasional offerings of the altar, the tithe of hay, the land at the fixed rent of four shillings and sixpence, one and a half farthings of sanctuary land immune from the payment of tithes, and thirty shillingsworth of the garb tithes, together with acceptance of the ordinary burdens, while the extraordinary ones are to be divided proportionately. Given at Cokesputt, 14 April.[t]

403 INSTITUTION AND ASSESSMENT OF COWICK VICARAGE. 15 October 1261, Exeter. The lord bishop assessed the vicarage of Cowick church in these terms: To all, etc. We wish it to be known to all of you by the tenor of these

[t] 1262 presumably; it seems unlikely to be later.

pervenire quod cum in ecclesia de Cowyk' in qua dilecti filii, prior et monachi
loci eiusdem, divino mancipantur obsequio, nullus ante tempora nostra
ordinatus esset vicarius qui plebis illius parochie curam gerere possit, dilectum
filium Henricum, presbiterum, per priorem et dictos monachos ad taxandam
ipsius ecclesie vicariam nobis presentatum, caritatis intuitu admittimus et
ipsum de ea investimus; fructuum ipsius ecclesie tenuitate et monachorum
ipsorum quam in eo loco iugiter exercent hospitalitate pensatis, ordinantes ut
omnibus fructibus et obventionibus ipsius ecclesie et capellarum ad eam
spectantium usibus dictorum monachorum qui omnia onera debita et
consueta subportabunt cedentibus, idem Henricus et vicarii successive post
ipsum ibidem instituendi quinque marcas argenti per manus prioris qui pro
tempore fuerit ad quatuor anni terminos principales equis portionibus nomine
vicarie percipiant annuatim, habeant[Fo.23]que mansum pro conditione loci
competentem; quare ne tractu temporis etc. Datum etc.

404   INFEODATIO AD VITAM. Anno et loco eisdem xvii Kalendas Novembris
dominus episcopus concessit Hamundo, servienti suo, de Tauton', unam
clawam terre cum pertinentiis, quam Thomas Daghelf et Matilda de Ponte
aliquando tenuerunt, habendam eidem Hamundo pro ii solidis ad quatuor
anni terminos, una cum secta curie sue.

405   CASSATIO ELECTIONE [sic] LANST'. Anno et loco eisdem in vigilia S.
Luce evangeliste dominus episcopus electiones in discordia factas in ecclesia
de Lansceveton' de fratribus Laurentio et Ricardo de Uppeton' propter
peccatum in forma earundem et alia que ob reverentiam personarum non
inseruntur cassavit, decernens potestatem providendi ad ipsum fore
devolutam.

406   FEUDUM PERPETUUM. Anno eodem die S. Luce apud Cokkespitte
dominus episcopus feodavit Willelmum de Broneston' in hac forma: Universis
etc. Walterus etc. Ad universitatis vestre notitiam volumus pervenire nos
dedisse concessisse [et] hac presenti carta confirmasse Willelmo, filio W. de
Bruneston', pro homagio et servicio unum ferlingum terre cum pertinentiis
quem Willelmus Penistrang aliquando de nobis tenuit in villa de Bruneston',
tenendum dicto W. etc. reddendo annuatim etc. tres solidos et novem
denarios ad Pascham et festum S. Michaelis equis portionibus et faciendo
forinsecum etc. Hiis testibus etc.

407   FEUDUM AD HEREDES DE CARNE. Anno et loco eisdem in crastino S.
Luce dominus episcopus concessit terram de Froggemere quam Henricus de
Cyrencestr', cantor Criditon', aliquando tenuit Roberto Franceys et heredibus de carne sua procreatis pro vi solidis et omnibus serviciis et
consuetudinibus ad dictam terram ab antiquo spectantibus, hoc excepto quod
iidem Robertus et heredes sui prepositi non fiant inviti; ita tamen quod si

presents that, since hitherto no vicar has been ordained to Cowick church, in which our beloved sons, the prior and monks of the same place, are committed to the divine office, who could undertake the cure [of souls] of the people of that parish, at the prompting of charity we have admitted our beloved son Henry, priest, who has been presented to us by the prior and the said monks to the vicarage – to be assessed – of the said church, and have invested him in it; laying down, after having considered the scantiness of the fruits of the said church and the hospitality constantly practised by the said monks in that place, that, while all the fruits and offerings of the said church and the chapels belonging to it are to be handed over for the use of the said monks, who shall bear all the due and customary burdens, the same Henry, and the vicars to be instituted in that same place in succession after him, shall receive annually five silver marks at the hands of the prior for the time being on the principal quarter days in equal instalments on account of the vicarage, and they shall have an adequate house for the needs of the place; wherefore, lest by the passage of time etc. Given etc.

404 INFEOFFMENT FOR LIFE. 16 October 1261, Exeter. The lord bishop granted to Hamund, his serjeant, of Tawton, one small plot of land with appurtenances, at one time held by Thomas Daghelf and Matilda de Ponte, to be held by the same Hamund for two shillings [payable] at the quarter days, together with suit of court.

405 ELECTIONS TO LAUNCESTON QUASHED. 17 October 1261, Exeter. The lord bishop quashed the disputed elections made of Brothers Laurence and Richard de Upton in the church of Launceston, on account of their defective form, and for other reasons which, out of respect for the persons, are not entered, decreeing that the power of provision should be devolved to him.

406 PERPETUAL FEE. 18 October 1261, Cokesputt. The lord bishop enfeoffed William de Broneston' in these terms: To all etc, Walter etc. We wish it to be known to all of you that we have given, granted, and by this present charter confirmed to William, son of W. de Bruneston, in return for his homage and service, one farthing of land with appurtenances, which William Penistrang at one time held from us in the vill of Bruneston,ᵘ to be held by the said William etc, paying annually etc, three shillings and nine pence at Easter and Michaelmas in equal instalments, and owing foreign service etc. Witnessed by etc.

407 FEE FOR THE HEIRS OF THE BODY. 19 October 1261, Cokesputt. The lord bishop granted land at '*Froggemere*',ᵛ at one time held by Henry de Cirencester, precentor of Crediton, to Robert Franceys and the heirs begotten of his body for six shillings and all services and customary dues relating to the said land from of old, with this exception, that the same Robert and his heirs

ᵘ Brownston? or Brownstone? there are five in Devon, of which the most likely seems to be the one in Modbury.
ᵛ There are five Frogmores in Devon, as well as Frogmire in the parish of Sandford.

idem Robertus sive heredes de carne sua decedat dicta terra ad dominum revertat.

408 COMMENDATIO. Anno eodem et loco in crastino S. Fritheswide dominus episcopus commendavit ecclesiam de Rokebear' Waltero de Ferndon' usque ad annum possidendam.

409 INSTITUTIO ET TAXATIO VICARIE. Anno et die et loco eisdem ad presentationem abbatis et conventus de Donekeswell' dominus episcopus admisit Iohannem de Wymple, presbiterum, ad taxandam vicariam ecclesie parochialis de Donekeswell ad instar illius de Cowyk' supra in proxima pagina; ordinans quod idem vicarius nomine vicarie percipiat per manum abbatis quinque marcas et dimidiam ad quatuor anni terminos et specialia legata sua et denarios missales in missis mortuorum et maioribus sollempnitatibus, et dictus abbas onera ordinaria agnoscet in toto.

410 INSTITUTIO. Anno die et loco eisdem ad presentationem abbatis et conventus de Lewes dominus admisit magistrum Nicholaum de Plympton' ad ecclesiam de Byri, et habet litteras in forma communi.

411 INSTITUTIO. Anno eodem in crastino S. Bricii apud Ferndon' ad presentationem Ricardi filii Bernardi dominus episcopus admisit Robertum de Hendevile ad vacantem ecclesiam de Ost Wlfrinton' sub pena Lateranensis et Oxoniensis Conciliorum, et habet litteras in eadem forma.

412 PREDICATIO. Anno et loco eisdem die S. Eadmundi confessoris dominus concessit litteras predicationis procuratoribus hospitalis de Roscidevall' in forma communi.

413[61] EXITUS. Anno et loco eisdem in octabis S. Martini exivit W. de Capella London' et rediit in vigilia S. Katerine, et die eiusdem virginis exivit et rediit iii Nonas Decembris. Item exivit die S. Lucie apud Chedeham' et rediit xviii Kalendas Ianuarii.

414 CARTA. Anno et loco eisdem die S. Saturnini in vigilia S. Andree apostoli facta fuit hec carta: Omnibus Christi fidelibus presentem cartam inspecturis vel audituris Walterus Dei gratia Exon' episcopus salutem. [Fo.23v] Noverit universitas vestra nos concessisse et hac presenti carta mea confirmasse Willelmo de la Rupe pro servicio suo et Agneti uxori sue et heredibus dicti Willelmi de carne sua procreandis unum mesuagium et unam virgatam terre que vocatur Stenekelaneslond' cum omnibus pertinentiis suis, que Matill' soror et heres Ade aurifabri petiit super nos in curia nostra de Ferndon' per breve domini regis, et ipsa postea totum ius et clamium quod in predicta terra habuit vel habere potuit pro se et heredibus suis dicto W. et A.

---

[61] This entry is heavily erased in parts

are not to become reeves against their will; on condition that if the same Robert or the heirs of his body depart, the said land is to revert to the lord [bishop].

408 COMMENDATION. 20 October 1261, Cokesputt. The lord bishop commended Walter de Ferndon to the church of Rockbeare, to be possessed for a year.

409 INSTITUTION AND ASSESSMENT OF A VICARAGE. 20 October 1261, Cokesputt. At the presentation of the abbot and convent of Dunkeswell the lord bishop admitted John de Whimple, priest, to the vicarage – to be assessed – of Dunkeswell parish church, after the example of [the admission] to Cowick, *supra* on the previous page;[w] laying down that the same vicar on account of the vicarage should receive from the hand of the abbot five and a half marks at the quarter days, and his private legacies, and the mass pennies from requiem masses and major solemnities, and the said abbot shall bear entirely the ordinary burdens.

410 INSTITUTION. 20 October 1261, Cokesputt. At the presentation of the abbot and convent of Lewes the bishop admitted Master Nicholas de Plympton to the church of Berrynarbor; and he has letters in common form.

411 INSTITUTION. 15[x] November 1261, Faringdon. At the presentation of Richard fitzBernard the lord bishop admitted Robert de Hendevile to the vacant church of East Worlington, under pain of the Lateran and Oxford Councils; and he has letters in the same form.

412 PREACHING. 16 November 1261, Faringdon. The bishop granted licence to preach to the proctors of the hospital of Roncesvalles, in common form.

413 DEPARTURE. 18 November 1261, William de Capella left London, and he returned on 24 November; on 25 November he left, and he returned on 3 December. Again, he left Chidham on 13 December, and returned on 15 December.

414 CHARTER. 29 November 1261, Faringdon. There was issued this charter: To all Christ's faithful who inspect or hear the present charter, Walter, by God's grace bishop of Exeter, greeting. Let all know that we have granted and by this present charter of mine confirmed to William de la Rupe, in return for his service, and to Agnes his wife and to the heirs to be begotten of the body of the said William, one dwelling house and one virgate of land, which is called '*Stenekelaneslond*', with all it appurtenances, which Matilda, sister and heir of Adam the goldsmith, claimed of us in our court of Faringdon by royal writ, and she afterwards yielded the entire right and claim which she had or could have in the aforesaid land for herself and for her heirs to the said

---

[w] **403**.

[x] Or possibly 14 November; the date of the feast varied.

uxori sue et heredibus suis pro fine inter ipsos facto in plena curia nostra de
Ferndon' absque omni retenemento per cartam suam dimisit: habenda et
tenenda dictis W. et A. uxori sue et heredibus dicti W. ex carne procreandis
de nobis et successoribus nostris libere integre quiete bene et in pace
inperpetuum; reddendo inde annuatim nobis et successoribus nostris iv
solidos argenti ad festum S. Michaelis pro omnibus serviciis et consuetudinibus et secularibus demandis, salvo servicio domini regis quantum pertinet
ad tantam liberam terram de eodem feodo. Ut autem hec nostra concessio et
presentis carte nostre confirmatio rata sint et stabiles inperpetuum ut
predictum est presenti carte nostre sigillum nostrum apponi fecimus. Hiis
testibus: dominis Thoma Makerel, Roberto de Popham, militibus, Ricardo de
Norton', Ricardo de la Wdecot', Roberto de Berlegh', Iohanne le Poer,
Roberto Mutun, Hugone de Westwde, et multis aliis. Datum apud Fernd',
anno et die supradictis.

415[62]　SOLUTIO. Anno eodem apud Cheddeham in vigilia Natalis Domini
Rogerus archidiaconus Exon' solvit de gratuito subsidio domini episcopi xxv
libras; et preterea de sequestro de Rokebear' i marcam; loco cuius dominus
episcopus prius recepit per manum abbatis de Dunekewill v marcas.

416　SOLUTIO. Anno eodem apud Horsleg' in festo S. Hilarii magister H. de
Bothleg' solvit de gratuito subsidio[63] archidiaconatus Cornub' viginti octo
libras et quatuor solidos.

417　ORDINATIO. Anno eodem in festo S. Agnetis ibidem Iohannes de
Bodrigan, rector ecclesie de Puntestok', pro variis contumaciis et offensis
excommunicatus, iuravit de parendo mandatis ecclesie super premissis et de
stando ordinationi et voluntati domini episcopi tam de persona sua simpliciter
quam de beneficio suo predicto usque ad triennium, et obtinuit absolutionem,
et, ea obtenta, de licentia eiusdem domini episcopi et voluntate tradidit
ecclesiam suam predictam ad firmam officiali archidiaconi Cornub' usque ad
terminum trium annorum singulis annis pro triginta sex marcis solvendis; et
ordinavit dominus episcopus ibidem de consensu predicti rectoris quod habeat
magistrum Reginaldum de Rostourec magistrum suum usque ad triennium et
ipsi duo habeant de predicta pecunie summa ad victum et alia necessaria et
debita dicti rectoris infra biennium acquietanda singulis annis triginta marcas.
Residuas vero sex marcas reservat idem dominus episcopus per ordinationem
suam in usus pauperum supletionem defectuum ipsius ecclesie et satisfactio-
nem emende sue convertendas. Debet etiam idem officialis agnoscere omnia
onera ordinaria debita et consueta et etiam extraordinaria usque ad viginti
solidos si infra idem tempus emerserint; debet etiam idem officialis preter
predicta ad supletionem defectuum apponere quadraginta solidos. Acta sunt
hec presentibus testibus infrascriptis: magistris I. Nobili, I. Engg', H. de
Bollegh', W. de Capella, [Fo.24] Thoma de Swynbrok', fratribus Ricardo de
Uppeton', Roberto le Verur, Iohanne de Brimcot, canonicis Lansceveton', et

---

[62] This entry has a marginal sign referring to **427**.
[63] MS has *subdiacono*.

William and Agnes his wife and his heirs in return for a fine made between them in our open court of Faringdon, without any reservation, through her own charter: the land to be had and held by the said William and Agnes his wife, and the heirs of the said William to be begotten of his body, from us and our successors freely, wholly, with immunity, well and peacefully forever; paying on that account annually to us and our successors four shillings of silver at Michaelmas for all services and customary dues and secular charges, save for such service due to the lord king as pertains to this much freehold land in the same fee. And in order that this our grant and the confirmation of our present charter may be approved and stand firm forever as aforesaid, we have had our seal affixed to our present charter. Witnessed by Sir Thomas Makerel, Sir Robert de Popham, knights, Richard de Norton, Richard de Woodcot, Robert de Berlegh, John le Poer, Robert Mutun, Hugh de Westwood, and many others.

415   PAYMENT. 24 December 1261, Chidham. Roger, archdeacon of Exeter, paid £25 pounds from the free subsidy of the lord bishop, and, moreover, one mark from the sequestration of Rockbeare, on the ground of which the lord bishop earlier received five marks from the hand of the abbot of Dunkeswell.

416   PAYMENT. 13 January 1262, Horsley. Master H. de Bothleg'ʸ paid £28 4s. from the free subsidy of the archdeaconry of Cornwall.

417   ORDINANCE. 21 January 1262, Horsley. John de Bodrigan, rector of Poundstock church, who had been excommunicated for various contumacies and offences, swore to obey the commands of the Church concerning the foregoing matters and to abide by the ordinance and will of the lord bishop, both completely as regards his own person and also in respect of his aforesaid benefice for a three-year period, and he obtained absolution. Having obtained this, by the leave and will of the same lord bishop, he handed over his aforesaid church to be farmed by the official of the archdeacon of Cornwall until the end of the three-year period, for a payment of 36 marks each year. And the lord bishop there ordered with the assent of the aforesaid rector that he should have Master Reginald de Rostourec as his supervisor for the three-year period, and that the two of them should have 30 marks each year from the aforesaid sum of money for their victuals and other necessities and for discharging the debts of the said rector within two years. The same lord bishop, however, by his ordinance reserves the remaining six marks a year to be used for the needs of the poor, making good defects in the church and payment for its repair. The same official must also bear all the ordinary due and customary charges, and also the extraordinary ones, up to 20 shillings, if they should arise during the same period. In addition to the aforesaid, the same official must also apply 40 shillings to making good the same defects. These things were done in the presence of the witnesses written below: Masters John Noble, John Engg', Henry de Bollegh, William de Capella,

ʸ Is this Henry de Bollegh?

aliis, fratre Henrico monacho Buffestr', magistro R[obert] de Polamford', Rogero de Derteford', senescallo domus, Roberto, et Willelmo, capellanis, Willelmo de Petresfeld', Hugone clerico.

418   RESIGNATIO. Anno et loco eisdem in vigilia Convertionis B. Pauli frater Laurentius resignavit electioni de se facte in priorem Lancevet': presentibus magistris Iohanne Nobili, Philippo de Cancell'.

419   INSTITUTIO. Anno eodem Idus Februarii apud Exon' ad presentationem Roberti de Crues, veri patroni ecclesie de Morcherd', dominus episcopus admisit Godefridum de Sowy, subdiaconum, ad eandem ecclesiam vacantem, et habet litteras.

420   INSTITUTIO. Anno eodem xv Kalendas Martii apud Crideton' ad presentationem Willelmi de Raleg', militis, veri patroni ecclesie de Alfrinton', dominus episcopus admisit Iohannem de Iplepenn', presbiterum, ad eandem ecclesiam vacantem, et habet litteras in forma communi.

421   INSTITUTIO. Anno die et loco eisdem, die S.Iuliane virginis,[64] dominus episcopus ad presentationem Walteri, archidiaconi Barn', ecclesie de Dunsidiok veri patroni, admisit Willelmum de Lappeflod', clericum et diaconum, ad eandem ecclesiam vacantem et habet litteras in forma communi.

422   COLLATIO. Anno die et loco eisdem dominus episcopus contulit Andree Prous, vicario de Cheddeham, prebendam que fuit Roberti, capellani, in ecclesia de Boseham cum eiusdem ecclesie sacristaria, consensu domini H de Bratton ad quem ipsius sacristarie collatio spectabat interveniente hac vice.

423   QUIETA CLAMANTIE. Omnibus Christi fidelibus ad quos presens scriptum pervenerit Walterus Hay salutem in Domino. Noveritis me concessisse remisisse et quietum clamasse pro me et heredibus meis imperpetuum venerabili in Christo patri Waltero Dei gratia Exon' episcopo et successoribus suis totum ius et clamium quod habui vel habere potui in terra de Kelly in manerio de Berner sine aliquo retenemento michi vel heredibus meis inposterum. In cuius rei testimonium presenti scripto sigillum meum apposui. Hiis testibus: S. Haym tunc senescallo Cornub', Radulpho Arundell' tunc vicecomite, Bernardo de Bodbran, Alexandro de Okeston', Rogero de Trelok', et aliis.

424   ORDINES. Anno eodem iv nonas Martii apud Polton' dominus episcopus ordinavit duos subdiaconos, scilicet Iohannem de Gyrelleston' et Hugonem Splot,[65] et unum accolitum.

---

[64] Added above the line.
[65] The names were added above the line, perhaps because Hugh Splot was a member of the bishop's household.

Thomas de Swinbrook, Brothers Richard de Upton, Robert le Verur, John de Brimcot, canons of Launceston, and others, Brother Henry, monk of Buckfast, Master Robert de Polamford, Roger de Dartford, steward of the household, Robert and William, chaplains, William de Petersfield, Hugh, clerk.[z]

418 RESIGNATION. 24 January 1262, Horsley. Brother Laurence renounced the election of himself as prior 'of Launceston in the presence of Master John Noble and Master Philip de Cancellis.

419 INSTITUTION. 13 February 1262, Exeter. At the presentation of Robert de Cruwys, true patron of [Cruwys] Morchard church, the lord bishop admitted Godfrey de Sowy, subdeacon, to the same vacant church; and he has letters.

420 INSTITUTION. 15 February 1262, Crediton. At the presentation of William de Raleigh, knight, true patron of Arlington church, the lord bishop admitted John de Ipplepen, priest, to the same vacant church; and he has letters in common form.

421 INSTITUTION. 23 February 1262, Crediton. At the presentation of Walter [de Pembroke], archdeacon of Barnstaple, true patron of Dunchideock church, the lord bishop admitted William de Lapford, clerk and deacon, to the same vacant church; and he has letters in common form.

422 COLLATION. 23 February 1262, Crediton. The lord bishop collated the prebend in Bosham church which Robert the chaplain held, together with the sacristy of the same church, to Andrew Pruz, vicar of Chidham, with the consent of Sir Henry de Bracton, to whom the collation of the said sacristy belonged for this turn.

423 QUITCLAIM. ?February/March 1262. To all Christ's faithful whom this present document shall reach, Walter Hay, greeting in the Lord. You are to know that I have granted, conveyed and quitclaimed on behalf of myself and my heirs in perpetuity to the venerable father in Christ, Walter by the grace of God bishop of Exeter, and to his successors, the whole right and claim which I had or could have had in the land at Kelly in the manor of Berner,[a] without any reservation for me or my heirs henceforward. In testimony whereof I have affixed my seal to this present document. Witnessed by S. Haym, then steward of Cornwall, Ralph Arundel, then sheriff, Bernard de Bodbran, Alexander de Oxton, Roger de Trelok', and others.

424 ORDINATION. 4 March 1262, Pawton. The lord bishop ordained two subdeacons, namely John de Grilstone and Hugh Splot,[b] and one acolyte.

---

[z] Probably Hugh Splot.
[a] The farm of Burniere in the parish of Egloshayle?
[b] Also known as Hugh de Plympton.

425 INSTITUTIO. Anno die et loco eisdem ad presentationem Mathei de Wulfrinton', veri patroni ecclesie de Westwlfrinton', dominus episcopus admisit Iohannem de Girelleston', subdiaconum, ad eandem ecclesiam vacantem et habet litteras in forma communi.

426 Anno eodem ibidem viii idus Martii magister I. de Esse' solvit Rogero de Derteford' de gratuito subsidio peculiaris iurisdictionis domini episcopi xii libras sine cautione.

427 QUIETA CLAMANTIE. Anno eodem xi kalendas Martii apud Lanceveton' magister Iohannes de Esse persolvit omnia arragia sui officii usque ad proximo transactum festum S. Michaelis, et habet litteras quiete clamantie domini episcopi de omnibus receptis et datis usque ad dictum festum S. Michaelis.

428 COMMENDATIO. Anno die et loco eisdem hoc est in vigilia Natalis Domini apud Chedeham ad presentationem domini Willelmi de Curtenay, veri patroni ecclesie S. Alluni in Cornub', ratione dotis Iohanne, uxoris sue, dominus episcopus commendavit magistro Willelmo de Capella dictam ecclesiam S. Alluni vacantem, et habet litteras inductionis et commendationis in forma communi.

[Fo.24v] **429** INSTITUTIO. Consecrationis eiusdem anno quinto die S. Cuthberti apud Exoniam magister R. de Tifford', officialis domini Exon', de mandato suo speciali ad presentationem prioris de Fromton', veri patroni ecclesie de Northam' vacantis, admisit Martinum de Litlebir' ad eandem, salvo iure cuiuslibet et habet litteras in forma communi.

430 INSTITUTIO. Anno eodem apud S. Germanum ad presentationem Margarete la Mahewe, vere patrone ecclesie de Pewrth', admisit Iohannem le Gras, subdiaconum, ad eandem vacantem et habet litteras in forma communi. Actum die Iovis ante Annunciationem Dominicam.

431 QUIETA CLAMANTIE. Anno eodem apud Exon' die Pasche dominus episcopus concessit magistro R. de Theford', officiali suo, litteras sub hac forma: W. miseratione divina Exon' episcopus dilecto filio magistro R. de Theford, officiali nostro, salutem gratiam et benedictionem. Firmum de preteritis obsequii vestri solatiis sumentes argumentum [. . .][66] devotioni vestre, quam probatam novimus, ut ratione gesti hactenus officii vestri de pecunia exinde qualitercumque proveniente[67]ad ratiocinia nullatenus teneamini, exnunc tenore presentium indulgemus onusque computandi de plano remittimus. In cuius rei testimonium presentes litteras vobis duximus concedendas. Datum Exon' die Pasche anno gratie mcclx secundo et consecrationis nostre quinto.

---

[66] More than half a line was here erased in the MS.
[67] The phrase from *de pecunia* . . . was inserted above the line.

425   INSTITUTION. 4 March 1262, Pawton. At the presentation of Matthew de Worlington, true patron of West Worlington church, the lord bishop admitted John de Grilstone, subdeacon, to the same vacant church; and he has letters in common form.

426   [PAYMENT]. 8 March 1262, Pawton. Master John de Esse paid to Roger de Dartford without security £12 of free subsidy from the bishop's peculiar jurisdiction.

427   QUITCLAIM. 19 February 1262, Launceston. Master John de Esse paid off all the arrears of his office up until the previous Michaelmas, and he has the lord bishop's letters of quittance for all receipts and payments up to the said Michaelmas.

428   COMMENDATION. 24 December 1261, Chidham. At the presentation of Sir William de Courtenay, true patron of the church of St Allen in Cornwall by reason of his wife Joan's dowry, the lord bishop commended Master William de Capella to the said vacant church of St Allen; and he has letters of induction and commendation in common form.

429   INSTITUTION. 20 March 1262, Exeter. At the presentation of the prior of Frampton, true patron of the vacant church of Northam, Master R. de Tyfford, the bishop of Exeter's official, at his particular command, admitted Martin de Littlebury to the same [church], saving the rights of any claimant; and he has letters in common form.

430   INSTITUTION. 23 March 1262, St Germans. At the presentation of Margaret la Mahewe, true patron of Pyworthy church, he[c] admitted John le Gras, subdeacon, to the same vacant [church]; and he has letters in common form.

431   QUITCLAIM. 9 April 1262, Exeter. The lord bishop granted to Master R. de Tyfford, his official, letters in these terms: Walter, by divine compassion bishop of Exeter, to our beloved son Master R. de Tyfford, our official, greeting, grace and benediction. Having clear proof of your dutifulness from past service . . . from now on, by the tenor of these presents, we concede to your devotion, which we know to be proven, that by reason of your performance thus far of your office, you shall in no way be bound to render account of the money yielded therein by whatsoever title, and we remit entirely the burden of drawing up accounts. In testimony whereof we have had granted to you the present letters. Dated etc.

---

c Presumably the bishop rather than his official.

432 INSTITUTIO. Anno eodem secundo die Pasche dominus episcopus instituit magistrum Thomam de Wymundeham' in ecclesia de Ken' ad presentationem domini I. de Curtenay per magistrum W. de Stanford', clericum, dicti magistri ad hoc specialiter deputatum procuratorem, et habet litteras. Actum Exonie.

433 INSTITUTIO. Anno loco et die eisdem dominus episcopus ad presentationem nobilis mulieris domine Iohanne Brewer' admisit Petrum de Bradeford', presbiterum, ad ecclesiam de Cadeleg' vacantem et habet litteras inductionis et institutionis cum onere residendi.

434 COLLATIO. Anno eodem feria v Pasche apud Coccespitt' dominus episcopus contulit Sywardo, presbitero, vacantem vicariam ecclesie de Syeftber', cuius collatio propter ineptam presentationem abbatis et conventus de Torr' ad ipsum est devoluta, et habet litteras institutionis et inductionis in forma communi.

435 INSTITUTIO. Anno eodem vi nonas Maii Londonie ad presentationem prioris et conventus de Tywerdrait, qui ecclesiam de Fawe in proprios usus obtinent pleno iure collatam, ad ipsius ecclesie vacantem vicariam Paulum de S. Uvele, presbiterum, admisit et habet litteras institutionis et inductionis in forma communi.

436 PRESENTATIO. Anno die et loco eisdem exivit littera continens quod dominus episcopus presentavit domino Wigorn' episcopo Henricum de Hertilond', presbiterum, ad de iure vacantem ecclesiam S. Michaelis Glouc' una cum capella S. Martini dependente ab eadem.

437 INSTITUTIO. Anno et loco eisdem iii nonas Maii ad presentationem prioris et conventus de Tywerdrait qui ecclesiam de Lanlivery in proprios usus obtinent pleno iure collatam ad ipsius ecclesie vacantem vicariam Randulphum, presbiterum, admisit et habet litteras institutionis et inductionis in forma communi.

438 INSTITUTIO. Anno die et loco eisdem ad presentationem Albrede de Botrell', vere patrone ecclesie de Plimtr' vacantis, dominus episcopus admisit Gundi [sic], presbiterum, ad eandem cum onere residendi et habet litteras in forma communi.

439 IURAMENTUM. Anno et loco eisdem in crastino S. Iohannis ante Portam Latinam Ricardus de Tregodh, Ricardus de Nanscuek', et Radulphus de Arundell', milites, tactis sacrosanctis, iuraverunt quod, super se quod duellum ineundum inter Willelmum Blundum, clericum, et Bartholomeum, sutorem, decreverunt et quod eidem interfuerunt illudque executi sunt, mandatis stabunt ecclesie eaque reverenter suscipient et adimplebunt, et quod nunquam [Fo.25] scienter et prudenter operam dabunt vel consentient quo honor ecclesie in persona clerici vituperetur. Hiis testibus: magistris I. Nobili, I. de Kernik', W. de Capella, R. de Pollamford', R. de Derteford', Roberto et Willelmo, capellanis, et aliis.

432 INSTITUTION. 11 April 1262, Exeter. At the presentation of Sir John de Courtenay, the lord bishop instituted Master Thomas de Wymondham to the church of Kenn through Master W. de Stanford, clerk, specially appointed proctor of the said Master [Thomas] for this purpose; and he has letters.

433 INSTITUTION. 11 April 1262, Exeter. At the presentation of the noble dame, the Lady Joan Brewer, the lord bishop admitted Peter de Bradeford', priest, to the vacant church of Cadeleigh; and he has letters of induction and institution, with the duty of residence.

434 COLLATION. 14 April 1262, Cokesputt. The lord bishop collated Siward, priest, to the vacant vicarage of Shebbear church, of which the collation had devolved upon him because of the invalid presentation of the abbot and convent of Torre; and he has letters of institution and induction in common form.

435 INSTITUTION. 2 May 1262, London. At the presentation of the prior and convent of Tywardreath, who have appropriated Fowey church, collated with full right, [the lord bishop] admitted Paul de St Eval, priest, to the vacant vicarage of the said church; and he has letters of institution and induction in common form.

436 PRESENTATION. 2 May 1262, London. A letter was issued stating that the lord bishop presented Henry de Hartland, priest, to the lord bishop of Worcester, for the church of St Michael, Gloucester, vacant de iure, together with its dependent chapel of St Martin.

437 INSTITUTION. 5 May 1262, London. At the presentation of the prior and convent of Tywardreath, who have appropriated Lanlivery church, collated with full right, [the lord bishop] admitted Randulph, priest, to the vacant vicarage of that church; and he has letters of institution and induction in common form.

438 INSTITUTION. 5 May 1262, London. At the presentation of Albreda de Bottreaux, true patroness of the vacant church of Plymtree, the lord bishop admitted Gundi [sic], priest, to the same with the duty of residence; and he has letters in common form.

439 OATH. 7 May 1262, London. Richard de Tregodh', Richard de Nanscuek', and Ralph de Arundel, knights, having taken a corporal oath, swore that, inasmuch as they had decreed the holding of a duel between William Blund, clerk, and Bartholomew, cobbler, and were present at the same and had seen it carried out, they shall abide by the commands of the Church and shall reverently receive and execute them, and that they shall never knowingly and wittingly cause or agree to anything whereby the honour of the Church may be insulted in the person of a clerk. Witnessed by Masters John Noble, J. de Kernik', William de Capella, R. de Polamford, R. de Dartford, Robert and William, chaplains, and others.

440 PENSIO. Anno eodem xii kalendas Iunii apud Horsleg' dominus episcopus concessit Waltero de Wylburham pensionem viginti solidorum infra quindenam S. Michaelis annuatim solvendorum et habet litteras patentes super hoc.

441 ORDINES: INSTITUTIO. Anno eodem iii nonas Iunii hoc est in vigilia Sancte Trinitatis Lond' dominus episcopus ordinavit Thomam de Molton', presentatum ad titulum ecclesie de Estboklond', in subdiaconum; et ad presentationem I. le Vinet, veri patroni ipsius ecclesie, ad eandem ecclesiam vacantem admisit, et habuit litteras inductionis.

442 COLLATIO. Anno die et loco eisdem dominus episcopus contulit vicariam ecclesie de Sydemue vacantem et ad presentationem prioris de Oteryton' spectantem que hac vice ad collationem suam extitit devoluta Radulpho de Cnolle, presbitero, et habet litteras inductionis.

443 INSTITUTIO. Anno et loco eisdem nonis Iunii dominus episcopus admisit dominum Alanum de Nimet ad ecclesiam de Samford' Curtenay ad presentationem domini I. de Curtenay et habet litteras inductionis.

444 LITTERA PENSIONIS RENOVATA. Anno eodem London' in vigilia apostolorum Petri et Pauli dominus episcopus precepit renovari litteram Petri de Vodonia in hec verba: Universis etc. Ad universitatis vestre notitiam tenore presentiam volumus pervenire quod nos ad instantiam venerabilis patris domini B., Cant' archiepiscopi, totius Anglie primatis, intuitu caritatis, dedimus et concessimus dilecto nostro Petro de Vodania, nepoti venerabilis patris domini .. Tarentas' archiepiscopi, decem libras sterlingorum de camera nostra in festo Resurrectionis Dominice annuatim percipiendas quousque eidem Petro ulterius duxerimus providendum. In cuius etc. Datum Cantuar' die Dominica proxima ante festum Gregorii pape anno gratie mcclvii et consecrationis die primo.

445 INSTALLATIO. Anno eodem die apostolorum Petri et Pauli London' ad presentationem fratris Roberti de Cumbwell', dudum prioris S. Nicholai, Exon', et procuratoris domini Reginaldi, abbatis de Bello, ad hoc specialiter deputati, dominus episcopus admisit fratrem Robertum de Rya, monachum, ad regimen prioratus ecclesie S. Nicholai predicte vacantis per resignationem eiusdem Roberti de Cumbwell', et habet litteras installationis. Datum in capitulo B. Marie de Swork', presentibus magistris Iohanne Noble, Roberto Pictaven', Randulpho de Naxinton', W. de Capella, R. de Polamefford, Henrico de Witemerse, item priore loci eiusdem, Rogero de Derteford', Roberto capellano, Willelmo capellano, Henrico monacho, Hugone Splot et aliis. Et remanet procuratorii et presentationis transcriptum sub sigillo magistri R. Pictaven' penes registrum.

440 PENSION. 21 May 1262, Horsley. The lord bishop granted Walter de Wylburham a pension of 20 shillings a year, payable within fifteen days of Michaelmas; and he has letters patent concerning this.

441 ORDINATION: INSTITUTION. 3 June 1262, London. The lord bishop ordained Thomas de Molton, presented to the title of East Buckland church, as subdeacon, and, at the presentation of J. le Vinet, true patron of that church, he admitted [him] to the same vacant church; and he had letters of induction.

442 COLLATION. 3 June 1262, London. The lord bishop collated Ralph de Knolle, priest, to the vacant vicarage of Sidmouth church, which was at the presentation of the prior of Otterton but on this occasion was devolved to his collation; and he has letters of induction.

443 INSTITUTION. 5 June 1262, London. At the presentation of Sir John de Courtenay, the lord bishop admitted Sir Alan de Nymet to Sampford Courtenay church; and he has letters of induction.

444 LETTER RENEWING A PENSION. 28 June 1262, London. The lord bishop ordered Peter de Vienne's letter to be renewed in these words: To all etc. We wish it to be known to all of you by the tenor of these presents that, at the instance of the venerable father the lord B[oniface], archbishop of Canterbury, primate of all England, at the prompting of charity, we have given and granted to our beloved Peter de Vienne, nephew of the venerable father the lord archbishop of Tarentaise, ten pounds sterling from our private purse, payable annually on the feast of the Lord's Resurrection until we have thought fit to make further provision for the same Peter. In testimony etc. Dated at Canterbury, 10 March 1258.

445 INSTALLATION. 29 June 1262, London. At the presentation of Brother Robert de Cumbwell, formerly prior of St Nicholas, Exeter, and specially appointed for this purpose as proctor of the lord Reginald, abbot of Battle, the lord bishop admitted Brother Robert de Rye, monk, to the rule of the aforesaid priory of the church of St Nicholas, vacant through the resignation of the same Robert de Cumbwell; and he has letters of installation. Dated in the chapter of St Mary [Overy Abbey] of Southwark, in the presence of Masters John Noble, Robert Pictavensis[d], Randulph de Naxinton, William de Capella, R. de Polamford, Henry de Witemerse, also the prior of the same place, Roger de Dartford, Robert, chaplain, William, chaplain, Henry, monk, Hugh Splot, and others. And the transcript of the proxy and of the presentation, under the seal of Master R. Pictavensis, remains in the registry.

d Perhaps Robert the Poitevin.

446 INSTITUTIO. Anno et loco eisdem die Translationis S. Thome martiris ad presentationem domini Philippi Basset, qui tunc habuit ius presentandi ad ecclesiam S. Melani in Kerior ratione custodie Iohannis de Rivariis, ipsius ecclesie veri patroni, dominus episcopus admisit Iohannem Quivel, presbiterum, ad eandem ecclesiam per resignationem magistri P. Quivel vacantem, et habet litteras inductionis.

447 INSTITUTIO. Anno eodem in crastino Assumptionis apud Crideton ad presentationem abbatis et conventus de Dunekewille dominus episcopus admisit Laurentium de Samford', presbiterum, ad vacantem vicariam ecclesie de Aulescumb', et habet litteras institutionis et inductionis in forma communi.

448 INSTALLATIO. Anno et die eisdem apud Frizelestok' dominus episcopus admisit Henricum Kaynnes ad regimen prioratus eiusdem loci et fecit eum vice et nomine archidiaconi Barnstap' installari.

449 VISITATIO. Anno eodem in vigilia Nativitatis S. Marie dominus episcopus visitavit priorem et monachos Pilton' et recepit procurationem xxs.[68]

450 COLLATIO. Anno eodem die Nativitatis S. Marie apud Tauton dominus episcopus contulit vacantem vicariam ecclesie de Lamerton' Willelmo [Fo.25v] de Stikelpathe, presbitero, per vacationem abbatie Tavistochie ad eum devolutam, et habet litteras inductionis.

451 CASSATIO ELECTIONIS ET PROVISIO. Anno die et loco eisdem cum in electione Tavistoke de fratre Iohanne Chubbe facta forma canonis non esset observata, dominus episcopus eam cassavit et de gratia speciali de eodem providit monasterio predicto.

452 Anno eodem die Sabbati proxima post festum Nativitatis S. Marie apud Nimeton' dominus episcopus recepit litteras magistrorum M. decani de Arcubus London' et Hugonis de la Motta officialis London', sede vacante; que penes eundem dominum resident sigillata.

453 RESIGNATIO: COLLATIO. Anno eodem in vigilia Exaltationis Sancte Crucis apud Cokespitt' magister Thomas de la Cnolle resignavit ecclesiam de Teygton' Episcopi, et dominus episcopus eandem sibi incontinenti contulit intuitu caritatis.

454 IURAMENTUM. Anno die et loco eisdem venit domina Rosemunda de Hevauton' petens a domino humiliter beneficium absolutionis sibi impendi et obtinuit in forma ecclesie: presentibus R. de Tefford', R. de Aveton', I. Wyger, I. de Blakedon', I. de Esse, R. de Polamford', Henrico monacho, Hugone Splot, Matheo de Eglosheyl', Durando serviente, Rogero Archiepiscopo, Thoma Caysho, Thoma Salvag', et aliis.

---

[68] The 'xxs.' was added, in a much paler ink.

446 INSTITUTION. 7 July 1262, London. At the presentation of Sir Philip Basset, who then had the right of presentation to Mullion in Kerrier church by reason of his wardship of John de Rivers, true patron of that church, the lord bishop admitted John Quinel, priest, to the same church, vacant through the resignation of Master Peter Quinel;[e] and he has letters of induction.

447 INSTITUTION. 16 August 1262, Crediton. At the presentation of the abbot and convent of Dunkeswell, the lord bishop admitted Laurence de Samford, priest, to the vacant vicarage of Awliscombe church; and he has letters of institution and induction in common form.

448 INSTALLATION. 16 August 1262, Frithelstock. The lord bishop admitted Henry Kaynnes to the rule of the priory of the same place, and had him installed in the place of and in the name of the archdeacon of Barnstaple.

449 VISITATION. 7 September 1262. The lord bishop visited the prior and monks of Pilton, and he received a procuration of 20 shillings.

450 COLLATION. 8 September 1262, Bishop's Tawton. The lord bishop collated William de Stikelpath', priest, to the vacant vicarage of Lamerton church, [of which the collation] had devolved on him because Tavistock Abbey was vacant; and he has letters of induction.

451 QUASHING OF AN ELECTION AND PROVISION. 8 September 1262, Bishop's Tawton. Since the terms of the canons had not been observed in the election of Brother John Chubbe [as abbot] of Tavistock, the lord bishop quashed it, but of special grace provided the same to the aforesaid monastery.

452 [LETTERS IN CANTERBURY'S VACANCY]. 9 September 1262, Bishop's Nympton. The lord bishop received letters from Masters M., Dean of Arches in London, and Hugh de la Motta, official of London, during the vacancy of the see [of Canterbury]; which sealed [letters] still stay with the same lord [bishop].

453 RESIGNATION: COLLATION. 13 September 1262, Cokesputt. Master Thomas de la Knolle resigned the church of Bishopsteignton and the lord bishop, at the prompting of charity, immediately collated him to the same.

454 OATH. 13 September 1262, Cokesputt. The lady Rosemunda de Heanton arrived, humbly seeking that the benefit of absolution be granted her by the bishop, and she obtained it in the Church's form, in the presence of R. de Tyfford, R. de Aveton, J. Wyger, J. de Blagdon, J. de Esse, R. de Polamford, Henry, monk, Hugh Splot, Matthew de Egloshayle, Durand, serjeant, Roger Arcevesk, Thomas Caysho, Thomas Salvage, and others.

e Bronescombe's successor as bishop of Exeter.

455 CUSTODIA. Anno die et loco eisdem dominus episcopus dedit tradidit et concessit magistro I. de Wig' et assignatis suis custodiam Iohannis, filii et heredis Thome de Bisscopleg', et terrarum ipsius Iohannis quas de eo tenere debet, et maritagium eiusdem Iohannis, pro xx marcis quas idem magister Iohannes premanibus ei solvit, et hoc usque ad legittimam etatem heredis. Et super hoc habet litteras eiusdem domini episcopi; Hiis testibus: W. decano Exon', E. decano Well', R. archidiacono Exon', Roberto cancellario Exon', et aliis.

456 APPROPRIATIO. Universis Christi fidelibus ad quos presens scriptum pervenerit Willelmus miseratione divina Exon' ecclesie minister humilis eternam in Domino salutem. Cupientes ecclesiam S. Nonne in Cornub' usibus illis integre cedere ad quos illam provida deliberatione duximus deputandam, nolentes etiam cellulam S. Cyrici que singulis annis de dicta ecclesia sex marcas quatuor solidos et tres obolos recipere consuevit quacunque ratione defraudari, nos, divine caritatis intuitu, de capituli consensu, dedimus et concessimus eidem cellule quinque marcas de bonis episcopatus nostri solvandas eidem singulis annis pro equis portionibus ad eosdem terminos, quibus dictam pensionem sex marcarum quatuor solidorum et trium obolorum recipere consuevit, donec eidem fuerit per nos vel aliquem successorum nostrorum competentius vel eque provisum. Quod quidem facere tenemur quam cito poterimus commode. Et ut hec nostra collatio futuribus temporibus rata et inconcussa permaneat, presens scriptum sigilli nostri necnon et decani et capituli cathedralis sigillorum munimine fecimus roborari. Datum Exon' anno gratie mccxxxvi ii kalendas Iunii consecrationis nostre anno xiii.

457 PREDICATIO. Anno eodem ix kalendas Novembris apud Exon' exivit littera predicationis pro ecclesia Bethleemitan' in forma communi.

458 INSTITUTIO. Anno die et loco eisdem dominus episcopus instituit Walterum de Farendon', presbiterum, in ecclesia de Rokeber' quam prius ei commendaverat et hoc ex vetere iure dudum ante sibi competente.

459 INSTITUTIO. Anno eodem in octabis S. Martini apud Horslegh ad presentationem domini Rogeri de Sanford, veri patroni ecclesie de Sokebroc, dominus episcopus admisit Iohannem Quivel, presbiterum, ad eandem ecclesiam vacantem, et habet litteras institutionis et inductionis in forma communi.

460 INSTITUTIO. Anno et loco eisdem die S. Clementis ad presentationem Rogeri de Toney, veri patroni ecclesie de Suth Tauton', dominus episcopus admisit Nicholaum Lungespeye ad eandem ecclesiam vacantem, salva vicaria, et habet litteras inductionis.

455 WARDSHIP. 13 September 1262, Cokesputt. The lord bishop gave, delivered and granted to Master J[ohn] Wyger and his assigns the wardship of John, son and heir of Thomas de Bishopsleigh, and of the lands of the said John which he should hold of him [the bishop], and the marriage of the same John, in return for 20 marks which the same Master John paid to him cash down, and this was to be until the heir came of lawful age. And concerning this he has letters of the same lord bishop; witnessed by W[illiam de Stanwey], dean of Exeter, E[dward de la Knolle], dean of Wells, R[oger de Thoriz], archdeacon of Exeter, Robert [de Tyfford], chancellor of Exeter, and others.

456 APPROPRIATION. 31 May 1236, Exeter. To all Christ's faithful whom this present document shall reach, William [Brewer], by the divine compassion humble minister of the church of Exeter, lifelong greeting in the Lord. Desiring to yield the church of Altarnun in Cornwall entirely to those purposes to which, after prudent deliberation, we have thought fit to appoint it, and at the same time not wishing the cell of St Cyricus, which has each year been accustomed to receive from the said church six marks, four shillings and three halfpence, to be deprived for any sort of reason, we, with the consent of our chapter, at the prompting of divine charity have given and granted to the same cell five marks from the property of our bishopric to be paid to the same each year in equal instalments at the same dates on which it has been accustomed to receive the said pension of six marks, four shillings and three halfpence, until more adequate or equal provision shall be made for the same by us or any of our successors. Which indeed we are bound to do as speedily as we conveniently can. And in order that this our collation may continue ratified and unshaken in future times, we have had this present document fortified with the corroboration of our seal and also of the seals of the dean and chapter of the cathedral.

457 PREACHING. 24 October 1262, Exeter. A licence to preach was issued in common form for the church of Bethlehem.

458 INSTITUTION. 24 October 1262, Exeter. The lord bishop instituted Walter de Farringdon, priest, in Rockbeare church, to which he had earlier commended him, this being appropriate for him from previous longstanding right.

459 INSTITUTION. 18 November 1262, Horsley. At the presentation of Sir Roger de Sanford, true patron of Shobrooke church, the lord bishop admitted John Quinel, priest, to the same vacant church; and he has letters of institution and induction in common form.

460 INSTITUTION. 23 November 1262, Horsley. At the presentation of Roger de Toney, true patron of South Tawton church, the lord bishop admitted Nicholas Longespee to the same vacant church, excepting the vicarage; and he has letters of induction.

461   INSTITUTIO. Anno die et loco eisdem ad presentationem Nicholai Lungespeye, rectoris ecclesie de Suthtauton', dominus episcopus admisit Alanum de Ieteminstr', presbiterum, ad ipsius ecclesie vacantem vicariam que ibi esse consuevit ab antiquo; que quidem consistit in [. . .][69]

462   SOLUTIO. Anno eodem London' iv kalendas Decembris dominus episcopus solvit procuratoribus Iohannis Guidonis de Anagnia [Fo.26] xl marcas de annua pensione xx marcarum pro annis gratie mcclx primo et secundo, et habet litteras.

463   INSTITUTIO. Anno eodem xiv kalendas Ianuarii apud Criditon' ad presentationem domini Philippi Basset, hac vice veri patroni ecclesie S. Melani in Cornub', dominus episcopus admisit Gregorium de S. Melano, subdiaconum, ad eandem ecclesiam vacantem et eam sibi concessit titulo commendationis possidendam ad beneplacitum sue voluntatis et super hoc habet cartam episcopi et litteras inductionis in forma communi.

464   ORDINES. Anno et loco eisdem x kalendas Ianuarii dominus episcopus celebravit ordines apud Criditon'.

465   INSTITUTIO. Anno et die et loco eisdem ad presentationem domini Willelmi de Widewrth', militis, veri patroni ecclesie de Lumsteleg', dominus episcopus admisit magistrum Petrum de Tauton', subdiaconum, ad eandem ecclesiam et super hoc habet cartam et litteras inductionis in forma communi.

466   INSTITUTIO. Anno eodem die S. Stephani apud Exon' ad presentationem Iohannis Peverel, veri patroni ecclesie de Herpaford', dominus episcopus admisit Robertum de Kyllebir', subdiaconum, ad eandem ecclesiam vacantem et habet litteras inductionis.

467   CONSOLIDATIO. Anno die et loco eisdem dominus episcopus admisit Willelmum de Membir', subdiaconum, ad totam ecclesiam de la Methe in qua prius percepit quinque marcas annuas nomine parsonatus.

468   CUSTODIA SEQUESTRI. Anno et loco eisdem iii kalendas Ianuarii dominus episcopus commisit custodiam ecclesie de Aufricumb magistro Olivero de Traci usque ad festum B. Petri ad Vincula, ita quod de fructibus et proventibus ipsius eidem domino respondeat cum fuerit requisitus, et hoc sub debito prestiti iuramenti fideliter repromisit.

469   REDDITIO LITTERARUM. Anno eodem in vigilia S. Hilarii apud Ferndon' W. de Capella reddidit domino litteras regis Alem' de sabulo Cornub', et litteras archidiaconi Totton' et magistri R. de Tefford' de decima

---

[69] A gap was left here for the taxation, and never filled.

461 INSTITUTION. 23 November 1262, Horsley. At the presentation of Nicholas Longespee, rector of South Tawton church, the lord bishop admitted Alan de Yetminster, priest, to the vacant vicarage of that church, which was accustomed to be there from of old; this indeed consists of . . .

462 PAYMENT. 28 November 1262, London. The lord bishop paid to the proctors of John Guido of Anágni 40 marks, from an annual pension of 20 marks for the years of grace 1261 and 1262,[f] and he has letters.

463 INSTITUTION. 19 December 1262, Crediton. At the presentation of Sir Philip Basset, for this time [g] true patron of the church of Mullion in Cornwall, the lord bishop admitted Gregory de S Melano, subdeacon, to the same vacant church, and granted it to him under title of commendation to be possessed at [the bishop's] pleasure; and concerning this he has the bishop's charter and letters of induction in common form.

464 ORDINATION. 23 December 1262, Crediton. The lord bishop held an ordination.

465 INSTITUTION. 23 December 1262, Crediton. At the presentation of Sir William de Widewrth', knight, true patron of Lustleigh church, the lord bishop admitted Master Peter de Tawton, subdeacon, to the same church; and concerning this he has a charter and letters of induction in common form.

466 INSTITUTION. 26 December 1262, Exeter. At the presentation of John Peverel, true patron of Harpford church, the lord bishop admitted Robert de Kyllebir', subdeacon, to the same vacant church; and he has letters of induction.

467 CONSOLIDATION. 26 December 1262, Exeter. The lord bishop admitted William de Membir', subdeacon, to the entire church of Meeth, from which previously he took five marks a year in the name of a parson's benefice.

468 CUSTODY OF A SEQUESTRATION. 30 December 1262, Exeter. The lord bishop committed the custody of Ilfracombe church to Master Oliver de Tracy until 1 August, on terms that he should answer, when required, to the same lord [bishop] for its fruits and proceeds, and he faithfully promised this again in virtue of an oath he took.

469 HANDING OVER OF LETTERS. 12 January 1263, Faringdon.[h] William de Capella handed over to the lord [bishop] letters of the king of Almayne [the earl of Cornwall] about the Cornish sand[-pits], and letters of the archdeacon

[f] Cf. **55** and **177**.
[g] The guardianship of John de Rivers, see **446**.
[h] Presumably the bishop's manor in Hampshire, rather than the Farringdon in Devon.

dominici domini episcopi in Chedeham, item litteras abbatis et conventus Westm' super serviciis manerii de Stokes in comitatu Sussex'.

470 INSTITUTIO. Anno eodem vi kalendas Februarii apud Horslegh dominus episcopus ad presentationem Nicholi filii Martini, ratione dotis uxoris sue veri patroni ecclesie de Mammeheved, admisit Nicholaum de Dunden', presbiterum, ad eandem ecclesiam vacantem et habet litteras institutionis et inductionis in forma communi.

471 Anno et loco eisdem in die Purificationis dominus episcopus benedixit abbatem de Tavistok'.

472 Anno eodem London' ii nonas Februarii dominus episcopus admisit fratrem [. . .] de Columbers ad regimen prioratus de Cowik' vacantis per resignationem fratris Thome, quondam prioris, factam in presentia domini Rothomagen' archiepiscopi cuius litteras exhibuit, et hoc ad presentationem abbatis et conventus de Becco.

473 Anno eodem iv nonas Martii obiit prior de Thywardrat Michael.

474[70] Anno Domini mcclx tertio in crastino Annuntiationis B. Marie mane obiit Baldewynus, prior de Plempton'.

475 Consecrationis domini episcopi anno sexto et gratie mcclx tertio die Dominica in crastino S. Egidii, hoc est iv nonas Septembris, pre foribus maioris ecclesie S. Petri Exon' comparuerunt fratres Iohannes Marker, sacrista, Robertus Spolt [sic] celerarius, et Britius, canonici Plympton, et de manibus domini decani Exon', habentis potestatem domini episcopi in hac parte, receperunt solempniter nomine prioris et ceterarum personarum de conventu Plympton' beneficium absolutionis a sententiis excommunicationis quibus, tam per dictum dominum episcopum quam eius officialem, propter manifestam offensam diversis temporibus fuerunt ligati.[71]

---

[70] After this entry the folio is erased for more than an inch.
[71] This paragraph was perhaps added later in a blank space at the foot of the folio, where is written *nota S. Ladoce*; there is also a marginal sign referring to the third folio on, **496**.

of Totnes and of Master R. de Tyfford about the tithe of the lord bishop's demesne in Chidham, and also letters of the abbot and convent of Westminster concerning the services of the manor of Stoke in the county of Sussex.

470 INSTITUTION. 27 January 1263, Horsley. At the presentation of Nicholas fitzMartin, true patron of Mamhead church by reason of his wife's dowry, the lord bishop admitted Nicholas de Dundon, priest, to the same vacant church; and he has letters of institution and induction in common form.

471 [BLESSING]. 2 February 1263, Horsley. The lord bishop blessed the abbot of Tavistock.

472 [NEW PRIOR]. 4 February 1263, London. The lord bishop admitted Brother [. . .] de Columbers to the rule of Cowick Priory, vacant through the resignation of Brother Thomas, formerly prior, made in the presence of the lord archbishop of Rouen, whose letters he showed; and this was at the presentation of the abbot and convent of Bec.

473 [DEATH]. 4 March 1263. Michael, prior of Tywardreath, died.

474 [DEATH]. 26 March 1263. Baldwin, prior of Plympton, died in the morning.

475 [ABSOLUTION]. 2 September 1263, Exeter. Brothers John Marker, sacristan, Robert Spolt, cellarer, and Britius, canons of Plympton, appeared before the doors of the cathedral church of St Peter, Exeter, and, in the name of the prior and other persons of the convent of Plympton, they solemnly received at the hands of the lord dean of Exeter, empowered by the lord bishop in this matter, the benefit of absolution from the sentences of excommunication by which they had been bound, both by the said lord bishop and by his official, on account of their manifest offence on various occasions.